A DICTIONARY OF WINES,
SPIRITS AND LIQUEURS

ANDRÉ L. SIMON

A Dictionary of Wines,
Spirits and Liqueurs

THE CITADEL PRESS · NEW YORK

INITIALS BY OTTOMAR STARKE

FIRST AMERICAN EDITION 1963

COPYRIGHT © 1958 BY ANDRÉ L. SIMON
LIBRARY OF CONGRESS CATALOG CARD NUMBER 63-21203
MANUFACTURED IN THE UNITED STATES OF AMERICA
PUBLISHED BY THE CITADEL PRESS
222 PARK AVENUE SOUTH, NEW YORK 3, N. Y.

INTRODUCTION

WHEREVER man settles, there must be water. Man must have water to live and ever since the Flood, when there was rather too much of it, man has had more than sufficient to quench his thirst. Yet despite this, from the dim-distant ages to the present day man has spent much of his time, ingenuity and labour in producing alternative draughts more pleasing to his palate. He early discovered how to make wine and for centuries the fermented juice of the grape was the beverage of all the civilized peoples of the earth from Cathay to Carthage. Then, as man began to migrate to more northern lands where the vine could not be depended upon to mature its fruit, he had to find some other alternative to the grape. Experiment in fermenting malted grain steeped in water resulted in ale and beer. Fermentation also gave him mead from honey, and cider from apples.

Very much later, barely five hundred years ago, he discovered that the alcohol in all fermented beverages could be 'vaporized' or separated from the 85 to 90 per cent residue of water: thus did spirits come upon the scene. Today spirits are used in ways beyond count: either by themselves; tempered with more or less water; blended with different wines, to which they add strength; or, flavoured with all kinds of herbs, barks, roots, seeds and flowers, as a basis for liqueurs and cordials.

As its title indicates, the present work is a dictionary. It is not, however, a directory and one must therefore not expect to find in it the names and addresses of the distillers and compounders of spirits, liqueurs and cordials, any more than the registered brands under which their products are marketed. The names which do appear are mostly the names of places where wines are produced every year, the birthplaces of wine.

In an age of mass-production and mass-suggestion, wine is still putting up a gallant fight for the survival of individuality. In a single *département* of France, admittedly the largest of all, La Gironde, there are over four thousand named vineyards which are listed in Féret's *Bordeaux et ses Vins*, known in France as the Bordeaux Bible. Many of these vineyards are very small; their wines may or may not differ greatly in appearance and quality, and may differ only very slightly in bouquet and flavour. Yet these small differences are of real importance to all who know and love the wines of Bordeaux.

In any dictionary such as this, wine is bound to occupy much greater space than the rest, not so much because of its greater antiquity, but because of its greater individuality. Every year an average of 3,500 million gallons of wine—real wine, the suitably fermented juice of freshly gathered ripe grapes—are made from the many vineyards of the world. (There are also a great many so-called wines made from fruit pulp or sterilized grape-juice, with which we are not concerned in this Dictionary.) All but about two per cent of the world's production of wine are plain beverage wines and are drunk within eighteen months of being made by the people of the countries where they are made. Such wines are very cheap, unremarkable, safe and healthful. They are safe because no germs live in wine—as they do in water and in milk—and they are healthful because their small percentage of alcohol is sufficient to stimulate the heart and digestive organs, but not sufficient to have any deleterious effect upon the brain.

The remaining two per cent of the world's annual production, a mere 70 million gallons, are quality wines and are in a very different category. Most, if not all, are of higher alcoholic strength. This enables them to stand the test of time and so gain greater grace with greater age, and also to travel without ill-effect and so reach a large number of wine-lovers in all parts of the civilized world. But their greater alcoholic strength is the least factor in their greater appeal and greater cost. Quality wines appeal to wine lovers chiefly because of their individuality. The alcohol they contain is the same in each case and its strength may be, and often is, identical; but their subtle perfume or *bouquet*, their flavour at their first impact upon the tongue, and the lingering after-taste of their last caress down the throat, vary from vineyard to vineyard and from vintage to vintage. Such wines are both a tonic and a joy, and many of them, though by no means all, are recorded in this Dictionary.

A DICTIONARY OF WINES, SPIRITS AND LIQUEURS

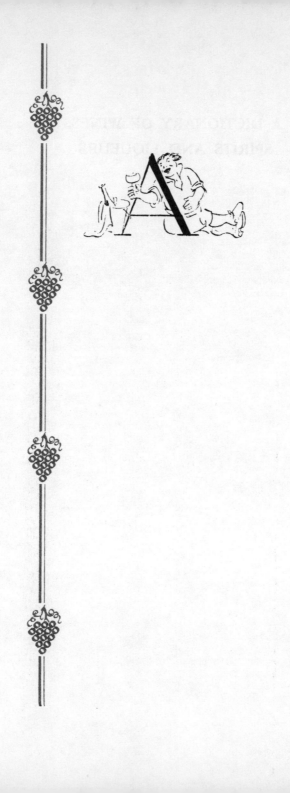

Dictionary of Wines, Spirits and Liqueurs

AARGAU
One of the minor wine-producing Cantons of Switzerland. Its chief vineyards are those of Villingen.

ABBAYE-SKINNER, Domaine de l'
Bourgeois growth of the Médoc; Vertheuil Commune.

ABBÉ-GORSSE-DE-GORSSE, Château de l'
Bourgeois Supérieur growth of the Médoc; Margaux Commune. Formerly known as Château Gorsse-Pérès.

ABBOCCATO
Sweet, in connection with the sweeter white wines of Italy, chiefly those of Orvieto.

ABEL-LAURENT, Château
Bourgeois Supérieur growth of the Médoc; Margaux Commune. Formerly known as Château Séguineau.

ABFÜLLUNG
'Bottled by', followed by the name of the vineyard owner or merchant who bottled the wine. German equivalent of the French 'Mise en bouteilles au Château'.

ABRAU
One of the best white wines of the Crimea.

ABRICOTINE
Liqueur made from the small apricots grown near Enghien-les-Bains, with the almond tang of the kernel.

ABSINTHE
A distilled product flavoured with wormwood, of definite tonic properties but dangerous when used indiscreetly owing to its potency. France and Switzerland, where it was consumed largely, have taken repressive measures resulting in the practical cessation of its manufacture in those countries.

ABTSWIND
One of the smaller wine-producing parishes of Franconia at the foot of the Steigerwald; mostly white wines.

ACERBE, Vin
An excessively sharp wine; usually one that was made from insufficiently ripe grapes.

ACETIC ACID. CH_3CO_2H
The most prevalent of all undesirable acids in wine. Acetic acid is due chiefly to the oxidation of ethylic alcohol in the presence of a fungoid catalyst known as *Mycoderma aceti*. Acetic acid is responsible for the sour, sharp taste of vinegar and 'pricked' wines. The lower the alcoholic strength of a wine, the greater the risk of oxidation of its alcohol into acetic acid, and the freer the access of air to a wine, the more rapid will be the formation of acetic acid. Vinegar should never be kept in the wine-cellar: it adds to the ever-present danger of acetification of wine.

ACHAIA
The third most important wine-producing Province of Greece.

ACHKARREN
A wine-producing parish of the Kaiserstuhl plateau; its vineyards produce the best white wine of Brisgau.

ACHTEL
A German wine-measure, one-eighth of the *Eimer*.

ACIDS
Acids are present in all wines, some being not only wholesome, but quite indispensable, whilst others are exactly the reverse.

To the first group belong the aldehyde-acids, which are chiefly responsible for the 'bouquet' of all wines; to the second belongs acetic acid, the principal cause of 'pricked' or 'vinegary' wines.

Free acids present in grape-juice before fermentation, and in wine after fermentation, in a more or less permanent or merely transitory state, are the following: carbonic, tartaric, tannic, malic and citric. Acids which are present in wine but not in grape-juice are: succinic, acetic, matapectic, lactic and butyric acids. The variety of acids in wine is due to differences existing in the soil of different vineyards, the species of grapes and the nature of Saccharomycetes and other micro-organisms present in the must, or introduced adventitiously in the wine after fermentation. The majority of those acids are only present in minute quantities, too minute, in most cases, to be measured, but the importance of the part they play as regards the degree of excellence of different wines is out of all proportion to their volume.

ACKERMAN
The most important wine-producing district of Bessarabia.

ADEGA
The Portuguese equivalent of the Spanish *Bodega* and French *Chai*.

ADLESBERG
One of the best red table wines of Hungary from the vineyards of Ofen-Pest; usually sold as *Ofen-Adlesberg*.

ADVOCAAT
Liqueur of Dutch origin, but now manufactured in other countries, including England and Australia. It has a thick creamy consistency produced by its ingredients of eggs, sugar and brandy, etc.

AFFENTHALER
One of the best red table wines of Baden (Germany).

AGAVE
The name of an American aloe (*Agave americana*), and also the name of a highly intoxicating drink distilled from its fermented sap. It is called *Maguey* in Mexico.

AGIOS GEORGIOS
A dark red and sweet dessert wine made at Nemea, in Greece.

AGLIANICO DEL VULTURE
A red table wine made from Aglianico grapes in the valley of the vulture, in the Basilicata, Italy.

AGRAFES
The metal clips which hold in place the temporary corks used in the first bottling of Champagne; later replaced by the final wire and cork of the finished article.

AGROS
The wine-producing district of Cyprus responsible for the best Muscat dessert wines of the island.

AGUARDIENTE
The Spanish name for Brandy.

AHM, AUM or OHM
The standard German barrel containing from 30¼ to 31 gallons of wine.

AHMCHEN
German wine measure: 6·3 gallons.

AHR
A tributary of the Rhine (left bank). The vineyards of the Ahr Valley produce both red and white table wines, the red wines being the more renowned.

AHRBLEICHERT
A German word deriving from *bleich* (bleach) applied to a pink or pale red wine from the district of the Ahr but not to any specific vineyard or location.

AIGLERIE, Château de l'
One of the more popular white table wines of Anjou.

AIGUEBELLE
Produce of the monastery Notre Dame d'Aiguebelle, founded by 12 monks of the Cistercian Order in 1137 at the confluence of the three streams *'belles eaux'* near Vallon in the Rhône Valley. They raise money for their charitable works by such industries as the manufacture of their liqueur Aiguebelle, which they claim contains over fifty different herbs. It is made in two varieties, green and yellow, the latter being the sweeter of the two.

AKVAVIT, AQUAVIT
Two Scandinavian forms of *Aqua vitae*. A highly rectified, colourless spirit distilled mostly from grain or potatoes and flavoured with caraway seeds.

ALBANA
A golden and rather sweet wine from the vineyards of Bertinoro, in the Province of Aemilia, Italy.

ALBANI, Colli
The Alban Hills, south of Rome, the vineyards of which produce table wines from fair to middling in quality, sold under different names, chiefly Frascati, Albano, Gonzano and Rocca di Papa.

ALBARIZA
The white, poor, chalky soil of some of the best vineyards between Jerez de la Frontera and San Lucar de Barrameda, the Sherryland of Andalucia.

ALBERTS, Château des
Premier Cru Bourgeois of the Blayais, producing much Claret and a little white Bordeaux.

ALBILLO
A Spanish grape used for dessert and also for wine-making.

ALBURY
One of the oldest of the wine-producing districts of New South Wales, Australia.

ALCOHOL
The name Alcohol covers a very large number of compounds of carbon, hydrogen and oxygen, but the member of the alcohol family which is such an important component part of all wines, beers and spirits is Ethyl Alcohol, or C_2H_6O, a colourless liquid with a faint and pleasant ethereal smell. There is absolutely nothing in the chemical composition of Ethyl Alcohol to warrant its description as a poison or a narcotic. Like other carbohydrates, it releases heat and supplies energy for muscular work; hence it is a food. But it is a food with a specific action upon the nervous system, an action which leads to perfectly normal functional changes, causing a gentle inner mental stimulation when taken in moderate quantities by normal subjects, but causing grave mental and physical deterioration when taken to excess or by subjects with undeveloped or impaired mental powers. In France, and in most wine-producing countries, the quantity of Ethyl Alcohol present in wine is reckoned in degrees of absolute alcohol, but in England it is reckoned in degrees of Proof spirit, 100 of absolute alcohol being equal to 175 of Proof spirit. The Ethyl Alcohol present in spirits is measured, in England, according to Sykes' method in degrees over or under 'Proof', which represent diluted alcohol equal to $57 \cdot 05°$ of absolute alcohol by volume, or $49 \cdot 85°$ by weight, at a temperature of 60°F.

ALCOHOLIC STRENGTH
The strength of wine refers to its alcoholic content, the greater the proportion

of alcohol there is in a wine, the stronger it is.

COMPARATIVE WINE STRENGTHS

In the United Kingdom the Duty is charged on the strength of Wines described as 'not exceeding 25 degrees or not exceeding 42 degrees of Proof Spirit'. The following Table shows the comparisons between degrees of alcohol and degrees of proof spirit.

Degrees of Alcohol	Degrees of Proof Spirit	Degrees of Alcohol	Degrees of Proof Spirit
1	1·8	13	23·1
2	3·7	14	24·7
3	5·6	15	26·4
4	7·2	16	28·1
5	8·9	17	29·9
6	10·7	18	31·6
7	12·4	19	33·4
8	14·2	20	35·2
9	15·9	21	37·0
10	17·7	22	38·9
11	19·4	23	40·7
12	21·2	24	42·6

ALDABO
A Cuban liqueur with Rum as its basis and orange its chief flavour.

ALDEGUND
One of the less important wine-producing parishes of the Lower Moselle.

ALE
The most popular beverage in all northern lands where there are no vineyards and where wine is accordingly too dear for daily consumption. *Ale* is made from barley, which is wetted, spread on a floor and allowed—or encouraged to germinate. It is then dried in a kiln and becomes malt. Malt is put in a tub with lots of warm water and some yeast, when fermentation soon starts and transforms the malt sugar into carbonic acid gas, which loses itself in the air, and alcohol, which remains in the liquid which may then be called *Ale*. It answers to Johnson's Dictionary's definition of *Ale: A liquor brewed from malt, to be drunk fresh*. This used to be known as *Common Ale*, in opposition to *Spiced Ale*, which used to be flavoured with a number of spices and herbs, other than hops. Hopped ale was called *Beer* (q.v.) and was meant to be matured. Since the nineteenth century, however, whatever differences there may be between *Ale* and *Beer* are due to purely local tradition in various parts of the country. According to the Shorter Oxford English Dictionary, *Ale and Beer were originally synonymous; but now 'beer' is the generic name for all malt liquors, 'ale' being the name for the lighter coloured kinds*. This is entirely wrong: hops made all the difference originally between *Ale* and *Beer*, and there are now *Ales* just as dark as the darkest *Beer*, other than *Stout*. Benskin's *Colne Valley Ale*, for instance, was a very dark and full strength *Ale* and one of the best 'bottled beers'. When *Ale* is stale it is often called *beery*, probably owing to a survival of the tradition that *Ale* was best freshly brewed, not having, like *Beer*, the benefit of hops, chiefly used originally as a preservative.

Stone Ale was not sold in stone bottles; it was *Ale* brewed originally at the monastery of Stone, in Staffordshire, which had the reputation of being the finest in the Midlands: the monks' skill in malting and brewing had probably something to do with it, but the excellence of the local water was mainly responsible then as it is to this day for the quality of the *Ale* brewed in Staffordshire.

March and October are the two best brewing months in England.

ALE FLIP or
ONE YARD OF FLANNEL
Put a quart of Bass & Co.'s Barley Wine, or Strong Ale, on the fire to warm, and beat up three or four eggs with 4 oz. of moist sugar, a teaspoonful of grated nutmeg or ginger and ¼ good old rum or brandy. When the ale is near to a boil,

put it into a pitcher, and the rum and eggs, etc., into another; turn it from one pitcher to the other till it is smooth as cream.

ALEATICO
A sweet, Italian red wine, made from the Aleatico grape, a species of black Muscat, grown in Apulia, Umbria, the Latium, and the island of Elba. There was a wine of Tuscany known in England by the name Aleatico as early as the time of Chaucer. Two of the best-known Aleatico wines of today are made in the Latium, from the Castelli Romani vineyards, the *Aleatico di Terracina* and the *Aleatico di Gradoli*. There are two others, the *Aleatico di Puglia* and the *Aleatico Elba*.

ALEBERRY
Mix two large spoonfuls of fine oatmeal in sufficient sweet small beer, two hours before using it; strain well, boil, and sweeten according to taste. Pour into a warm jug, add wine, lemon juice, and nutmeg to taste, and serve hot with thin slips of toast or rusks.

ALELLA
The name of a village of Catalonia (Spain) and also that of the wine— mostly white, made from the vineyards which surround Alella; they are sold in long, fluted bottles resembling Hock bottles, but the wine has neither the bouquet nor any other characteristic of Hock; it is just a plain, refreshing, dry, white wine.

ALEMBIC
From an old Arabic word meaning a still for distillation.

ALEYOR
A very dark red, almost black, table wine from the vineyards of Majorca.

ALF-BULLAY
One of the less distinguished white wines of the Moselle Valley.

ALGARINEJO
One of the wine-producing districts of Spain (Granada) where a great deal of undistinguished table wine is made, much of it being distilled into Spanish brandy.

ALGERIA, the wines of
Within a hundred years of the French occupation and pacification of Algeria, its vineyards produced close upon 500 million gallons of wines, mostly red and of the *ordinaire* class. Algeria has become one of the largest wine-producing countries in the world, in spite of the fact that practically the whole of the labour needed to grow the grapes had to be Muslim non-drinking labour.

ALGHERI
A wine-producing area in Sardinia.

ALICANTE
A sweet, red dessert wine from the vineyards of the Levante Province of Spain.

ALIGOTÉ
White grape used for wine-making in Burgundy.

ALKERMÈS
A French cordial which was once upon a time very popular. Its attractive red colour is due to the Alkermes berries used as a dye; these are not berries at all, but insects of the cochineal genus.

ALLASCH
A certain type of kummel.

ALMERIA
A part of Andalucia famous for the excellence of its table grapes and raisins.

ALMISSA
The best dessert red wine of Dalmatia.

ALMUDE
A Portuguese wine measure equal to two *alqueiras*, i.e. 3·641 gallons, at Lisbon;

3·901 gallons in Madeira; 5·519 gallons at Oporto; and 7·05 gallons in Brazil.

ALMUS
A sweet white wine made from the grapes grown upon the slopes of the Trieffeinstein hill, outside Aschaffenburg, in Bavaria.

ALOUPKA
A wine-growing district of the Crimea which produces both red and white wines.

ALOXE-CORTON
An important wine-producing Commune of the Côte d'Or (Burgundy). Its best vineyards are *Le Corton* and *Le Charlemagne* for both red and white wines; *Clos du Roi, Bressandes, Chaumes, Combes, Fiètres, Grèves, Languettes, Maréchaudes, Meix, Pougets, Renardes* and *La Vigne au Saint* for red wines only.

ALSACE
The easternmost Province of France between the Vosges and the Rhine, now divided into two Départements, Haut-Rhin and Bas-Rhin. All the best vineyards of Alsace are south of Strasbourg and north of Mulhouse, in the Colmar region. They produce almost exclusively white wines which are mostly sold under the names of the grapes from which different wines are made, chiefly Sylvaner for the lighter and cheaper wines, Riesling, Traminer and Gewurztraminer for the finer ones. Other species of wine-making grapes are the Elbing and Burger, for the commoner wines, Gentil, Pinot Gris or Tokay and Muscadel for the better ones. A few only of the Alsace wines are sold under the name of a Château or of a registered brand, but all bear the name of their shipper or seller and his address, either Colmar, Riquewihr, Ribeauvillé, Mittlebergheim, Guebwiller, Eguisheim, Mittelwihr, Ammerschwihr, Kientsheim Hunawihr, etc.

ALSENZ
One of the two tributaries of the Nahe along the valley of which are vineyards producing pleasant, but not outstanding wines.

ALSHEIM
A wine-producing parish of Rhine-Hesse more renowned for the quantity of its wines than for their quality.

ALTAR WINE
The unadulterated fermented juice of fresh grapes used for sacramental purposes. Fortified wines may be and sometimes are considered suitable; they are 'assisted' but not 'adulterated'.

ALTENAHR
A village of the Upper Ahr Valley; its vineyards produce some fair red table wines.

ALTENBAMBERG
One of the Palatinate villages surrounded by vineyards which produce a fair quantity of both red and white wines.

ALTESSES, Vin des
One of the (locally) best-known white wines of French Savoy; it is made from grapes grown at Yenne.

ALTKIRCH
On the Haut-Rhin, producing red and white table wines.

ALTO DOURO
The Upper Valley of the Douro from Regoa to the Spanish frontier. Its vineyards produce the only wine which is entitled to the name of Port.

ALZEY
A wine-producing locality of Rhine-Hesse responsible for a fair quantity of white wines of average quality.

AMARANTE
A Portuguese white table wine.

AMARILLO CHARTRES
A Cuban Liqueur.

AMBARÈS
A Commune of the Gironde Département; its vineyards produce a fairly large quantity of useful but by no means great red wines.

AMBÈS, Bec d'
The westernmost part of the Médoc at the mouth of the Gironde; its vineyards produce a fair quantity of the more *ordinaire* type of Claret.

AMBONNAY
A first growth of the Marne Département, Champagne. The red table wine made from Ambonnay-grown grapes is considered the peer of the Red Bouzy, the best still red wine of Champagne.

AMBROSIA
The mystical tipple of the gods in Olympus according to Greek mythology. It was said (by the poets) to be 'nine times as sweet as honey'.

AMER PICON
A brand of Orange Bitters used in France as an *Apéritif*.

AMERICAN VINE STOCKS
These became important to Europe after the destruction of the French and other European vineyards by the dread phylloxera pest at the end of the nineteenth and beginning of the twentieth centuries. The vineyards were replanted with the disease-resistant American stocks on to which slips from the old vines were grafted.

AMERICAN WINES
Grapes grow and wine is made in many parts of both North and South America, such as the Argentine, Brazil, California, Canada, Chile, Mexico, New York State and Uruguay.

AMMERSCHWIHR
One of the more important wine-producing villages of Alsace.

AMOLTERN
One of the lesser wine-producing localities of the Kaiserstuhl, in Baden (white wines).

AMONTILLADO
Originally a Montilla-type of Sherry, but now the name of many different kinds of *Fino* quality Sherries.

AMOROSO
A 'medium' type of Sherry, the quality of which varies with each Sherry Shipper.

AMOUREUSES, Les
One of the best vineyards of Chambolle-Musigny; it produces a red Burgundy of great charm and distinction.

AMPHORAE
Ancient wine containers in the form of earthenware jars, often of very beautiful, simple design.

AMPUIS
A small town on the right bank of the Rhône at the foot of a hill covered with vineyards which produce the Côte Rôtie wines.

ANACREON
A lyric Greek poet (*c.* 532 B.C.) who had the reputation of being a great drinker, and who died of a grape-pip in his windpipe. He wrote the 'Ode to Wine' which Abraham Cowley translated, beginning:

The thirsty Earth drinks up the Rain,
And drinks, and gapes for drink again.
The plants suck in the Earth, and are
With constant drinking fresh and fair.
The sea itself, which one would think
Should have but little need of Drink,
Drinks ten thousand rivers up.

and ending:

> Nothing in Nature's sober found,
> But an eternal Health goes round.
> Fill up the bowl, then, fill it high,
> Fill all the glasses there, and why
> Should every creature drink but I,
> Why, man of morals, tell me why?

AÑADA
Spanish word for the young 'wine of the year' before blending; the next stage of development after being 'mostos'.

ANCY
A white wine of no particular distinction, but one of the best of Lorraine.

ANDALUCIA
The eighth wine-producing Province of Spain as regards quantity, but the first for quality wines. Jerez-de-la-Frontera, the metropolis of the Sherry vinelands, is in Andalucia.

ANDRON, Château
Bourgeois growth of the Médoc; Commune of Civrac.

ANEY, Cru
Bourgeois growth of the Médoc; Commune of Cussac.

ANFORA
Italian wine measure equal to 114 gallons.

ANGELICA
(*a*) A Basque Liqueur of the *Chartreuse* type; it is pale yellow in colour, very sweet and highly aromatic. The best is made by Izarra.
(*b*) A very sweet white wine originally made in the San Joaquin Valley of California by the Mission Fathers. It is now mostly made in various parts of Southern California from grape-juice the fermentation of which is checked by the addition of spirit. It is more a *Mistelle* than a wine, that is a sweet and alcoholic basis for the making of cordials and

'aperitifs'. The name also applies to highly fortified dessert Californian wines, made in the same way as white Port, that is fortified after fermentation has started.

ANGELUS, Clos de l'
A first growth of Saint-Emilion (Claret)

ANGLADE, Château d'
An important growth of the Entre-deux-Mers district of the Gironde; mostly red but also a little white wine.

ANGLUDET, Château
Bourgeois Supérieur growth of the Médoc; Cantenac Commune.

ANGOSTURA
A very popular brand of Bitters from the island of Trinidad.

ANIS
French for Aniseed. Used to flavour a number of liqueurs in France, Spain and Italy.

ANISETTE
The name of a number of French aniseed liqueurs.

ANJOU
One of the former Provinces of France now mostly the Maine-et-Loire Département. Its vineyards produce some red wines but a much greater quantity of white wines, some of which are wines of great distinction, as well as the most popular of French sparkling wines, after Champagne. See *Layon, Quarts de Chaume* and *Saumur*.

ANKER
The German and Dutch name of a wine measure equal to 7·561 gallons.

ANNEREAUX, Domaine des
An important growth of the Lalande-Pomerol district of the Gironde Départe-

ment, mostly red but also some white wines.

ANSEILLAN, Château d'
Bourgeois growth of the Médoc; Pauillac Commune.

ANTIGUA
One of the West Indies noted for its rum.

APÉRITIFS
A generic French name for all manner of fairly potent and often bitter drinks which are taken to stimulate one's appetite before meals.

APOSTLES
The twelve huge casks, containing old Hocks, in the municipal cellars of the town of Bremen.

APPELLATIONS CONTRÔLÉES
French quality wines, the standard of quality of which must conform to official ruling.

APPLE BRANDY or APPLE JACK
A colourless or pale-straw potable spirit distilled, usually at high strength, from cider. That which is distilled in Normandy is called *Calvados.*

APRE
French for 'hard', referring to a wine with an excess of tannin.

APREMONT
One of the lesser-known but most acceptable white wines of French Savoy.

APRICOT BRANDY
The national liqueur of Hungary. It is also made in England, France, Holland and Australia.

APRICOT GIN
Made in England from the ingredients named.

APRY
Distilled in Bordeaux from old brandy as a basis and flavouring of apricots.

APULIA
One of the more important wine-producing provinces of Italy.

AQUAVIT
See *Akvavit.*

ARAGON
One of the more important wine-producing parts of northern Spain.

ARBANATS, Château d'
One of the good white wine growths of the Graves de Bordeaux district; Arbanats Commune.

ARBIN
One of the few red wines of French Savoy; not particularly attractive.

ARBOIS
An attractive little town at the foot of the Juras; it is surrounded by vineyards which produce both white and *rosés* table wines; also some sparkling wines and dessert wines.

ARCHBISHOP
Sugared Claret made hot, with a clove-ridden apple steeped in. A cold winter's night comfort.

ARCHE, Château d'
A second growth of Sauternes.

ARCHE-PUGNEAU, Cru d'
One of the lesser growths of Sauternes, in the Commune of Preignac.

ARCHE-VIMENEY, Château d'
One of the smallest growths of Sauternes, in the Commune of Preignac.

ARCINS, Château d'
Bourgeois growth of the Médoc; Commune Arcins.

ARCINS, Domaine d'
Bourgeois growth of the Médoc; Commune Arcins.

ARDENAY
One of the few red wines of Lorraine; an *ordinaire*.

ARDILLATS
One of the red wines of Beaujolais which is popular locally.

ARENAS
The characteristic sandy soil in the area around Jerez where the lighter sherries are produced.

ARGENTINE WINES
The wines of the Argentine come mostly from the Provinces of Mendoza and San Juan, close to the Andes. There are red, white and *rosés* table wines, sparkling wines and dessert wines made in the Argentine, most of them from fair to middling in quality.

ARGILLIÉRES, Les
One of the best vineyards of two Communes of the Côte d'Or, Prémeaux and Pommard.

ARINTO
The name of the white grape from which Bucellas are made in the Tagus Valley, near Lisbon. It is also the name usually given in Portugal to *Bucellas*.

ARISTOPHANES (450–385 B.C.)
And dare you rail at wine's inventiveness?
I tell you nothing has such go as wine.
Why, look you now; 'tis when men drink they thrive,
Grow wealthy, speed their business, win their suits,
Make themselves happy, benefit their friends.
Go, fetch me out a stoup of wine, and let me
Moisten my wits, and utter something bright.
                Aristophanes, *The Knights*

ARISTOTLE (384–322 B.C.).
Founder of literary criticism, for twenty years Plato's disciple and a firm believer in wine. 'To know how to apply them (wine and honey) for the purposes of health, and to whom, and at what time, is as difficult as to be a physician.' *Nic. Ethics.* V. ix. 16 (Bohn).

ARMAGNAC
The Brandy distilled from wine of the Gers Département of France. The centre of the Armagnac district is Condom. The best Armagnac Brandies are distilled from the Bas-Armagnac wines, and are divided into three classes: *Grands, Fins,* and *Petits* Armagnacs. The Armagnac district is divided into (1) BAS-ARMAGNAC, from the Landes to the Gelize; (2) TANAREZE, from the Gelize to the Baize; (3) HAUT-ARMAGNAC, from the Baize to the Gers. Armagnac Brandy is usually distilled at lower strength than Cognac. Good Armagnac can be very good and much better than ordinary Cognac, but the best Armagnac cannot hope to approach—let alone rival the best Cognac.

ARMENS, Château d'
One of the minor growths of Saint-Emilion (Claret).

ARMSHEIM
One of the lesser growths of Rhine-Hesse, in the Oppenheim district (Hock).

ARNAUD-BLANC, Château
An important *Palus* growth of the Médoc, in the Commune of Margaux.

ARNAUD-JOUAN, Clos
A white wine growth of the Entre-deux-Mers district of the Gironde, in the Commune of Cadillac-sur-Garonne.

ARNAULD, Cru
Bourgeois growth of the Médoc; Commune Arcins.

ARNAVILLE
A Lorraine red wine from fair to middling in quality.

ARÔME or AROMA
Usually called bouquet.

ARRACK, ARACK
A fiery spirit distilled, formerly in the Dutch Indies and British India, from rice. But the name, qualified or not, has also often been used for 'native spirits'. Thus the *Pariah Arrack*, a spirit distilled from *Toddy*, the juice of the palm, drunk by the half-castes and lowest classes in India; *Batavia Arrack*, a spirit distilled from molasses with little cakes of dried Javanese rice added to the molasses. The worst *Arrack* of all is the *Tungusian Arrack*; it is distilled by the Tartars of Tungusia from fermented sour mare's milk. Although some *Arrack* is much worse than others, there is no *Arrack* pleasing to a cultivated palate.

ARROBA
A Spanish wine-measure equal to about 3½ gallons, except at Alicante where the Arroba is smaller (2½ gallons).

ARROPE
A syrup made from unfermented grape-juice (*must*) gently brought up to boiling point so that it can never ferment. It is used for sweetening Brown Sherries and other dessert wines.

ARROSÉE, Cru l'
A *premier cru* of Saint-Emilion (Claret).

ARS
One of the quite *ordinaire* white wines of Lorraine.

ARSAC, Château d'
Bourgeois growth of the Médoc; Arsac Commune, which adjoins Margaux. The vines of Château d'Arsac produce both red and white wines.

ARTABA
A Persian wine measure equal to 14·53 gallons.

ARVELETS, Les
One of the best vineyards of two Côte d'Or Communes, Fixin and Pommard (Red Burgundy).

ARVISIO
A Greek island producing a very potent wine.

ARZHEIM
One of the minor growths of the Palatinate producing both red and white wines of no great distinction.

ASPISHEIM
One of the less important growths of Rhine-Hesse, a little to the south-west of Bingen (Hock).

ASSMANNHAUSEN
One of the more important wine-producing parishes on the right bank of the Rhine (Rhinegau). It produces the best-known red wine of Germany.

ASTI
A town of Piedmont surrounded by a great many vineyards which produce very large quantities of white wines, both still and sparkling, but Asti is chiefly famous all the world over for its sparkling wine; *Asti Spumante*.

ASZTALI
Hungarian for *Vin ordinaire*.

ASZÚ
Hungarian for the better and sweeter grades of Tokay.

ATHOL-BROSE
Scotch liqueur-like drink made with whisky, honey, cream, etc., said to have been enjoyed by Queen Victoria and recently revived.

ATHOS, Mount (Hagion Oros)
A mountain of Greece where there has been, for many centuries, a monastery and a vineyard attached to it. The wine which is made by the monks from their own grapes may be tasted and purchased by visitors.

AUBANCE, Coteaux de l'
Some very fair, and often rather sweet, white wines are made from the grapes grown upon the hills on both banks of the Aubance river, one of the tributaries of the Loire.

AUBE
A French Département, which adjoins the Marne Département. Its vineyards produce mostly white wines, some of which are quite acceptable as sparkling wines, less distinguished and much less costly than Champagne.

AUDE
One of the three more important wine-producing Départements of France. Its vineyards produce enormous quantities of *ordinaires* wines, but also some of fine quality, both still and sparkling, mostly those of Limoux (sparkling), Corbières and Minervois.

AUENSTEIN
A Wurttemberg village, the vineyards of which produce a little white wine, a little more red wine, and a great deal of *Schillerwein*.

AUGENSCHEIMER
One of the minor growths of the Moselle opposite Trier.

AUGGEN
The largest wine-producing part of the Markgraflerland, in Baden.

AUM or OHM
Two names for the same German cask, similar to the French *barrique* or *pièce*, but rather smaller (160 litres or 35¼ gallons).

AUROS, Château d'
One of the more important Estates of the Bazadais (Gironde), producing both red and white Bordeaux, three times more white than red.

AURUM
A pale-gold liqueur with a brandy-cum-orange basis and flavoured with some of the wild flowers of the Abbruzzi. It is made at Pescara, Italy.

AUSBRUCH
A fine quality Tokay wine, although the word is German.

AUSLESE
German for 'selected', referring to the quality of the grapes specially chosen for picking and pressing at the time of the Vintage.

AUSONE, Châteaux
The *Premier* growth of Saint-Emilion (Claret).

AUSTRALIA
New South Wales is the cradle of the Australian viticulture, but it has been outpaced by Victoria, and above all by South Australia, which is responsible for nearly three-fourths of the Australian wine production. In both Queensland and Western Australia a little wine is also made, but not on a sufficiently important scale to provide wines for export. The principal types of Australian wines and

the chief centres of production are as follows:

(a) The Hunter River district (New South Wales); the Great Western and the Lilydale districts (Victoria) produce chiefly light beverage wines, suitable for local consumption.

(b) The Irrigation Areas, all along the borders of New South Wales, Victoria and South Australia, where the greatest quantities of wines are produced, mostly distilled into Brandy for fortifying 'sweet' wines.

(c) The Rutherglen and Corowa district, partly in New South Wales and partly in Victoria, which produce some of the best 'sweet' wines.

(d) The Watervale (Springvale) and other districts of South Australia, which produce the largest quantities of both sweet and dry wines suitable for export.

(e) The Queensland and Perth vineyards, which produce a limited quantity of both light and fortified wines.

AUSTRIA, Wines of

Although Austria does not produce any really great wines, there are many Austrian red and white table wines which are very attractive. The vineyards of Austria which are responsible for the best wines are those of Niederosterreich, Steiermark and Burgenland. The best Austrian red table wines are the *Voslauer* and *Falkensteiner*; the best-known white table wines those of *Grinzing, Kremser, Sievering, Nussdorf, Anninger, Perle* and *Gumpoldskirchen.*

AUVERNIER

One of the better-known vineyards of the Neuchatel Canton of Switzerland. It produces mostly white wines but also a tawny wine known as *Oeil de Perdrix.*

AUXERRE

The chief city of the Yonne Département; its vineyards produce a fair quantity of both red and white wines which are highly prized locally.

AUXEY-DURESSES

One of the smaller Communes of the Côte d'Or, adjoining that of Monthelie. It produces some red wines of fair quality.

AVELSBACHER

A pleasant, light, white Moselle wine from the vineyards of the Valley of the Avelsbach where this small river joins the Moselle, close to Trier.

AVENAY

A first growth of Champagne, upon the right bank of the river Marne above Epernay.

AVENSAN, Château d'

Bourgeois growth of the Médoc, in the Commune of Avensan which adjoins Margaux.

AVIZE

A first growth of Champagne, and the most important township of the white grapes district, known as Montagne des Blancs, east of Epernay.

AY

A first growth of Champagne and a quaint old little town on the right bank of the river Marne almost opposite Epernay.

AYLER

A white Saar wine from the vineyards of Ayl in the Saar Valley, immediately west of Saarburg.

AYSE

A small township of French Savoy; its vineyards produce a dry white wine highly prized locally.

AZUMBRE

A Spanish wine measure equal to one-eighth of the Arroba, or about two-thirds of a gallon.

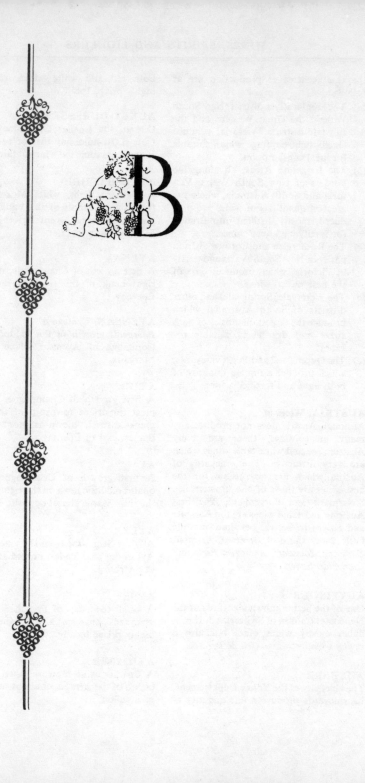

BACARDI
A brand of Cuban Rum.

BACHARACH
An ancient city on the left bank of the Rhine: white wines of moderate quality (Hock).

BADACSONY
A hilly district of Hungary which has long been famous for its wines, both white and red: these are usually sold with the name of the grape from which each is made, tacked on to *Badacsony*, their native vineyard, such as *Badacsony Rizling*, *Kéknyelu* or *Auvergnas Gris*, for the white wines, and *Badacsony Burgunder* for the red.

BADEN
A former Grand Duchy of Germany where there are still many vineyards but not as many as in the past. The vineyards responsible for the best wines of Baden are those of the Kaiserstuhl, of Brisgau, and of the Swiss frontier, which are known as *Seeweine*.

BAGATELLE, Château
There are two Châteaux of this name, one in the Commune of Saint-Estèphe, which produces none but White Bordeaux; the other is a small vineyard of the Graves de Bordeaux, in the Commune of Mérignac.

BAGATELLE, Domaine de
An Estate of the Entre-deux-Mers district of the Gironde Département, producing both Red and White Bordeaux.

BAGES
Bourgeois growth of the Médoc; Pauillac (Claret).

BAHLINGHEN
White wine from the Kaiserstuhl ridge, in Baden.

BALAC, Château
Bourgeois growth of the Médoc; Saint-Laurent. Mostly red, but also a little white wine.

BALATON, LAKE (Plattensee)
The centre of one of the more important white wine vineyards areas of Hungary.

BALEAU, Château
First growth of Saint-Emilion (Claret).

BALESTARD-LA-TONNELLE, Château
First growth of Saint-Emilion (Claret).

BALESTEY, Château
An Estate of the Cérons Commune, in the Graves de Bordeaux district, producing both white and red wines.

BALLAN
Red Touraine wine of fair quality from the Commune of Joué.

BALOGUES-HAUT-BAGES, Château
Bourgeois growth of the Médoc; Pauillac (Claret).

BALTHAZAR
A fancy name for a glass bottle large enough to hold sixteen ordinary bottles, or 2·75 gallons: it is mostly used as a 'dummy', empty, for show purposes.

BANDOL
A small port of the French Riviera, at the foot of a vineclad hill: its white wines are highly prized locally.

BANYULS
One of the best and better-known dessert wines of France; it is made from over-ripe grapes from the vineyards of Banyuls, a quaint and ancient little town by the Mediterranean at the eastern end of the Pyrénées, close to the Spanish frontier. There is a red wine and a *rosé* wine made from black grapes from the Banyuls vineyards, but both wines must be sold as *Grenache*; the name *Banyuls* is kept exclusively for the wine made from the white grapes of Banyuls.

BARACK PÁLINKA
An unsweetened spirit distilled in Hungary from apricots.

BARATEAU, Château
Bourgeois growth of the Médoc; Saint-Laurent (Claret).

BARBARESCO
A stoutish Italian red table wine made mostly from Niebbolo grapes from the hillside vineyards of the Monferrato district in Piedmont.

BARBERA
The name of a black grape extensively grown in Northern Italy, and also the name of the red table wines made therefrom. The best *Barbera* wine is made in the Province of Alessandria.

BARBERA AMABILE
A sweet red Italian wine which may or may not be made from Barbera grapes; it is not a wine of fine quality.

BARBERATI
Italian red table wines of the more *ordinaire* type; they are said to be made with *some* Barbera and other grapes.

BARBERONE
California red table wine made from Barbera grapes.

BARDOLINO
Italian red wine from the vineyards of the eastern shore of Lake Garda, in the Veneto Province.

BARI
Fairly dry white table wine of the *ordinaire* class, but the best white wine of Apulia (Italy).

BAROLO
Italian red table wine which has little nose but good body and an attractive quality. It is made from grapes grown in a district of Piedmont known as *Le Langhe*, which comprises the vineyards of Barolo and those of a few other localities in the immediate vicinity of Barolo.

BARRAIL, Château du
Bourgeois growth of the Médoc; Bégadan (Claret).

BARRAIL DE GORSSE, Château
Palus growth of the Médoc; Soussans (Claret).

BARREL
English wine cask, the contents of which differ a little in different parts of the country. In London, the Barrel is reckoned at 26¼ gallons, or two barrels to the hogshead.

BARRICA
Portuguese and Spanish for *Hogshead*.

BARRIL
Portuguese and Spanish for *Barrel*.

BARRIQUE
French for *Hogshead*. The contents of the Barrique vary from 56 gallons in Anjou to 50·246 gallons at Sauternes; 49·786 gallons at Bordeaux, for Claret; and 45·221 gallons in Burgundy, Champagne and the Charentes. In England, a Barrique is usually reckoned to contain roughly 50 gallons.

BARSAC
Important wine-producing Commune of the Gironde, much larger than the Commune of Sauternes, which it adjoins. The vineyards of Barsac produce a large quantity of sweet white wines of the Sauternes type, fair, fine and great in quality. The two great wines of Barsac are those of Château Coutet and Château Climens, which were placed among the *Premiers Crus* of Sauternes in the 1855 Classification. Second to these in point of excellence, the wines of Châteaux Doisy-Dubroca, Doisy-Daëne, Doisy-Védrines, de Myrat, Broustet-Nairac, Cantegril, Suau and Caillou rank as fine

wines. Among the less exalted and expensive white wines of Barsac, the following are well deserving of notice: Châteaux Camperos et Mayne-Bert, de Carles, de Rolland, Guiteronde, Piada and de Bastard.

BARTHEZ, Château
First growth of the Graves de Bordeaux; Gradignan (Claret).

BARTHEZ-PIAN-MÉDOC, Château
Bourgeois growth of the Médoc; Le Pian-Médoc (Claret).

BASILICATA
The southernmost wine-growing district of Continental Italy.

BASQUE, Le
Important wine-growing estate attached to the Château de Virelade, in the Arbanats Commune (Graves de Bordeaux).

BASQUE, Château le
Bourgeois growth of Puisseguin-Saint-Emilion (Claret).

BASTARD
A sweet Peninsular wine, either white or tawny, probably blended and sweetened by the vintners, who sold it in England, in Elizabethan days and earlier.
  Bastard was one of the wines familiar to Shakespeare:
Elbow. Nay, if there be no remedy for it, but that you will needs buy and sell men and women like beasts, we shall have all the world drink brown and white bastard.
        Measure for Measure,
            Act III, Scene ii.
Prince Henry. Why, then, your brown bastard is your only drink . . .
        First Part *Henry IV,*
            Act II, Scene iv.
Prince Henry. Score a pint of bastard in the Half-moon.
        First Part *Henry IV,*
            Act II, Scene iv.

BASTIA
The chief wine-producing centre of Corsica.

BASTOR-LAMONTAGNE, Château
Bourgeois Supérieur gɪ ɔwth of Sauternes; Preignac (white wine).

BATAILLEY, Château
Fifth 'Classed' growth of the Médoc; Pauillac (Claret).

BÂTARD-MONTRACHET
The name of a group of small vineyards partly in the Commune of Puligny-Montrachet (24 acres) and partly in the Commune of Chassagne-Montrachet (32 acres), which produce one of the best white Burgundies. The Bâtard-Montrachet vineyards are shared by a number of different owners, which accounts for the fact that some Bâtards-Montrachet of the same vintage may be and often are of different degrees of excellence.

BAUBENS-MONTAGNE, Château
Palus growth of the Médoc; Blanquefort (Claret).

BAVARIA
One of the more important wine-producing areas of Germany: its best vineyards are those of the Palatinate and Franconia.

BAZADAIS
Canton of the Gironde Département with many vineyards which are responsible for a great deal of *Bordeaux rouge.*

BÉARN
One of the smaller former Provinces of France, now the Département of the Basses Pyrénées, stretching from Pau to the Spanish frontier. Its many vineyards produce much wine, the best of which is the Jurançon.

BEAUCAIRE
One of the wine-producing localities of

the lower Rhône Valley (right bank). Its best-known wine is *Canteperdrix*.

BEAUGENCY
A wine-producing locality some twelve miles south-west of Orléans (Loire). Its red wines are today of the *ordinaire* class, but there was a time when they ranked among the best wines of France.

BEAUJEU
Formerly the metropolis of the Beaujolais and still an important mart for the Beaujolais wines. The *Hospice de Beaujeu* owns vineyards, like the *Hospices de Beaune*.

BEAUJOLAIS
A large wine-producing area which stretches south of the Mâconnais from Romanèche-Thorins (Saône-et-Loire) to below Villefranche (Rhône). Beaujolais produces a great deal of both red and white wines from middling to fair quality, but nothing like the quantities of wines sold, in Paris alone, under the immensely popular name of Beaujolais. The best known of the quality wines of Beaujolais are those of Moulin-à-Vent (red) and Pouilly-Fuissé (white).

BEAULIEU, Château
Bourgeois growth of the Médoc; Saint-Germain d'Esteuil; both red and white Bordeaux.

BEAULIEU, Château
Bourgeois growth of the Graves de Bordeaux; Cérons; White Graves.

BEAULIEU-sur-LAYON
A Commune of Maine-et-Loire; its vineyards produce some fine and rather sweet white wines sold as *Coteaux du Layon*.

BEAUMONT, Château
Bourgeois growth of the Médoc; Cussac (Claret).

BEAUMONT-en-VERNON
Loire Valley; red Touraine wine.

BEAUNE
An old walled city, in the heart of the Côte d'Or vineyards, and the home town of many important firms of Burgundy wine-merchants. The vineyards of Beaune produce a very large quantity of fine red wines and a very small quantity of white wines. Beaune has given its name to the Côte de Beaune, immediately south of the Côte de Nuits, as far and a little beyond Santenay, where the Côte d'Or Département ends and the Saône-et-Loire begins. Among the many fine red wines of the vineyards of Beaune, some of the better known are: Grèves, Fèves, Clos des Mouches, Clos du Roi, Marconnets, Bressandes, Cent-Vignes, Clos de la Mousse, Champimonts, Teurons, Aigrots, and a number of others. (See also *Hospices de Beaune*.) The less distinguished wines of Beaune and of other vineyards of the Côte de Beaune may be sold under the *Appellation Controlée Beaune-Villages*.

BEAUREGARD, Château
First growth of Pomerol (Claret).

BEAUSÉJOUR, Château
First growth of Saint-Emilion (Claret), now split into two Estates, one known as *Beauséjour* and the other as *Beauséjour-Duffau*. There are other Châteaux Beauséjour in the Gironde Département, two in the Médoc (Saint-Estèphe and Listrac); one in the Graves de Bordeaux (Villenave d'Ornon); and two in the Saint-Emilionnais.

BEAU-SITE, Château
Bourgeois growth of the Médoc; Saint-Estèphe (Claret).

BEBERAGEM
The rough red Portuguese wine given to

the men who work in the Wine Lodges (Oporto).

BECHTHEIM
A minor growth of Rhine-Hesse; Worms district (Hock).

BEER
The most popular thirst quenching beverage in all lands where there are no vineyards and where wine is accordingly too dear for most people for daily use. Beer is fermented from malted and hopped barley, and filtered or fined before being drunk. The taste, flavour and gravity (or alcoholic strength) of *Beer* depend upon the quality of the malt and that of the water used, in the first instance; then upon the manner and method of brewing, bottling and keeping.

Malt is obtained by wetting and spreading Barley on a floor, allowing it to germinate, when it is dried in a kiln. The method of drying the malt has much to do with the colour of the beer. The malt is then ground in a mill and becomes grist; the grist and plenty of hot water are mixed in a tub and become the mash —in the mash tub; hops are then put in, the wort is extracted from the mash and boiled with it, then cooled. The wort passes on into the fermenting tank. Yeast is then added and fermentation sets in; it produces carbonic acid gas, which loses itself in the air, and alcohol, which remains in what was the wort and now becomes *Beer*. Beer is then racked into casks or filled in bottles, and each brewer has his own method for fining, filtering, sweetening or not, dry-hopping or not, and otherwise giving the last 'finishing touch' to the Beer he is going to sell. The strength of the beer, of course, depends upon the proportion of water to malt; the more malt the greater the strength; the more water the milder the beer. The result of the late A. Chaston Chapman's analysis of a number of London and country brews of beer shows great differences in the strength of pre-war beers:

Alcoholic content by weight		
Type of Beer	*London*	*Country*
Strong ale and old ale	8·43	5·36
Bitter and pale ale ..	3·92	3·62
Stout and porter ..	3·75	3·45
	English	*Foreign*
Lager	4·03	3·54
Mild ale and table beer	3·03	3·33

BEERENAUSLESE
German for 'Selected berries', referring to a fine white wine made from the ripest and soundest berries picked out from each bunch of grapes at the time of the vintage.

BEESWING
Very fine floating crust peculiar to some old bottled Ports.

BEE WINE
The name given to a country home-made drink which was usually accepted as a 'soft' drink by teetotallers in spite of the fact that its alcoholic strength was higher than that of any Mild Ale. It was fermented from the *Ginger beer plant*, which is described in Johnson's Gardeners' Dictionary (1917) as a 'minute fungus capable of setting up alcoholic fermentation, and in different forms known as *Saccharomyces cervisiae* and *S. mycoderma*.'

BEILSTEIN
Important wine-producing locality of Wurttemberg; some white and some red wines, but mostly Schillerwein.

BEL-AIR
There are twenty-four Châteaux Bel-Air in the Gironde Département, including one in the Médoc (Blanquefort); five in the Graves de Bordeaux; six in the Saint-Emilionnais, Lalande-de-Pomerol and Frondsadais; and seven in the Entre-deux-Mers district.

BEL-AIR-MARQUIS-d'ALIGRE, Château
Bourgeois Supérieur growth of the Médoc; Soussans (Claret).

BELGRAVE, Château
Fifth *Cru Classé* of the Médoc; Saint-Laurent (Claret).

BELLEGRAVE
There are three *Bourgeois* growths Châteaux Bellegrave in the Médoc, in the Communes of Listrac, Pauillac and Valeyrac; and one in the Graves de Bordeaux, in the Commune of Pessac (Claret).

BELLET
The Commune of the Alpes-Maritimes Département which produces some fair red and white wines generally considered as the best of Provence.

BELLEVUE
There are several Châteaux Bellevue in the Gironde Département, one a *Bourgeois* growth of the Médoc, Macau; one a first growth of Saint-Emilion; one in the Blayais; one in the Commune of Saint-Magne, Saint-Emilionnais; and one in the Commune of La Brède, in the Graves de Bordeaux.

BELLEVUE-CORDEILLAN-BAGES, Château
Bourgeois growth of the Médoc; Pauillac (Claret).

BELLEVUE-SAINT-LAMBERT, Château
Bourgeois growth of the Médoc; Pauillac (Claret).

BEL-ORME-TRONQUOY-de-LALANDE, Château
Bourgeois growth of the Médoc; Saint-Seurin-de-Cadourne (Claret).

BÉNÉDICTINE
French liqueur which enjoys a world-wide reputation; it is made at Fécamp, in Normandy.

BENICARLOS
Very dark red wine of high-alcoholic strength from the vineyards of Castellon de la Plana, in the Province of Valencia, Eastern Spain.

BENSSE, Château de
Bourgeois growth of the Médoc; Prignac (Claret). Close to the Château, there is a *Cru* de Bensse vineyard.

BERGERAC
The centre of the best vineyards of the Dordogne Département. The wines of Bergerac are mostly dark red table wines, rather stout of body, satisfying but undistinguished.

BERGHEIM
Important village of Alsace; its vineyards produce much good white wine.

BERLIQUET, Château
First growth of Saint-Emilion (Claret).

BERNKASTEL
One of the most famous as well as one of the most picturesque little towns of the Middle Moselle, on the right bank of the river, joined by a bridge to its twin town of Cues on the opposite bank. The vineyards of Bernkastel produce much fine white wines, none better nor better known than the *Bernkasteler Doktor*. The famous *Doktor* vineyard (13 acres) is divided among three owners, the heirs of the late Dr. Thanish, Messrs. Deinhard, of Coblenz, and Messrs. Lauerberg. Other Bernkastel vineyards of repute: Schlossberg, Graben, Badstube, Pfaffenberg, Altenwald, Rosenberg and Lay.

BERNEX
A white Swiss wine of no particular distinction from the Canton of Geneva.

BERNON, Château
Bourgeois growth of the Médoc; Queyrac (Claret).

BERNONES, Château
Bourgeois growth of the Médoc; Cussac (Claret).

BESIGHEIM
Wine-producing locality of Wurttemberg, where the rivers Neckar and Enz meet (Hock).

BEYCHEVELLE, Château
Fourth *Cru Classé* of the Médoc; Saint-Julien-Beychevelle. In the seventeenth century, Château Beychevelle was the residence of the Grand Admiral of France, and all ships on their way to or from Bordeaux had to 'dip sail' as they sailed by, hence the name of *Baisse Voile*, or *Beychevelle*.

BÉZE, Clos de
The twin vineyard of Chambertin. The red wines of both Chambertin (32 acres) and Clos de Bèze (37 acres) are the best of the Commune of Gevrey-Chambertin, in the Côte d'Or, and are the peers of the greatest red Burgundies.

BIBLE WINES
The different wines which are named in the Bible are as follows:

Ahsis—A name used five times in Holy Writ for 'perfumed wine', or aromatic wine (Song of Songs viii, 2).

Khemer, Khamar—The poetical form of Yayin, Wine, used on eight different occasions (see Deut. xxxii, 14).

Khometz—The name for 'small wine', 'poor wine' or 'vinegar'.

Mesech—The Hebrew name for a mixture of wine and water, or wine and anything else.

Mimsach—A name which appears twice only; it has been translated as wine in Prov. xxiii, 30, and liqueur in Isaiah lxv, 11.

Schechar—A name used 23 times in Holy Writ for wine, more particularly in the sense of an intoxicating beverage (see Prov. xxxi, 6 and 7).

Soveh—A name used but three times for wine, but what type of wine was intended is not clear (see Isaiah i, 22).

Tirosh—Wine in the sense of new wine or sweet wine. It appears 38 times (see Joel ii, 24; Isaiah lxii, 8 and 9, etc.).

Yayin—The most commonly used name of wine; it appears 140 times (from Gen. ix, 21, the wine from Noah's vineyard, to Prov. xxi, 17).

BICHON-BAGES, Château
Bourgeois growth of the Médoc; Pauillac (Claret).

BIKADER
One of the darker and stouter of the red table wines of Hungary; from the vineyards of the Eger Valley.

BIN
The home given to bottled wines from the moment they have been bottled until wanted. When a wine is sold 'in bin' or 'ex bin', it means that the cost of packing and delivery are to be borne by the purchaser.

BINGEN
An important centre of the wine trade of Rhine-Hesse. The town stands on the left bank of the Rhine, where the Nahe flows into the Rhine, opposite Rüdesheim. The vineyards of Bingen produce some white wines from middling to fair in quality (Hock).

BIRKWEILER
One of the minor wine-producing localities of the Palatinate, in the Landau district (Hock).

BISHOP
The name given to a comforting wintertime drink, consisting of red Port made hot, sweetened with sugar-candy and flavoured with an orange, stuck with cloves, steeped in it.

BISMARCK
Another name for *Black Velvet*—half Champagne and half stout; a pick-me-up which Bismarck is said to have favoured.

BISSERSHEIM
A small but very ancient wine-producing locality of the Palatinate (Hock).

BITTERS
The generic name of a number of highly flavoured, pungent and bitter liquid compounds which are prepared from the roots, bark, fruits or leaves of various trees and plants, mostly from tropical or sub-tropical countries. Bitters are used to flavour drinks, long and short, and they bear the name either of whatever flavour may be their outstanding one (such as in *Orange Bitters*), or the registered name of the people who make them, such as *Dr. Siegert's Angostura*; *Amer Picon*, well-known French Bitter; *Fernet Branca*, well-known Italian Bitter.

BIZEAUDUN, Cru de
Bourgeois growth of the Médoc; Ludon (Claret).

BLACKBERRY CORDIAL
A Cordial compounded with spirit, crushed Blackberries and sugar.

Mash and strain berries through sieve; to 1 gallon juice add 1lb. sugar. Boil and add 1 tablespoon allspice and 1 tablespoon of cloves; cook till thick; when nearly cold, add 1 quart whisky or brandy; bottle and seal.

BLACKBERRY WINE
Take blackberries when they are fully ripe, bruise them, and put to every quart of berries a quart of water; mix them well, and let them stand one night; then strain them through a sieve, and to every gallon of liquor add two pounds and a half of sugar. When your sugar is dissolved, put it into your cask: to every 20 gallons of which add a gill of finings, and the next day bung it up. In two months bottle it.

BLACKCURRANT LIQUEUR
A Liqueur prepared from black currants, brandy and sugar: it is better known under its French name of *Cassis* (q.v.).

BLACK STRIPE
One wine glass of Santa Cruz rum; one tablespoonful of molasses. This drink can either be made in summer or winter. If the former season, mix in one tablespoonful of water, and cool with chipped ice; if in the latter, fill up the tumbler with boiling water. Grate a little nutmeg on top in either case.

BLAGNY
One of the quality white wines of Burgundy, from Puligny-Montrachet (Côte d'Or).

BLANC de BLANCS
A white sparkling Champagne made exclusively from white Pinot grapes.

BLANC FUMÉ
The best white wine of Pouilly-sur-Loire; made exclusively from Sauvignon grapes.

BLANCHOT
First growth of Chablis (White Burgundy).

BLANQUETTE de LIMOUX
One of the oldest sparkling white wines of France, from the vineyards of Limoux, near Carcassonne.

BLAYAIS
A large strip of vineyards below and above the town of Blaye, on the right bank of the River Gironde, some 30 miles from Bordeaux, opposite the Haut-Médoc. The vineyards of Blaye, or Blayais, produce a great deal of table wines, mostly red wines, of middling to fair quality.

BLEICHERT
The name of what little *Schillerwein* is made in Silesia.

BLOCKESBERG
Hungarian red table wine from the vineyards of Alderberg, near Budapest.

BOA VISTA
One of the famous Quintas or Estates of the Alto Douro. Its Ports of many classical vintages of the past were not blended with other wines of the Upper Douro, and they were sold under the Quinta's name with or without the Shipper's name.

BOAL
The Portuguese spelling of the Madeira grape and of the wine made from it, known in England as *Bual*.

BOCCALE
Italian wine measure which varies from place to place; the Turin *Boccale* holds 1·2 pint; the Florence *Boccale* 2 pints.

BOCK
The name, in Paris and many parts of France, for a half-pint of light beer served in a thick glass mug or tankard.

BOCK BEER
The name given in some States of the U.S.A. to a special brew of beer, brewed in the winter to be drunk in the following Spring. The first day of Spring is sometimes called—but not in strict temperance circles—*Bock Beer Day*.

BOCKELHEIMER
See *Niederhausen - Schlossbockelheimer a.d. Nahe*.

BOCKSBEUTEL
The flat-sided glass flagon of dark green glass in which most white wines of Franconia are bottled. It is often called *Boxbeutel* in England.

BOCKSTEIN
A very fine quality white wine from vineyards in the parish of Ockfen, in the Saar Valley; usually listed in England as a Moselle wine.

BODEGA
The Spanish name of a wine store or cellar. In England the name is often used for a wine bar.

BODENHEIM
One of the more important townships of Rhinehesse; its vineyards produce a great deal of white wines of fair quality.

BODY
In reference to wine, *body* (Fr. *Corps*) is a complimentary term; a wine lacking in body is light and dumb; a wine which has plenty of body possesses the right proportion of alcoholic strength and 'fruit'.

BOISMARTIN, Château
First growth of the Graves de Bordeaux; Léognan (Claret).

BOLZANO
See *Bozen*.

BOMMES
Commune of the Gironde which adjoins the Commune of Sauternes. Its best white wines are those of Châteaux La Tour Blanche, de Rayne-Vigneau, Lafaurie-Peyraguey, Rabaud-Promis, Sigalas-Rabaud, and Clos Haut-Peyraguey. Its less distinguished wines are sold as plain *Sauternes*.

BON-AIR-LA-TOUR-DU-PAPE, Château
Bourgeois growth of the Graves de Bordeaux; Mérignac (Claret).

BOND
With reference to wine, a *Bond* is not a contract but a cellar, store or vault, where wine and spirits are kept under Customs

and Excise supervision until such time as duty shall be paid when delivery will be granted.

BONNES MARES, Les
One of the larger and better vineyards of the Côte de Nuits, partly in the Commune of Morey-Saint-Denis, partly in the adjoining Commune of Chambolle-Musigny. *Bonnes Mares* of a good vintage is a very fine red Burgundy.

BONNEZEAUX
One of the best white wines of the Coteaux du Layon (Anjou).

BONNIGHEIM
A fair red table wine from the Besigheim district of Wurttemberg at the foot of the Michelsberg.

BORDEAUX
The metropolis of the Gironde Département, an important port of western France on the river Garonne, and the centre of the Bordeaux wine trade. *Bordeaux* is also the name of the less distinguished red (*Bordeaux rouge*) and white (*Bordeaux blanc*) wines of the Gironde. All the better quality wines of the Gironde are sold under the name of their native Commune (*Margaux, Saint-Estèphe, Saint-Julien, Saint-Emilion*, etc.), and all the best wines are sold under the name of their native Château, Clos, Cru or Domain.

BORJA
Full-bodied red wine from north-east Spain (Catalonia).

BOSA
A fair red wine of Sardinia.

BOSCO di CATANIA
One of the few red table wines of Sicily.

BOSENHEIM
A moderate quality growth of Rhinehesse (Hock).

BOTA
Spanish for *Butt*; the Sherry *Bota* or Butt holds 108 gallons.

BOTELHA
Portuguese for Bottle.

BOTELLA
Spanish for Bottle.

BOTTLES
Bottles are containers in which to store and carry liquids. The earliest bottles were made of skins sewn together, but the Ancients also had bottles made of stone, alabaster, glass, ivory, horn, silver and common earthenware. Modern wine-bottles are made of glass composed chiefly of silica, soda and lime in varying proportions. The shades of green of wine-bottles, other than plain white ones, are imparted by iron oxide. *Quart* and *Pint* bottles must, by law, contain a fourth and an eighth of a gallon, but the actual liquid contents of a 'bottle', 'half-bottle' or 'quarter-bottle' are not legally defined, a fact taken advantage of by some unscrupulous dealers in wine. According to current commercial usage, wine bottles should never appreciably vary from the accepted standard of contents of 26⅔ fluid ounces per reputed quart, or 6 quarts to the gallon, equal to 4 imperial quarts of 40 fluid ounces each. The more usual names of bottles in Great Britain, besides half-bottles and quarter-bottles, are the magnum (two bottles), double-magnum (four bottles), tappithen (three imperial quarts), imperial pint (three-quarters of the reputed quart or ordinary bottle). Outsize bottles, for show purposes more than for practical use:

	Bottles	Litres	Gallons
Jeroboam or Double-Magnum -	4	3·20	0·70
Rehoboam - - -	6	4·80	1·05
Methuselah - - -	8	6·40	1·40
Salmanazar - - -	12	9·60	2·10
Balthazar - - -	16	12·80	2·80
Nebuchadnezzar -	20	16·00	3·50

In France, the fluid contents of various bottles are fixed by law as follows:

	Centilitres	Gallon
Litre - - -	100	0·220
Champagne - -	80	0·176
Burgundy - -	80	0·176
Bordeaux - - -	75	0·165
Anjou - - -	75	0·165
Alsace - - -	72	0·158
St. Galmier - -	90	0·193
Vichy - - -	80	0·176
Vittel - - -	75	0·165

BOTTLE SICKNESS
A kind of distemper to which many red wines are subject from three to six months after being bottled; there is no other remedy for bottle sickness than *time*; leave the wine alone and it will soon pull itself together and get used to what is its first taste of close confinement.

BOTTLESCREW
The first name given to the Corkscrew in England.

BOTTOMS
The name of wine *lees* in the Wine Trade.

BOTZINGEN
One of the better growths of the Kaiserstuhl ridge, in Baden (Hock).

BOUCHÉ
French for bottled wine, literally *stoppered* or *corked wine*, but not *corky*.

BOUCHEAU, Ile
One of the islands of the river Gironde. There is in the island a Château Boucheau; undistinguished and inexpensive red wine (Claret).

BOUCHON
French for Cork.

BOUCHONNÉ
French for Corky, i.e., a wine tainted by a musty or otherwise defective cork.

BOUQUET
French for the discreet but very attractive fragrance which is one of the chief assets of all fine quality wines. Common wines have no *bouquet* and so long as they have no objectionable smell—musty, corky or vinegary—they are acceptable. Fine wines all should have not only a sweet fragrance but the characteristic *bouquet* of their grape and native vineyard.

BOUQUEYRAN, Château
Bourgeois growth of the Médoc; Moulis (Claret).

BOURBON WHISKY
A potable spirit which is distilled in Kentucky (U.S.A.) from a fermented mash of grain of which not less than 51 per cent must be maize.

BOURG. BOURGEAIS
Bourg is an ancient fortified city on the right bank of the Dordogne just before it joins the Gironde. *Bourgeais* is the name of the vineyards and other lands within the administrative bounds of Bourg. The better wines of the Bourgeais may be sold as *Vins de Bourg*, *Côtes de Bourg* or *Bourgeais*; the others as *Bordeaux rouge* and *Bordeaux blanc*.

BOURGOGNE
French for Burgundy, the French Province of that name and the wines from its vineyards.

BOURGUEIL
Usually considered to be the best red wine of Touraine; the best Bourgueil is from the vineyards of Saint-Nicolas-de-Bourgueil, in the Loire Valley, 25 miles west of Tours. Red Bourgueil should be drunk, like Beaujolais, fresh, not *chambré*

BOUSCAUT, Château du
First growth of the Graves de Bordeaux; Cadaujac (Claret and White Graves).

BOUTYLKA
Russian liquid measure: 1·35 pint.

BOUZERON
One of the lesser white Burgundies (Côte Chalonnaise).

BOUZY
First growth of Champagne, long famous for the excellence of its still red Champagne.

BOXBEUTEL
The usual English spelling of the German *Bocksbeutel* (q.v.).

BOYD-CANTENAC, Château
Third *Cru Classé* of the Médoc; Margaux (Claret).

BOZEN
An Austrian village of the Upper Adige Valley which became Italian after World War I and has been renamed Bolzano. Its best wine is a dry white wine formerly known as *Leitacher* and now called *Santa Giustina* or *Giustina-Leitach*.

BRACHETTO
One of the red *ordinaires* (table wines) of Piedmont.

BRACKENHEIM
One of the smaller wine-producing localities of Wurttemberg; mostly red wine.

BRANDY
A potable spirit distilled from wine, any wine, anywhere. In the British Isles, where French Brandy was the first and for a long time the only Brandy obtainable, *Brandy*, when not otherwise qualified, means French Brandy. Other Brandies are sold as Spanish, South African, etc. All the good, better and best Brandies are sold under the names or brands of the distillers responsible for the brandy in the bottle. (See also *Armagnac* and *Cognac*.)

Brandy Blazer—A glass of brandy, a lump of sugar, a piece of orange peel and one of lemon peel in a small pan; set alight for a few moments, stir and strain in a small, thick glass.

Brandy Cocktail—A glass of brandy, two dashes of Angostura Bitters, shake with cracked ice in a shaker and pour into a cocktail glass.

Brandy Crusta—Three parts brandy to one of *Maraschino*; add the juice of a lemon; shake with cracked ice and pour into a wine-glass; decorate with fresh fruit in season.

Brandy Daisy—Three parts brandy to one of raspberry syrup; add juice of half a lemon, half an orange, and half a lime; shake with cracked ice and pour in large tumbler, adding iced soda or fizzy lemonade according to taste before drinking.

Brandy Fix—A tablespoon of sugar, half a wineglass of water, the juice of half a lemon, in a large tumbler; add a wine-glass of brandy and some cracked ice; stir well with a spoon and decorate with fruit in season.

Brandy Flip—There are two versions, one cold and one hot. *Cold Brandy Flip*—Shake with cracked ice a glass of brandy, a tablespoon of sugar and one raw egg. Strain in a wine-glass and add a little grated nutmeg before serving. *Hot Brandy Flip*—Heat a wine-glass of brandy, one of water and sugar to taste; stir and when very hot pour into a thick tumbler; place a piece of toasted biscuit or pulled bread on top and grate a little nutmeg on it.

Brandy High-Ball—A large thick glass with a few lumps of ice in it; add as much brandy as desired, and fill with plain or aerated water to taste.

Brandy Julep—A tablespoon of sugar in a tall tumbler and a little water to dissolve the sugar; add four sprigs of fresh mint; then a wine-glass of brandy and a dash of rum; fill the glass with cracked ice; decorate with fruit in season; serve with straws.

Brandy Punch—One teaspoon of sugar; a little water to dissolve; one tablespoon of raspberry syrup; one-and-a-half glasses of brandy; the juice of a lemon; two slices of orange; a piece of pineapple. Fill the glass with cracked ice; stir well; dress with fruits in season; serve with straws.

Brandy Rickey—A wine-glass of brandy poured on ice in a tumbler; add juice of a lime; fill the glass with iced soda water; stir well; serve with straws.

Brandy Sangaree—Three parts of brandy to one of Port, poured upon cracked ice in a tumbler; sweeten to taste; stir well and strain into wine-glass.

Brandy Scaffa—Half brandy and half *Maraschino* with a dash or two of Angostura on top; serve in a cocktail glass.

Brandy Sling—A long iced drink of brandy and water, plain or aerated, with sugar to taste.

Brandy Sour—A tablespoon of sugar in a tumbler and enough water to dissolve it; add wine-glass of brandy and the juice of a lemon; a piece of ice or some shaved ice; stir well and serve in small tumblers.

Brandy Toddy—Brandy, with as much or as little sugar and hot water as each person may prefer.

BRANE-CANTENAC, Château
Second *Cru Classé* of the Médoc; Cantenac (Claret).

BRASENOSE ALE
The name given to a bowl containing three quarts of Ale, made hot, sweetened with sifted sugar, and with six roasted apples floating in it: it used to be brought in the refectory after dinner, and passed round, at Brasenose College, Oxford, on Shrove Tuesday.

BRANNTWEIN
German for *Brandy*.

BRAUNEBERGER
One of the most renowned white wines of the Mittel Mosel (Moselle).

BRAZZA
A small island off the Dalmatian coast; its vineyards produce a fair red table wine.

BREED
The quality of a fine wine which is the most difficult to describe; a wine which possesses 'breed', has a discreet but fragrant 'bouquet', perfect poise of 'body' and an attractively lingering 'farewell'.

BRESCIA
Lombardy city, the vineyards of which produce some of the best table wines of northern Italy.

BRESSANDES, Les
One of the better vineyards of Aloxe-Corton and also of Beaune (Red Burgundy).

BRETZENHEIM
One of the lesser growths of the Nahe Valley, near Kreuznach (Hock).

BREUIL, Château du
Bourgeois growth of the Médoc; Cissac (Claret). There is also a Château du Breuil in Anjou, which produces some fair white wines.

BRÉZÉ
Village near Saumur, in Anjou; its white wines are highly prized locally.

BRIEDEL
Village near Zell, Mittel Mosel; its wines are the peers of those of Zell (Moselle).

BRILLETTE, Château
Bourgeois growth of the Médoc; Moulis (Claret).

BRISACH
A little town of the Kaiserstuhl, in Baden; it gives its name to the district of Brisachgau (Anglice *Brisgau*). The Brisgau wines belong mostly to the *ordinaire* class.

BRISTOL CREAM
A dessert Sherry, of fine quality, sold by a Bristol firm, who have registered the name as one of their brands of Sherry.

BRISTOL MILK
A dessert Sherry of good quality sold by all Bristol wine-merchants.

BRITISH WINES
Imitation wines manufactured in the British Isles from grape-juice, raisins and other imported materials. They are known to the Excise authorities, for taxation purposes, as *Sweets*. The oldest *British Wines* were the *Home-made Wines*, which, in olden days, were the pride of the still-room in all great, and even modest, households. *Home-made Wines*, when they were made on a commercial scale, were first offered for sale under the name of *English Wines*. Both were made from the same materials, mostly the fruits, leaves, flowers, seeds and roots of English grown plants, such as elderberry, apples and pears, cowslips and gooseberries; but also from oversea produce, such as oranges and ginger, which were imported on a commercial scale into England from an early date. All such wines were mostly known under the names of the fruit or plant which formed their basis, but it was not at all uncommon to call some of them by the better-known or better-sounding name of some imported wine which they were intended to approximate. Thus was the *Gooseberry Wine* called *English Champagne*, and *Elderberry Wine*, *English Port*.

At present, however, the name *British Wines*, although it still covers *Home-*

made Wines and *English Wines*, applies chiefly to a more modern type of alcoholic beverages made in England on more scientific lines, since the early part of the twentieth century. These, the latest form of *British Wines*, are made from either grapes, raisins, grape-juice or grape-sugar, imported in various forms—solid, liquid or semi-liquid—to which water is added, then some form of yeast to secure the fermentation of the sugar content of the brew; the resulting alcoholic liquid is then coloured and flavoured to taste and with such skill that it has been calculated that not less than three out of every four bottles of wine sold in the British Isles are of this particular form of *British Wines*. Be that as it may, the figures published by the Treasury are there to show that the small Excise duty charged on *Sweets* brought in a greater revenue than the very high duties charged on imported wines.

BROCHON
A minor wine-producing Commune of the Côte d'Or, adjoining Gevrey-Chambertin; its wines are red, from middling to fair in quality (Burgundy).

BROLIO CHIANTI
One of the more dependable brands of Chianti (Italian red wine).

BRONI
One of the more popular table wines of Lombardy (red Italian wine).

BRONTE
The Sicilian locality from which Lord Nelson took his title; there used to be a brand of *Marsala* wine known as *Bronte*.

BROUILLY—Well-known Beaujolais red wine from the vineyards of *Brouilly*; the better quality of Brouilly wine is sold under the name of *Côte de Brouilly*.

BROUSTET-NAIRAC, Château
Second growth of Sauternes in the Commune of Barsac (white wines).

BROUZAC, Château
Palus growth of the Médoc; Cantenac (Claret).

BROWN, Domaine de
Bourgeois growth of the Graves de Bordeaux; Léognan (both red and white wines).

BROWN-CANTENAC, Château
See *Cantenac-Brown.*

BRUT
French for 'unsweetened', in reference to very dry Champagne. In practice, however, *Brut* Champagne may not be wholly unsweetened, but it should be drier than Champagne labelled Extra Dry or Dry.

BRUTTIG
A small village of the Lower Moselle, near Cochem; its vineyards produce white wines from middling to fair in quality.

BUAL
The usual English spelling of the Portuguese *Boal*, the name of one of the better quality grapes grown in the island of Madeira; also of the wine made from them.

BUCELLAS
A golden wine made from Arinto white grapes grown in the vineyards of Bucellas, a village near Lisbon.

BUCHERBURGER
One of the few red wines of Switzerland; St. Gall Canton.

BUCKHOLZ
One of the best white wines of Brisgau, in Baden (Hock).

BUDESHEIM
A village of Rhinenesse, in the foothills of the Scharlachberg Mountains overlooking Bingen, where the Nahe joins the Rhine. The wines of Budesheim are white and are sold as *Scharlachberger.*

BUHLERTAL
Red wine from the vineyards nearest to Baden-Baden.

BULLAY
A minor wine-producing locality of the Lower Moselle, near Zell.

BURCKHEIM
Ordinaire red wine from Baden (Germany).

BURGER
The name of a white grape extensively grown in Germany. Also the name of the white wine from the vineyards of Burg, in the Lower Moselle, near Zell.

BURGERBERG
A red wine from the Adlesberg mountain, near Budapest (Hungary).

BURGSPONHEIM
A village of the Nahe Valley, in the Kreuznach district (Hock).

BURGUNDY
The name of one of the more illustrious Provinces of France, and of the wines— red, white and *rosés*, still and sparkling— from its vineyards. When the former French Provinces were cut up into smaller Départements, Burgundy was divided into three Départements, the Yonne, in the north, where Chablis comes from; the Côte d'Or, in the centre, where the best red and white Burgundies come from; and the Saône-et-Loire, in the south, as well as a small part of the Rhône Département, where the Mâcon, Beaujolais and the less expensive red and white Burgundies come from.

The finest red Burgundies are usually accepted to be the following:

	Commune of
La Romanée Conti	Vosne-Romanée
Le Clos Vougeot	Vougeot
La Tâche ..	Vosne-Romanée
Le Richebourg ..	,,
La Romanée ..	,,

	Commune of
Le Chambertin ..	Gevrey-Chambertin
Le Musigny ..	Chambolle-Musigny
Le Clos de Tart..	Morey
Le Corton ..	Aloxe-Corton
Les St. Georges..	Nuits-St. Georges

Next come: *Les Bonnes Mares* and *Les Lambrays*, in the Commune of Morey; *Le Clos de Bèze*, in the Commune of Gevrey-Chambertin; and *Les Grands Echézeaux*, in the Commune of Flagey. Then come all the best vineyards of the Communes of the Côte de Beaune, i.e. Aloxe-Corton, Savigny, Beaune, Pommard, Volnay, Chassagne, Meursault, and Santenay.

BURGY
A white wine of the *ordinaire* class from Mâconnais vineyards (White Burgundy).

BURIGNON
A fair quality white wine from a vineyard of Chardonnes, in the Vaud Canton, which is the property of the City of Lausanne.

BURKHEIM
One of the wine-producing parishes of the Kaiserstuhl, in Brisgau (Baden).

BURRWEILER
A minor wine-producing parish of the Palatinate (Oberhaardt).

BUSHMILLS WHISKEY
A whiskey with a peculiar smoky flavour which is distilled in Northern Ireland.

BUTT
The English name of a Spanish and Portuguese cask holding 126 gallons; also the name of an English beer cask holding 108 gallons.

BUTTAFUOCO
A brilliant red Italian wine from vineyards in South Lombardy; it is rather sweet and quite undistinguished.

BUXY
One of the fair white wines of the Côte Chalonnaise (Burgundy).

BUZAU
One of the best wine-producing districts of Wallachia (Roumania).

BYRRH
A popular French *apéritif* made at Thuir, eastern Pyrénées.

BZENEC
One of the few important wine-producing localities of Czechoslovakia.

CABANNE, Cru
Palus growth of the Médoc; Macau (Claret).

CABANNIEUX, Château de
Bourgeois growth of the Graves de Bordeaux; Portets (Claret).

CABERNET
The family name of a number of black grapes extensively grown in many vinelands of the world for making quality red wines.

CABINET or KABINETTWEIN
Used for some of the finer Hocks, meaning 'Private Reserve'.

CADAUJAC, Château
Bourgeois growth of the Graves de Bordeaux; Cadaujac (Claret).

CADET, Château
Bourgeois growth of the Saint-Emilionnais; Saint-Geniès (Claret).

CADET-BON, Château
A first growth of Saint-Emilion (Claret).

CADET-PIOLA, Château
A first growth of Saint-Emilion (Claret)

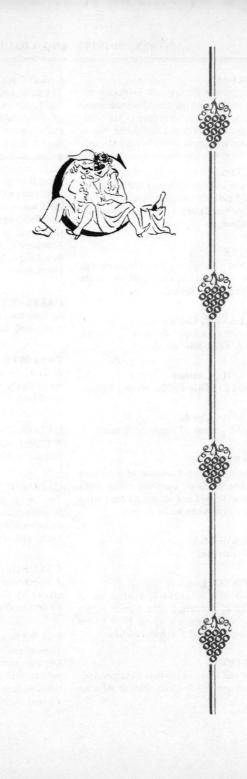

CADILLAC

A Commune of the Gironde Département on the right bank of the Garonne some 24 miles S.S.-E. of Bordeaux. Its vineyards produce both red and white wines, but more and better white wines than red.

CAGLIARI

The more important wine-producing district of Southern Sardinia; the best wines of its vineyards are known as *Rossi del Campidano*

CAHORS

The chief city of the Lot Département and the name of the very dark red table wine from the vineyards of the Lot.

CAILLAVET, Château de

Premières Côtes de Bordeaux; Capian (mostly White Bordeaux).

CAILLOU, Château

A second *Cru Classé* of Sauternes; Barsac.

CAILLOU, Cru de

A second growth of Pomerol (Claret).

CALABRIA

A wine-producing Province of southern Italy; the wines of Calabria range from *ordinaires* to *très ordinaires;* its only wine of any merit is the white *Gerace*.

CALCAVELLA

See *Carcavellos*.

CALDARO, Largo di

The red wine from the vineyards facing the lake of Caldero in the Upper Adige Valley; it was known up to 1919 by its Austrian name of *Kaltererseewein*.

CALEDON

One of the more important wine-producing districts of the Cape. (South African wines.)

CALIFORNIA

The most important of the wine-producing States of the U.S.A. The vineyards of California cover more than half a million acres given up to growing grapes to be dried for raisins, wine-making grapes and table or dessert grapes. The more important parts of California as regards viticulture are: the Coastal Range of northern California, where all the best table wines come from; the San Joaquin and the Sacramento Valleys of Southern California, as well as the counties of San Bernardino, Riverside, Los Angeles and San Diego, for raisins, table grapes and sweet wines.

CALISAYA

A Catalan digestive liqueur which is excessively bitter and full of quinine.

CALLISTE

A dark, sweetish and rather heavy wine which is the pride (vinously speaking) of the island of Santorin (Greece).

CALON-SÉGUR, Château

A third *Cru Classé* of the Médoc; Saint-Estèphe (Claret).

CALORIC PUNSCH

The most popular 'tonic' liqueur in Scandinavian countries. It is made in different manners, but rum is always its basis, and sugar.

CALUSO

A sweet white wine made from over-ripe grapes at Cana Vesano, near Ivrea, in Piedmont (Italy).

CALVADOS

The name of one of the Normandy Départements, and also the name of a potent spirit distilled from cider, in Normandy; it is the French version of the English *Applejack*.

CALVÉ-CROIZET-BAGES, Château
A fifth *Cru Classé* of the Médoc; Pauillac (Claret).

CALVI
One of the more important wine-producing parts of Corsica; its vineyards produce red, white and *rosés* table wines.

CAMA DE LOBOS
One of the best vineyards of Madeira.

CAMBON-LA-PELOUSE, Château
Bourgeois growth of the Médoc; Macau (Claret).

CAMENSAC, Château
A fifth *Cru Classé* of the Médoc; Saint-Laurent (Claret).

CAMPANIA
An important wine-producing Province of southern Italy; the most famous wine of Campania in Roman literature was the *Falernum*.

CAMPARI
One of the more popular Italian Bitters, and the bitterest of all. It is made in Milan.

CAMPEROS, Château
Bourgeois Supérieur growth of Barsac (White Bordeaux).

CAMPIDANO
One of the best wines of Sardinia from vineyards near Cagliari.

CANADA
Viticulture in Canada is severely hampered by the severity and length of the winters, which limit the choice of the vines and the ambition of the vintners; they make as good wine as they can, but they cannot hope to make any wine of real distinction.

CAÑADA
A Spanish liquid measure equal to 8·684 gallons.

CANARY ISLANDS
The Spaniards introduced viticulture in the Canary Islands in the sixteenth century and wine has been made ever since, more particularly in the larger islands. The wine of Palma was popular in England during the seventeenth century under the name of *Canary Sack*, and in the eighteenth as *Palma* and *Teneriffe* wines. There is much less wine made now in the Canary Islands and none of a quality that justifies its export to overseas markets.

CANARY WINE
One of the favourite wines of Shakespeare and Ben Jonson.

> *Host. . . . .* but, i'faith, you have drunk too much canaries; and that's a marvellous searching wine, and it perfumes the blood ere one can say, What's this?
> Second Part *King Henry IV*,
> Act II, Scene iv.

> *Host.* Farewell, my hearts, I will to my honest knight
> Falstaff, and drink canary with him.
> *Merry Wives of Windsor*,
> Act III, Scene ii.

> *Sir Andrew Ague-cheek.* Never in your life, I think; unless you see canary put me down.
> *Twelfth Night*, Act I, Scene iii.

CANDIA
See *Crete*.

CANELLI
One of the best wine-producing parts of the Monferrato hills; *Canelli* is one of the better red wines of Piedmont.

CANETTE or CANNETTE
A measure for bottled beer and wine in northern France and Belgium; equal to 1·842 pint at Lille; 1·583 at Valenciennes; and 1·388 at Tournai.

CANNETTO PAVESE
A small town of southern Lombardy and the name of a rather sweet red wine emanating from its vineyards.

CANON, Château
A first growth of Saint-Emilion (Claret). There is also a Château Canon in the Fronsac district which produces a red Bordeaux of more *ordinaire* quality.

CANON-LA-GAFFELIÈRE
A first growth of Saint-Emilion (Claret).

CANTARA
Another name for the Spanish wine measure *Arroba*; also for the Portuguese wine measure *Alquiera*.

CANTEBAU-COUHINS, Château
A first growth of Graves de Bordeaux; Villenave d'Ornon (White Bordeaux).

CANTEGRIL, Château
A second *Cru Classé* of Sauternes; Barsac. There is also a *Clos Cantegril* in the Cabanac Commune, Graves; its wines are white, drier and of the *ordinaire* class.

CANTEGRIVE, Cru
Palus growth of the Médoc; Macau (Claret).

CANTELOUP, Château
Bourgeois growth of the Médoc; Saint-Estèphe (Claret). There are six other Canteloup vineyards in the Gironde: Château Canteloup in the Graves de Bordeaux, which produces a little red and more white wine; Château Canteloup in the Entre-deux-Mers district, which produces some quite *ordinaire* red wines; another Château Canteloup in the Entre-deux-Mers, which produces a little red and much more white wines, both of the *ordinaire* class; Château de Canteloup also in the Entre-deux-Mers, which produces about the same quantity of both red and white *ordinaire* wines; and two *Crus Canteloup* in the Médoc, in the Communes of Arsac and Saint-Yzans, producing none but red wines, the first *ordinaire* and the second *très ordinaire*.

CANTEMERLE, Château
A fifth *Cru Classé* du Médoc; Macau. None but the finest Claret of the Cantemerle vineyards is sold under the name of Château Cantemerle; the next best is sold under the registered brand *Château Royal-Médoc*.

CANTENAC
A Commune of the Haut-Médoc. All the best wines of Cantenac are sold under the names of the Château of their birth; the others are sold under the better-known name of the adjoining Commune of Margaux.

CANTENAC, Château
A second growth of Saint-Emilion (Claret).

CANTENAC-BROWN, Château
A third *Cru Classé* du Médoc; Cantenac (Claret).

CANTEPERDRIX
The name of the best red table wine of Beaucaire (Languedoc).

CANZEM or KANZEM
A first growth of the Saar, in the Saarburg district (Moselle).

CAP CORSE
A French *Apéritif* made from some red wines of Cap Corse, in Corsica, doctored with quinine and herbs.

CAPBERN, Château
Bourgeois growth of the Médoc; Saint-Estèphe (Claret).

CAPBRETON
A red wine of the *ordinaire* class from the Dax district, south of Bordeaux.

CAP-DE-HAUT-BERGERON, Château
Bourgeois growth of the Médoc; Lamarque (Claret).

CAP-DE-MOURLIN, Château
A first growth of Saint-Emilion, the property of the Capdemourlin family to-day and during the past five hundred years (Claret).

CAPE WINES
See *South Africa*.

CAPERITIF
A South African *Apéritif* from the Cape; it is golden in colour.

CAPILLAIRE
French for Maidenhair Fern and also for a syrup flavoured with this fern, or some herbs; it is used to sweeten the commoner types of white wines, and various drinks.

CAPITEUX
French for 'heady' as applied to a wine not necessarily of exceptionally high strength, but aromatic and more likely to 'go to the head'. (*Caput*).

CAPRI
The white wines from the Italian isle of Capri; also from the mainland vineyards opposite Capri and from the neighbouring islands.

CAPRICOT
An English cordial or liqueur, golden in colour and with an apricot flavour.

CAPSULE
The metal cap which protects the cork of bottled wines from damp and insects.

CARAFFA
An Italian wine-measure equal to 1·164 pint, except at Naples where the Napolitan *Caraffa* is a little larger, i.e. 1·28 pint.

CARATELLO
One of the Italian (local) names for a *barile*, a barrel.

CARBONNIEUX, Château
A first growth of the Graves de Bordeaux in both the Léognan and Villenave d'Ornon Communes; its vineyards produce a great deal of both red and white wines of fine quality.

CARCAVELLOS
Both red and white wines from vineyards along the southern bank of the Tagus estuary, facing Lisbon.

CARDINAL, Clos du
Palus growth of the Médoc; Blanquefort (Claret).

CARDINAL-VILLEMAURINE, Château
A first growth of Saint-Emilion (Claret).

CAREMA
One of the better red wines of Piedmont; it is made from some of the Val d'Aosta vineyards.

CARIGLIANO
A Sicilian wine which enjoys some repute locally.

CARIGNANE
The name of a white grape, and also of a sweet white wine made from it in the eastern Pyrénées district of France.

CARIÑENA
A fairly sweet white dessert wine of the Madeira type which is made in the district of Saragossa (Spain).

CARLES, Château de
A second *Cru Classé* of Sauternes;
Barsac (White).

CARLOWITZ
The only Hungarian table wine which
was ever popular in England during the
'Sixties'.

CARMEIL, Château
A *Cru* of the Île du Nord of the Gironde,
producing mostly red wine; also a little
white wine, both in the *Bordeaux supérieur*
category. There is also a *Cru Carmeil* in
the Île du Nord producing red wine in
the plain *Bordeaux* class.

CARMEILH, Château
A *Cru* of the Île du Nord, in the Gironde,
producing more red wine than any of the
other growths of the Île du Nord. There
is also a *Cru Carmeilh* in the Île du Nord;
it produces about half the quantity of
red wine produced by the Château Carmeilh vineyards; the wines of both
Château and *Cru* Carmeilh are entitled
to the *Appellations controlées Bordeaux
supérieur* and *Bordeaux*.

CARMÉLINE
A French digestive liqueur, golden in
colour, of the Chartreuse type.

CARMES-HAUT-BRION, Château des
A first growth of the Graves de Bordeaux;
Pessac (Claret).

**CARONNE-SAINTE-JEMME,
Château**
Bourgeois growth of the Médoc; Saint-
Laurent (Claret).

CARRASSET, Château de
Bourgeois growth of the Médoc; Lamarque (Claret).

CARRUADES
The name of that part of the Château
Lafite vineyards which occupies the
higher ground and produces a wine not
always considered to be deserving of the
name of Château Lafite; it is then sold as
Carruades de Lafite and it costs less but
it is by no means an undistinguished wine
(Claret).

**CARRUADES D'ARMAILHACQ,
Cru des**
The wine of the Château Mouton-
d'Armailhacq which is not considered
quite up to the quality of the Château's
wine and is sold at a lower price (Claret).

CARTILLON, Château du
Bourgeois growth of the Médoc; Lamarque (Claret).

CASEL or KASEL
A first growth of the Ruwer Valley, near
Trèves or Trier (Moselle).

CASK
The generic name for a wine container
made of assembled and 'coopered' staves
of wood. The casks mostly used for storing wine are named Barrel, Butt, Hogshead, Pipe and Tun, in England.

CASSIS
The wine-producing Commune of the
Bouches-du-Rhône Département nearest
to Marseilles; it produces table wines,
red, white and *rosés* not of remarkable
quality but very pleasing and in great
demand on the Riviera.

CASSIS
French for black-currants, also the name
of a well-known French black-currant
liqueur and of a black-currant syrup.
The *Cassis de Dijon* is the most popular
Cassis in France.

CASTELL TOBLINO
The best *Vino Santo* of the Tyrol; a sweet
dessert wine.

CASTELLI DI JESI
An Italian table wine from some of the
Marche vineyards.

CASTELLI ROMANI
Italian table wines, mostly red, from the hillside vineyards of the hills nearest to Rome.

CASTELLO DI CANELLI
One of the few white table wines from the Monteferrato vineyards (Piedmont).

CASTELNAU
A Commune of the Haut-Médoc, the wines of which have acquired by long usage the right to be sold under the better-known name of the adjoining Commune of Listrac.

CASTELNAU-RIVIÈRE-BASSE
One of the best table wines of the Basque country, on the French side of the Pyrénées, from the vineyards of the Madiran district.

CASTELNAUD, Château
The name of the red table wine made from some black grapes of the Château de Suduiraut vineyards; one of the very few red wines of Sauternes.

CASTÉRA, Château du
Bourgeois growth of the Médoc; Saint-Germain d'Esteuil; its vineyards produce a great deal of white wine and a greater quantity of red, both entitled to the *Appellation Controlée Médoc*.

CASTIGLIONE FALETTO
The best red table wine of the parish of Faletto in the Le Langue district of Piedmont; it is entitled to be sold as *Barolo*.

CATALONIA
The second largest wine-producing Province of Spain. *Tarragona* is the best-known of the Catalan wines, in England, but the white wine of Alella, which is one of the favourite table wines in Barcelona, is now also exported.

CATAWBA
The name of one of the indigenous American vines, and also the name of the wine made from it in the Eastern States of the U.S.A.

CAUB or KAUB
One of the oldest wine marts of the Middle Rhine: its vineyards produce rather undistinguished white wines.

CAUDLE
Spiced hot wine given to women in childbed, in Shakespeare's time. It is also given to anybody suffering from a bad cold.

CELLAR
An underground storing place for wine; it is the anglicized form of the French *Cellier*, which is an overground store for wine as distinct from 'cave', a name used in English for a cavity or cavern. The necessity for wine to be stored underground is due to the fact that changes of temperature are bad for wine and a cellar should be deep enough not to be affected by heat in the summer and cold in the winter. Cellars in which wine is kept for any length of time should be airy and scrupulously clean; provided they possess both those qualities, it matters little whether they be damp or dry: damp encourages moulds, which hang to the roof of the cellar and may even grow on the bottles; but it does not encourage cork weevils which bore the corks and do irreparable harm.

CENTERBE
An Italian digestive liqueur in the making of which it is claimed a hundred different herbs are used.

CENTILITRE
French measure for the hundredth part of a litre, or 9·670 gills (British) and 0·358 fluid ounce (U.S.A.).

CEP
French for a vine-stock.

CÉPAGE
French for a species of vine.

CEPHALONIA
A Greek island the vineyards of which produce some light and fair red wines.

CERASELLA
A popular Italian Cherry Brandy Liqueur.

CERDON
A Commune of the Ain Département, the vineyards of which produce quite undistinguished table wines, and also a slightly sparkling *rosé* wine which looks like raspberry vinegar but is sweet and pleasant.

CERES
One of the important wine-growing districts of the Cape Province (South Africa).

CERIGO
A Greek island of the Ægean sea, off Cape Matapan, noted for its wines.

CÉRONS
The last Commune of the Graves de Bordeaux before coming to Barsac. Its vineyards produce mostly white wines, by no means dry but not so sweet as those of the adjoining Commune of Barsac.

CÉRONS, Château de et
CALVIMONT, Château de
Bourgeois growth of the Graves de Bordeaux; its vineyards, together with those of the adjoining *Grand Enclos du Château de Cérons*, are the most important of the Commune of Cérons: they produce some red wine but much more and better white.

CERTAN, Château
A first growth of Pomerol (Claret).

CESTAS, Château de
Bourgeois growth of the Graves de Bordeaux; Cestas (Claret).

CHABLIS
A small town of the Yonne Département. Its name is better known than most French towns of much greater importance: it owes this to the excellence and personality of the white wines of its vineyards. In France, Chablis is sold under four different *Appellations contrôlées*, according to their standard of quality:

1. *Chablis Grand Cru* or *Grands Chablis;*
2. *Chablis Premier Cru;*
3. *Chablis;*
4. *Petit Chablis*, or *Bourgogne des environs de Chablis.*

The *Grands Chablis* vineyards are *Blanchot, Les Clos, Valmur, Grenouilles* and *Vaudésir*; the *Premiers Crus* are *Preuze, La Moutonne, Vaulorent, Bougros, Fourchaume, Chapelot, Montée de Tonnerre* and *Mont de Milieu.*

CHACOLI
A sharp white wine made in Viscaya (Spain) from which some of the best Spanish Brandy is distilled.

CHAGNY
The northernmost Commune of Saône-et-Loire; its vineyards produce a little red wine, *très ordinaire*; also more and much better white wine (Burgundy).

CHAI
The Bordeaux name for *cellier*, above-ground cellar, where wine is stored before it is bottled.

CHAINTRÉ
Two white wines bear this name, a dry white Burgundy from Saône-et-Loire, and an Anjou wine which is a little sweeter from the Maine-et-Loire: both are wines of very fair quality.

CHALKIS
One of the more important wine-producing districts of Greece: its white wines are best.

CHALONS-SUR-SAÔNE
An industrial town on the river Saône, above Mâcon, and the metropolis of the Saône-et-Loire Département, immediately south of the Côte d'Or and north of the Rhône.

CHALONNAISE, La Côte
The continuation of the Côte de Beaune hills, in the north, as far as the hills of the Côte Mâconnaise, in the south. The vineyards of the Côte Chalonnaise produce a considerable quantity of *ordinaire* wines, mostly red, as well as some red and white wines of fine quality, none better than those of *Mercurey* (red), *Chagny* and *Rully* (white).

CHÂLONS-SUR-MARNE
The metropolis of the Marne Département and one of the more important centres of the Champagne Trade.

CHAMBERTIN
One of the more famous red Burgundies. A *Tête de Cuvée* of the Gevrey-Chambertin Commune; the Chambertin vineyards cover 32 acres divided among a dozen owners, which accounts for differences in the quality of *Chambertins* of the same vintage.

CHAMBÉRY
One of the old cities of Savoy: its vineyards produce mostly white wines, the best of them being the *Montmelian*, but Chambéry is better known for its Vermouth, the driest there is.

CHAMBOLLE-MUSIGNY
One of the more famous Communes of the Côte d'Or. Its most illustrious vineyard is Les Musigny, one vineyard only but divided into two very unequal parts by a small country road.

CHAMBRAY
A red wine of quite fair quality from the vineyards of Joué, in Touraine.

CHAMBRER
French for bringing up the temperature of a red table wine to the temperature of the dining-room. All too often, however, the English equivalent of *chambrer*, 'to take the chill off', means plunging a bottle of red wine into hot water, or putting it in front of a three-bar electric fire—which is murder: there is nought but a dull, flat, dead mulled wine left. A red wine which is too cold can always be warmed up gradually in the hollow of a warm human hand; but a wine which has been warmed up too much is ruined past all help.

CHAMPAGNE, La
One of the great Provinces of France which was cut up at the time of the French Revolution into smaller Départements, the Marne and Aube wholly, and parts of two others. The vineyards of the Marne produce wines of far higher standard of quality than all other Champagne vineyards.

CHAMPAGNE
The most famous of all sparkling wines. It is made from grapes grown within the limits of the four Champagne Départements, exclusively from Pinots grapes, and most of them black Pinots. The juice of black Pinots is white, and when the grapes are picked and pressed, at the vintage time, their white juice is run off immediately so as not to remain in contact with the bruised skins which contain the colouring red pigment responsible for the colour of all red wines. The bubbles in Champagne are not put into the wine: they are due to the fact that Champagne is made to go on fermenting after being bottled, and one of the by-products of fermentation is carbonic acid gas: as it cannot escape

it remains in solution in the wine of the securely corked Champagne bottle, but as soon as the cork is removed, the gas leaves the wine and escapes in the air: it carries with it the tiniest droplets of wine which are the 'bubbles'. Other wines, red, white and *rosés*, can be made and are made 'sparkling' by the *méthode champenoise*, that is in the same way as Champagne; or by pumping gas into them at the time of bottling. In all cases, the carbonic acid gas is the same, but everything else is different and the real Champagne, the sparkling wine from the Champagne vineyards, when good, is better than the best sparkling wines made anywhere else in the world, which usually cost less and are worth less.

CHAMPAGNE, Fine
French for a Cognac Brandy of fine quality.

CHAMPAGNE, Grande
That part of the Cognac vineyards responsible for the finest Brandy.

CHAMPAGNE, Petite
That part of the Cognac vineyards responsible for the next finest Brandy to the Grande Champagne Brandy.

CHAMPIGNY
A Touraine Commune, the vineyards of which produce a very fair red wine.

CHANTE-ALOUETTE
A vineyard of the Hermitage Hill, at Tain l'Ermitage; it produces a very good white Hermitage wine.

CHANTELLE
One of the more acceptable red wines of Auvergne.

CHANTURGNE
The red wine reputed to be the best of Auvergne wines.

CHAPTALISÉS, Vins (German: *Chaptalisieren Weine*)
Wines which have been 'assisted' at the vintage time by the addition of sugar to grapes considered lacking in sweetness, in order to raise the alcoholic strength of the wine after fermentation: the whole of the added sugar is eventually fermented so that it does not impart any degree of 'sweetness' to the wine. The process was introduced by Jean Antoine Chaptal (b. 1756, d. 1852), hence its name.

CHARLEMAGNE, Le
A *Tête de Cuvée* of the Aloxe-Corton Commune: its white wine is sold as Corton-Charlemagne. Le Charlemagne vineyard (42·5 acres) is shared by at least a dozen different owners.

CHARMES, Les
The name of two red Burgundy vineyards; the larger of the two is in the Commune of Gevrey-Chambertin (31 acres), and the smaller in the Commune of Chambolle-Musigny (14·5 acres): both are *Premières Cuvées* (Red Burgundy). There is also a *Première Cuvée* of Meursault usually known as *Meursault-Charmes*, but its real name is *Les Charmes Dessus* (39 acres). There is no Charmes vineyard in the Chablis country, and the wine sold as *Chablis Charmes* is just a nice name with no roots in any vineyard.

CHARNU
French for 'fleshy' in the sense of a wine which has a fairly big 'body' but sufficient acidity to avoid being coarse or corpulent.

CHARTREUSE
One of the most famous of all French liqueurs, which was made for a very long time by the Carthusian Monks of La Grande Chartreuse, near Grenoble: it is made in two colours, the yellow which is sweeter, and the green which is of a higher alcoholic strength than the yellow.

CHARTRONS, Clos des
A part of the vineyards of Château Lagrange, in the Commune of Saint-Julien, which produces red wine which is not entitled to the name of the Château and is sold under the name of this Clos (Claret).

CHASSAGNE-MONTRACHET
A Commune of the Côte d'Or, towards the southern end of the Côte de Beaune; its vineyards produce a small quantity of fine red Burgundy but a great deal more of very fine white Burgundy, including part of Le Montrachet and Bâtard-Montrachet.

CHASSELAS
The French name of one of the best white eating grapes and also of a white wine-making grape known in Germany as *Gutedel*, and in Switzerland as *Fendant*.

CHÂTEAU
French for Castle, in the vernacular; in the Gironde, however, *château* means the homestead of a wine-producing Estate, however modest it may be, sometimes even when there is no longer any homestead but only vineyards.

CHÂTEAU-BOTTLED
A wine which has been bottled where it was made, a fact which is recorded upon the wine's label as *Mise en bouteille du Château*, or *Mis en bouteilles au Château*. The Château bottling is a certificate of authenticity but not necessarily of better quality.

CHÂTEAU CHALON
The best and best-known white wines of the Jura Département; they are the best wines of the Communes of L'Étoile, Voiteur and Ménétrue, and in two styles, either as *Vin jaune*, which are austerely dry, or *Vin de paille*, which are rich and luscious.

CHÂTEAU GRILLET
A very fine white table wine from the vineyards of Condrieu, on the right bank of the Rhône, below Lyons.

CHÂTEAUMEILLANT
One of the few good red table wines of the former Province of Berry, now the Cher Département.

CHÂTEAUNEUF, Domaine de
Bourgeois growth of the Graves de Bordeaux; Léognan (Claret).

CHÂTEAUNEUF
Bourgeois growth of the Médoc; Lesparre (Claret).

CHÂTEAUNEUF-DU-PAPE
A very small town on the left bank of the Rhône, near Avignon, surrounded by very extensive vineyards which produce a considerable quantity of wines, mostly red, from fair to fine in quality.

CHÂTEAU-RENARD
One of the few red wines of Provence, from Arles vineyards, a little above the *ordinaire* class.

CHATELET, Cru le
A second growth of Saint-Emilion (Claret).

CHATELET, Domaine du
A first growth of Saint-Emilion (Claret).

CHATOLLE, Cru de la
Bourgeois growth of the Médoc; Saint-Laurent (Claret and a little White Bordeaux).

CHAUCER
Chaucer, the son of the King's Butler, loved wine and knew all about the wines of his day; as a matter of fact, it is to Chaucer that we owe much of what we know of the wines which were popular in England during the latter part of the

fourteenth century and early fifteenth century.

There were then, according to Chaucer, three distinct categories of wine, viz. beverage wines, dessert wines, and made or medicinal wines.

The beverage wines were known chiefly by their colour, as red, white, and claret. Red wines were mostly the very dark wines of Languedoc, whilst white wines came from La Rochelle or Nantes, being the produce of Angoumois, i.e. Charente, and Anjou vineyards. Claret, or Clairet, was the name given to the wines of Bordeaux, red wines which were not nearly so deep in colour as other red wines.

Must, or very new wine, is also considered by Chaucer as one of the beverage wines, wines for the thirsty, wines not to be sipped but swilled.

The dessert wines mentioned by Chaucer were, on the contrary, wines to be enjoyed when friend met friend, for pleasure's sake or hospitality. They were richer, stronger, and very much dearer than any of the red, white, or claret wines. They were brought chiefly by Venetians and Genoese to Southampton, Deal or London, where they were known under the following names:

Malvoisie or *Malmsey*, or *Candye*, from Cyprus.

Romany, Ribolle, Grenache, from Spain and Portugal.

Vernage from Florence.

Lepe, from Lepe, in Spain, between Moguer and Seville, now called Niebla.

In the third category we may include all the wines which were made up in England, being invariably sweetened with honey and flavoured with any and every kind of herb, seed or root; some of these had, and still have, marked medicinal properties, whilst others were supposed to possess, in Chaucer's time, the most uncanny virtues.

Chief among these queer wines was *Hippocras*, a name which covered a multitude of concoctions of which wine and honey were always at the base. Two other kinds of made or medicinal wines often named by Chaucer, *Piement* and *Clary* or *Clarree*, were also used chiefly for health's sake or for some dark ulterior motive.

CHAVIGNOL

One of the few white wines of distinction from the vineyards of the former Berry Province, now the Cher Département. There is also a Chavignol *rosé*.

CHEILLE

A fair Touraine red wine from the vineyards of Cheille, a Commune of the Indre-et-Loire Département.

CHÉNAS

A fair Beaujolais red wine from the vineyards of the Chénas Commune, which adjoins Romanêche-Thorins, in the Saône-et-Loire Département.

CHENÔVE

One of the less important Communes of the Côte d'Or: its vineyards produce some Red Burgundy from middling to fair in quality.

CHERRY BOUNCE

The name appears for the first time in William Robertson's *Phraseologia generalis*, in 1693, and, according to R. G. Latham's *Dictionary* (1866), *Cherry Bounce* was really *Cherry Brandy* renamed in order to avoid the Excise duty on Brandy. Thus, in *Poor Robin's Almanak* for 1740:

'Brandy ... if you chuse to drink it raw,
Mix sugar which it down will draw;
When men together these do flounce,
The call the liquor Cherry Bounce.'

N.M.P.

Cherry Bounce has ceased to be made or sold under that name for many years past, in England, but the name survives in the U.S.A., where it is given to a Cordial made as follows:

Strain the juice of the cherries through a coarse cloth, then boil it, and put in cinnamon, lemon peel, cloves, allspice, mace, and sugar (you are to be governed in the quantity of each by your taste). Then add one gallon of brandy to four of juice—at first it will be very strong, but in two months it will lose the strength and it will be necessary to add a quart of brandy to every four gallons of the bounce.—*Mrs. William Courtland Hart, Somerset County.*

CHERRY BRANDY
A Liqueur distilled from the juice of ripe cherries fermented with some of the cherry stones, crushed, as it is from these that a valuable oil is obtained which gives to *Cherry Brandy* its distinctive bitter almond finish. Cherry Brandy is more or less sweetened with sugar or glucose, according to methods favoured by different distillers, and it is also made without Brandy and Cherries, with any kind of spirit and flavouring essences. The best Cherry Brandy is made where cherries are most plentiful and cheapest, in Kent, and in Alsace and Germany, where it is called *Kirsch* or *Kirschwasser*. The best-known brand of Riga *Cherry Brandy* is called *Nalivka*.

CHERRY WHISKY
A liqueur or cordial made with whisky and cherries by a number of distillers and liqueurs compounders in England and in France.

CHEVAL BLANC, Château
The most famous first growth of Saint-Emilion, with Château Ausone (Claret).

CHEVALIER, Domaine de
A first growth of the Graves de Bordeaux: Léognan (Claret). There is also some white wine made which is good but not so fine a wine as the red: the white *Chevalier* is sold as *Château Chevalier.*

CHEVALIER-MONTRACHET
A vineyard (15·3 acres) of the Commune of Puligny-Montrachet producing some of the best white wines of Burgundy.

CHEVELU
A semi-sparkling white wine of Savoy, from the Ambérieu district.

CHIANTI
The best-known of Italian wines in Great Britain. It is made from a strictly de-limitated area of the Province of Siena, known as Chianti Ferrese. Chianti is mostly red, but a small quantity of white is made.

CHICHÉE
A small Commune of the Auxerre district in the Yonne Département; its vineyards produce a pleasant, light white wine of Chablis character.

CHICLANA
A white Cadiz wine of the *Manzanilla* type.

CHIGNIN
A white table wine from *ordinaire* to fair in quality from the vineyards of Chignin, south of Chambéry, in Savoy.

CHIGNY
A first growth of the Montagne de Reims (Champagne).

CHILE
The vineyards of Chile produce the best wines of South America, and a greater quantity of wine than all other South American Republics, the Argentine excepted.

CHINON
A picturesque old town some 30 miles west of Tours; its many vineyards produce some very fair red wines which are best served at cellar temperature rather than *Chambrés.*

CHIOS
A Greek island still producing much wine, none of which, however, deserves today the high praises which the Chian wines received from the poets of ancient Greece and Rome.

CHIROUBLES
A popular growth of the Beaujolais (Red Burgundy).

CHOPINE
French for Pint.

CHOPPIN
Old Scotch wine measure equal to a pint and a half.

CHOUILLY
A first growth of the Marne, between Épernay and Cramant (Champagne).

CHUSCLAN
A light red or *rosé* wine of the Côtes de Tavel vineyards, upon the right bank of the Rhône, in the Gard Département.

CINQUE-TERRE, Vini di
The only white wines of Liguria (Italy) of any distinction.

CISSAC
A Commune of the Haut-Médoc; its wines have acquired by long usage the right to be sold under the better-known name of the nearby Commune of Saint-Estèphe.

CITRAN, Château
Bourgeois growth of the Médoc; Avensan (Claret).

CITTA di SANT ANGELO
One of the best wine-producing areas of the Pescara Valley in the Abruzzi (Italy).

CLAIRET
A bastard Claret introduced after World War II, to compete with the red wines of Beaujolais which are acceptable at a very much earlier age than any Claret.

CLAIRETTE de DIE
A semi-sparkling light red wine from Die on the river Drôme in the Vaucluse Département.

CLAIRETTE de GAILLAC
A semi-sparkling rose-red wine from Gaillac, near Albi, in the Tarn Département of France.

CLARET
The name by which the red wines of Bordeaux have been known in England ever since the twelfth century. The name is also used to designate natural, red beverage wines from other wine-producing districts, but in all such cases Claret should be qualified, as Australian Claret, Spanish Claret, etc. Used without any such geographical qualification, the name Claret only applies to the red wines of Bordeaux, the most natural and the most wholesome of all wines. There is no wine other than Claret to possess so great a variety of styles and types, such perfection of poise and harmony between all that a wine should have: colour, bouquet, flavour and savour. (See *Bordeaux*.)

What was considered perfection in Claret in Shakespeare's time has been described by Gervase Markham in the *English House-Wife*: 'See that in your choice of Gascoine wines, you observe, that your Claret wines be faire coloured, and bright as a Ruby, not deep as an Amethest; for though it may show strength, yet it wanteth neatness: also let it be sweet as a Rose or a Violet, and in any case let it be short, for if it be long, then in no case meddle with it.'

> *Cade* . . . And here, sitting upon London stone, I charge and command that, at the city's cost, the pissing-conduit run nothing but claret wine this first year of our reign. . . .
> Second Part *Henry VI*.
> Act IV, Scene vi.

CLARETE
Spanish name for red table wines of Claret type.

CLARKE, Château
Bourgeois growth of the Médoc; Listrac (Claret).

CLARKE-MERLE-BLANC, Château
Bourgeois growth of the Médoc; Listrac (White Bordeaux).

CLERC-MILON-MONDOT, Château
Fifth *Cru Classé* of the Médoc; Pauillac (Claret).

CLIMAT
The Burgundy equivalent of the Bordeaux *Cru*, or Growth, i.e. an individual vineyard with a name of its own.

CLIMENS, Château
First *Cru Classé* of Sauternes; Barsac.

CLINET, Château
A first growth of Pomerol (Claret).

CLINET, Château de
Bourgeois growth of the Entre-duex-Mers (Red and White Bordeaux).

CLOCHER, Clos du
Bourgeois growth of the Médoc; Bégadan (Claret).

CLOS
The prefix to French vineyards which are or were once upon a time 'enclosed' by a wall or a fence. There is but one famous Claret *Clos*, the Clos Fourtet, at Saint-Emilion, but there are many *Clos* in Burgundy, such as:

Les Clos—One of the best wines of Chablis.
Clos Arlot—In the Prémeaux Commune, but entitled to be sold as Nuits-Saint-Georges.
Clos Blanc—First growth of Pommard (Red Burgundy).

Clos de Bèze—One of the two outstanding growths of Gevrey-Chambertin.
Clos des Mouches—One of the largest vineyards of Beaune; mostly red and a little white Burgundy.
Clos de Tart—One of the best growths of Morey-Saint-Denis.
Clos de Vougeot—The largest and most famous growth of the Côte de Nuits.
Clos de la Mousse—A small but very good growth of Beaune.
Clos des Lambrays—One of the best growths of Morey-Saint-Denis.
Clos du Roi—One of the best growths of Aloxe-Corton.
Clos Saint - Denis—Two Burgundy growths bear this name; in Morey-Saint-Denis and Flagey-Echézeaux.
Clos Saint-Jean—One of the best red wine growths of Chassagne-Montrachet.

CLOSERIE, La
Bourgeois growth of the Médoc; Moulis (Claret).

CLOSIOT, Château du
Bourgeois growth of Sauternes; Barsac.

CLÜSSERATH
One of the minor wine-producing parishes of the Upper Moselle, Trier district.

COBBLERS
The American name of iced and sweetened summer drinks made up with various wines or spirits and usually decorated with fruit or foliage.
'There are cobblers to eat and cobblers to drink, both as all-American as pie and circus lemonade, and made with many different kinds of fruits and berries.'
Here is a selection of 'Cobblers to drink':

Applejack Cobbler.
  1 jigger Applejack
  ½ teaspoonful lemon juice
  1 tablespoon orange juice
  1 tablespoon maraschino cherry liquor

Mix and serve in old-fashioned cocktail glass partly filled with shaved ice.

Champagne Cobbler. Put into a large tumbler 1 tablespoonful of icing sugar, then add a thin paring of lemon and orange peel; fill the tumbler one-third full of shaved or pounded ice, and the balance with champagne; stir with spoon, ornament with slices of lemon and berries in season, and place two straws in the glass.

Claret Cobbler. Fill goblet with fine ice; add ½ jigger Claret and ½ jigger syrup; stir and decorate with fruit.

Monongahela Cobbler. Put into a large tumbler one wine-glass of Bourbon whisky, one tablespoonful of icing or pounded sugar, one slice of lemon, and a slice of orange; fill up with shaved ice, shake well, and imbibe through two straws.—F.D.S.D.

Port Wine Cobbler. Fill goblet with fine ice; add ½ jigger syrup and 1½ jigger Port Wine. Stir and decorate with fruit.

Sherry Cobbler.
    2 oranges, sliced thin
    1 lemon, sliced thin
    Pineapple wedges
    1 cup powdered sugar
    Shaved ice
    1 cup Sherry
    2 cups cold water
    Berries to garnish
Lay oranges, lemon and pineapple in bottom of a bowl, alternating layers of fruit with sugar and shaved ice. Pour in Sherry and water. Stir well. Serve in goblets with a bit of each fruit in each drink, and an extra garnish of berries.

Whisky Cobbler. Fill goblet with fine ice; add 1 jigger Bourbon and ½ jigger Curaçao; also 1 slice lemon; stir and decorate with fruit.

COBLENCE
Also Coblenz and Koblenz. The chief centre, with Trier, of the Moselle Wine Trade. It stands on the Rhine and Moselle, where those two rivers meet.

COCHEM
Also Kochem. An important wine-producing parish of the Lower Moselle.

COCHYLIS
One of the worst scourges of European vineyards. The Cochylis moth lays its eggs in the wood of the vine and presently the grubs will attack one berry after another in each bunch of grapes.

COCK ALE
Take 10 gallons of Ale and a large cock, the older the better, parboil the cock, flay him, and stamp him in a stone mortar till his bones are broken (you must craw and gut him when you flay him), then put the cock into 2 quarts of Sack, and put to it 3 pounds of raisins of the sun, stoned, some blades of mace, and a few cloves; put all these into a canvas bag, and a little before you find the Ale has done working, put the bag and Ale together into a vessel; in a week or nine days' time bottle it up; fill the bottle but just above the neck, and give it the same time to ripen as other Ale.

COCKTAILS
The cocktail is intended to be like unto a bugle call to meals: it must not be sweet, nor warm, nor long, nor soft, but, on the contrary, in order to whet the appetite as well as stimulate conversation, it should be flavoursome, cold, spirity, and served in small glasses, one sip or two, and no more. One cocktail helps, two do not, and three harm the flow of gastric juices which should be summoned at the beginning of a meal. The difference between *Cocktails* and *Apéritifs* is chiefly that *Cocktails* are always mixtures of a number of different ingredients, so well blended together that not any one of them overshadows the other. This is why most *Cocktails* are energetically shaken in a specially-constructed 'shaker' before serving. The most popular *Cocktail* is probably the *Martini*, one of the simplest being half Gin and half French Vermouth

mixed. There are variants, however, such as the *Dry Martini*, with two-thirds Gin and one French Vermouth, and a dash of orange Bitters; the *Very Dry Martini*, with three-fourths Gin and one-fourth French Vermouth, and a dash of orange Bitters; the *Sweet Martini*, half Gin and half Italian Vermouth. Another simple Cocktail which is very popular in the U.S.A. is the *Manhattan*, two parts rye Whisky to one of Italian Vermouth, and a dash of Bitters. But the number of *Cocktails* has positively no limits since everyone is free to use one's imagination in the blending of various spirits, wines, flavourings and potable liquids of every description in the making of *Cocktails*.

Alabazam. One teaspoonful of Angostura bitters; 2 teaspoonfuls of orange Curaçao; 1 teaspoonful of white sugar; 1 teaspoonful of lemon juice; ½ a wine glass of brandy. Shake up well with fine ice and strain in a claret glass.

Alaska. A dash of Orange Bitters; ⅓ Yellow Chartreuse; ⅔ Old Tom Gin.

Alexander

(1) ⅓ Gin; ⅓ Crème de Cacao; ⅓ cream. Frappé.

(2) ¾ jigger Rye Whisky; ¼ jigger Bénédictine; twist orange peel on top. Stir.

Anderson. ¼ jigger Italian Vermouth; ¾ jigger Dry Gin. Orange peel; stir well.

Ardsley. Half Sloe Gin and half Calisaya well shaken together.

Astoria. 1 dash Orange Bitters; 1 jigger Apple Brandy; squeeze piece of lemon in mixing glass. Frappé.

Atta Boy. ½ French Vermouth; ⅔ dry Gin; 4 dashes Grenadine. Shake well and strain into cocktail glass.

Bacardi

½ Teaspoon granulated sugar
½ large or 1 small green lime (juice)
1 jigger Bacardi Gold Label Rum
Dash of Grenadine

First shake up lime juice, sugar and Grenadine until cold. Then put in the rum and shake until shaker frosts. Strain and serve.

Barney Barnato. Dash Angostura Bitters; 1 dash Curaçao; ½ Caperitif; ½ Brandy. Stir well and strain into cocktail glass.

Barracas. One-third Fernet-Branca and two-thirds Italian Vermouth well shaken.

Bishop Potter Cocktail. ½ dry Gin; ¼ French Vermouth; ¼ Italian Vermouth. Two dashes Orange Bitters and two dashes Calisaya. Shake well.

Biter. Four glasses of gin, two glasses of sweetened lemon-juice and two of *Chartreuse*. Add a dash of *Absinthe* just before shaking.

Black Hawk. 50 per cent Rye Whisky; 50 per cent Sloe Gin. Fill glass with ice. Stir, strain and serve in cocktail glass.

Black Mammy. To the juice of one grapefruit and one lemon add a strip of thin orange peel and a strip of thin lemon peel, one heaping teaspoonful of sugar, two cloves, three glasses of Santa Cruz Rum and one glass of Brandy. Ice well and shake.

Blackstone. ¼ jigger Italian Vermouth; ¼ jigger French Vermouth; ½ jigger Dry Gin; 1 piece orange peel; shake.

Blackthorne. 1 dash Orange Bitters; ⅓ jigger Italian Vermouth; ⅔ jigger Sloe Gin. Lemon Peel.

Blanche. ⅓ Cointreau; ⅓ Anisette; ⅓ White Curaçao. Shake well and strain into cocktail glass.

Blue Blazer.

1 teaspoon powdered sugar
2 jiggers Scotch Whisky
2 jiggers boiling water
Twist of lemon peel

Put sugar and Whisky in one metal mug and boiling water in another. Touch a match to the Whisky, and when it's blazing well pour rapidly into the boiling water, then back and forth between the mugs in one running flame of fire, 5 or 6 times, until the blaze dies down. Serve in a small thick glass and twist a tail of lemon over for zest.

Blue Train Special. Fill the shaker with cracked ice and pour into it 1 glass of Brandy and 1 glass of pineapple syrup. Shake carefully, and then add 3 glasses of Champagne. Give one or two more shakes and serve without further delay.

Booby. 1 jigger Gin; ½ jigger Grenadine Syrup; ¼ jigger Lime Juice; shake well.

Brant. 1 dash Angostura; ¼ jigger White Mint; ¾ jigger Brandy; lemon peel on top; shake.

Bronx. One of the most popular Cocktails. It was first compounded by Johnnie Solon at the Old Waldorf Bar, New York, and named by him after the Bronx Zoo. The original *Bronx* was made up of one-third orange juice and two-thirds Gin, and a dash of Italian and French Vermouths, but it has since become a blend of one-fourth French Vermouth, one-fourth Italian and one-half Gin; a piece of orange peel and iced.

Bronx Dry. ½ Dry Gin; ½ French Vermouth; 1 barspoonful orange juice; shake.

Brooklyn. 1 dash Amer Picon Bitters; 1 dash Maraschino; 50 per cent Rye Whisky; 50 per cent Italian Vermouth. Fill glass with ice. Stir, strain and serve.

Champagne. Place 1 lump of sugar saturated with dash of aromatic bitters in glass. Add cube of ice. Fill glass with chilled Champagne. Twist small piece of lemon rind over glass and insert.

Champs Elysées. Three glasses of Brandy, one of *Chartreuse* and one and a half of sweetened lemon juice, put in the shaker with a dash of *Angostura* Bitters.

Chantecler. A Bronx Cocktail with 4 dashes of Grenadine Syrup.—L.T.C.R.

Church Parade. ⅔ Plymouth Gin; ⅓ French Vermouth; 1 dash Orange Curaçao; 4 dashes orange juice. Shake well and strain into cocktail glass.

Clare. ½ jigger Sloe Gin; ½ jigger Italian Vermouth; dash of Brandy. Stir well.

Clove Leaf. Juice of half a lemon; white of 1 egg; 1 jigger Dry Gin; 1 barspoon raspberry syrup; shake well; serve with a spray of mint on top.

Clover Club.
   ½ jigger lemon juice
   1 jigger Dry Gin
   White of 1 egg
   1 teaspoonful Grenadine
Shake thoroughly with cracked ice and strain.

Columbus. ⅔ jigger French Vermouth; ⅓ Angostura Bitters; shake well.

Coomassie. Break the yolk of a new-laid egg into a small tumbler, and mix with it a teaspoonful of icing sugar; add 6 drops of Angostura Bitters, two-thirds of a wine-glass of Sherry, and one-third of a wine-glass of Brandy; fill the tumbler with shaved ice; shake well and strain; dust with a little nutmeg and cinnamon.

Covered Wagon.
   1 jigger Tequila
   1 pony French Vermouth
   ½ lime
   Dash of Grenadine
This modern Border Cocktail, with its romantic name, depends on the Mexican cactus or century plant liquor 'Tequila' for its kick, and that, in turn, has the kick of a new Mexican burro. It's a nice tipple if you can take it.

Cushman. 25 per cent French Vermouth; 75 per cent Dry Gin. Fill glass with ice, shake, strain and serve.

Daiquiri:
   Juice of ½ green lime, freshly expressed
   1 barspoon granulated sugar
Put some cracked ice in the shaker and shake until it gets cold. Add 1½ oz. White Label Cuban or Puerto Rico Rum. Shake until the shaker frosts. Strain and serve. *Important*: This Cocktail should be drunk immediately because the rum, lime and sugar tend to separate if the drink is allowed to stand.

Diana. Use Port Wine glass. Fill with shaved ice; fill glass ¾ full with white Crème de Menthe and top with Brandy.

Down. ⅔ Dry Gin; ¼ Italian Vermouth; 1 dash Orange Bitters. Stir and serve with an olive in the glass.

Dry Martini. ½ French Vermouth and ½ Dry Gin.

Dubonnet. ½ Dubonnet; ½ Dry Gin; 1 dash Orange Bitters.

Duchess. ⅓ French Vermouth; ⅓ Italian Vermouth; ⅓ Absinthe. Shake well.

Emmerson. ½ Italian Vermouth; ½ Old Tom Gin; 3 dashes of Maraschino and the juice of half a lime. Shake well.

Express. 1 dash Orange Bitters; ½ jigger Italian Vermouth; ½ jigger Scotch Whisky. Stir.

Fairbank's. Ten dashes Apricot Brandy; 1 jigger Rye Whisky; 1 dash Angostura Bitters; serve in old-fashioned glass.

Feather. ⅓ French Vermouth; ¾ Italian Vermouth; ½ Absinthe. Shake well.

Fifty-fifty. ½ Dry Gin; ½ French Vermouth. Shake well and strain into cocktail glass.

Frank Hill. ½ Cherry Brandy; ½ Cognac Brandy; a twist of lemon peel. Shake well.

Futurity. ½ Italian Vermouth; ½ Sloe Gin, 2 dashes Angostura Bitters. Stir well.

Gin. Dry Gin with a dash or two of Angostura Bitters.

Graham. ¼ French Vermouth; ¾ Italian Vermouth. Stir well, strain and serve.

Guggenheim. French Vermouth with two dashes of Fernet Branca and one of Orange Bitters.

Harvard.

⅔ Gin
⅓ French Vermouth
2 dashes Grenadine
1 dash Absinthe

Like Harvard Beets and Harvard Soup, the Harvard Cocktail carries out the crimson colour note, here furnished by Grenadine.

Holstein. ½ Cognac Brandy; ½ Blackberry Brandy; 1 dash Amer Picon.

Hunter. ⅔ Rye Whisky; ⅓ Cherry Brandy.

Iris. ⅓ lemon juice; ⅔ Gin; 1 barspoon sugar; shake well and serve with a sprig or two of mint.

Irving. ½ Dry Gin; ¼ French Vermouth; ¼ Calisaya; 1 slice orange.

Jack Rose.

½ large green lime (juice)
1 teaspoonful Grenadine
1 jigger Applejack

Shake thoroughly with cracked ice and strain.

Jack Zeller. ½ Old Tom Gin; ½ Dubonnet; stir.

Jenks. 1 dash Bénédictine; 50 per cent Italian Vermouth; 50 per cent Dry Gin. Fill glass with ice. Stir, strain and serve.

Jersey Lily: A *Martini* Cocktail served with a sprig or two of mint.

Jersey.

½ cup Cider
½ teaspoon sugar
3 or 4 dashes Bitters
Lemon peel

Mix and shake with ice. Twist lemon peel over top.

Jockey Club. 1 dash Orange Bitters; 1 dash Angostura Bitters; 2 dashes Crème de Noyeau; 4 dashes lemon juice; ¾ glass dry gin. Shake well and strain into cocktail glass.

Knickerbocker. 1 dash Italian Vermouth; ⅓ French Vermouth; ⅔ Dry Gin. Shake well and strain into cocktail glass. Squeeze lemon peel on top.

La Louisiane.

½ jigger simple syrup
1 dash Peychaud Bitters
1 dash Angostura Bitters
3 or 4 drops Absinthe
½ oz. Bénédictine
½ oz. Italian Vermouth
1 oz. Whisky

This is one of the reasons that people

still flock to La Louisiane Restaurant, founded in 1861.

Leonora. ½ Dry Gin; ¼ orange juice; ¼ raspberry syrup.

Loevi. ¼ jigger French Vermouth; ¼ jigger Orange Gin; ¼ jigger Dry Gin. Frappé.

Lone Tree. 2 dashes Orange Bitters; ⅓ Italian Vermouth; ⅓ French Vermouth; ⅓ Dry Gin. Shake well and strain into cocktail glass.

Lusitania. ⅔ French Vermouth; ⅓ Brandy; 1 dash Absinthe; 1 dash Orange Bitters.

McHenry. ½ Italian Vermouth; ½ Dry Gin; and 1 barspoonful Hungarian Apricot Brandy.

Manhattan.

1 jigger Rye Whisky
½ jigger Italian Vermouth
Dash of aromatic Bitters

Stir well with cracked ice and strain into cocktail glasses. Decorate with maraschino cherry.

Marquette. ⅓ Italian Vermouth; ⅔ Dry Gin; 1 dash Crème de Noyau.

Martini. ½ Italian Vermouth, ½ Dry Gin and a dash of Orange Bitters. Fill glass with cracked ice, stir, strain and serve.

Martini, Dry. ½ French Vermouth and ½ Dry Gin. Cracked ice; stir, strain and serve.

Merry Widow. 50 per cent Byrrh Wine; 50 per cent Dry Gin. Fill glass with ice; stir and strain in cocktail glass; twist of orange peel and serve.

Montana Club.

1 part Brandy
1 part French Vermouth
2 dashes Anisette

Half fill barglass with cracked ice, stir in ingredients, strain into cocktail glass and garnish with an olive.

Nicholas. 50 per cent Orange Gin; 50 per cent Sloe Gin. Fill glass with ice; stir, strain and serve.

Nielka. Put three glasses of Vodka into the shaker with two glasses of orange juice and one of French Vermouth. This is meant to be a very dry Cocktail but sugar may be added if desired.

North Pole. ½ jigger Dry Gin; ½ jigger Maraschino; the juice of half a lemon; the white of one egg well beaten. Shake well, strain and serve with whipped cream on top.

Old Fashioned. Put in an old-fashioned glass: 1 lump sugar muddled with ½ jigger water; 3 dashes aromatic Bitters and 1 jigger Rye Whisky. Add cube of ice. Stir a little. Garnish with slice of orange and a maraschino cherry. Twist thin pieces of lemon rind over glass and insert. Serve with stirrer.

Olympic. ⅓ orange juice; ⅓ Curaçao; ⅓ Brandy. Shake well and strain into cocktail glass.

Opera. ½ jigger Dubonnet; ½ jigger Dry Gin; 2 barspoons Crème de Mandarine; twist orange on top; shake, strain and serve.

Orgeat.

2 oz. Dry Gin
1 oz. Orgeat
1 oz. lemon juice
1 teaspoon sugar

Shake with ice, strain and serve.

Oyster Bay. 50 per cent Curaçao; 50 per cent Dry Gin; ½ glass ice. Shake, strain and serve.

Paradise. ⅔ Apricot Brandy; ⅓ gin; shake.

Peter Pan. ¼ Peach Bitters; ¼ Orange Juice; ¼ French Vermouth; ¼ Dry Gin. Shake well and strain into cocktail glass.

Ping Pong. ½ jigger Sloe Gin; ½ jigger Crème Yvette; 3 dashes lemon juice. Shake well.

Pink Gin. A glass of Dry Gin with a dash of Angostura Bitters. (No shaking.)

Pink Lady. ½ jigger Gin; ½ jigger Apple Jack; ½ jigger lime juice; 5 dashes Grenadine. Shake well.

Planter's Cocktails. Rum, lime juice, orange juice or lemon juice mixed in varying proportion and sweetened or not according to the taste or fancy of the mixer. Such are the different Cocktails known as *Planter's Cocktail* in the West Indies, where they are the most popular form of *Cocktail.*

Plaza. ¾ jigger Dry Gin; ¼ jigger Italian Vermouth; 1 slice pineapple. Shake.

Presidente.

1 jigger White Label rum
2 dashes Orange Curaçao
½ jigger French Vermouth
Dash of Grenadine

Add ice, shake well, and strain.

Prince. ⅓ jigger White Crème de Menthe; ⅓ jigger Dry Gin; ⅓ jigger Italian Vermouth. Shake.

Princeton. ⅔ Gin; ⅓ Port; 2 dashes Orange Bitters; 1 lemon peel, twisted over. Shake with ice.

Rob Roy. ½ jigger Scotch Whisky; ½ jigger Italian Vermouth; 2 dashes aromatic Bitters. Stir well with cracked ice and strain.

Ruby. ½ Sloe Gin; ½ French Vermouth; 2 dashes raspberry syrup.

Rue Royale. 2 ounces Dry Gin; 1 teaspoon milk; 3 dashes Anisette; 1 egg white. Shake with ice, strain and serve.

Salome. ¼ French Vermouth; ¼ Italian Vermouth; ½ Dry Gin; 2 dashes Orange Bitters. Well iced and served with 2 or 3 celery leaves.

Sazerac. Muddle ½ cube of sugar with a little water in mixing glass. Add ice, 1 jigger of rye whisky, 2 dashes Peychaud Bitters, and a twist of lemon peel. Stir until cold, then remove ice, add several drops of absinthe, and stir a little. Strain into a chilled glass and serve with iced water on the side.

Side Car. A Cocktail made up of ⅓ Cointreau Triple Sec, ⅓ Brandy and ⅓ Lemon Juice, all three well shaken with shaved ice, and strained into cocktail glasses.

Stinger. ½ jigger brandy; ½ jigger Crème de Menthe (white). Twist a thin piece of lemon rind over the mixing glass and insert. Shake thoroughly with cracked ice and strain.

Tango. 2 dashes Curaçao; the juice of ¼ Orange; ¼ French Vermouth; ¼ Italian Vermouth; ½ Dry Gin. Shake well and strain into cocktail glass.

Thorp Cocktail. 1 teaspoon sugar syrup; 1 teaspoon Orange Bitters; 5 teaspoons Old Tom Gin; 5 drops Noyau or Maraschino. Stir on ice with a spoon until thoroughly chilled and blended. The mixture must not be shaken, as that fills it with air. Lastly, take a piece of lemon just the size of a ten-cent piece, hold it over the cocktail and express a little of the oil, then drop it in the glass.

Tom and Gerry. 1 doz. eggs; 1 tablespoon sugar; 1½ tablespoons ground cloves; 1 tablespoon Allspice; 1½ tablespoons cinnamon; ½ cup Jamaica Rum.

Beat yolks and whites separately. Mix sugar with beaten yolks, whip in the whites, add spices and lastly rum. This is only the foundation. Put one tablespoon of it in a small thick cup, add 1 jigger of Bourbon whisky, and the same amount of boiling water. Stir until it froths, dust lightly with nutmeg.

Van Wyck. ½ jigger Sloe Gin; ½ jigger Dry Gin; 2 dashes Orange Bitters; Shake well.

Van Zondt. ½ jigger French Vermouth; jigger Dry Gin; 1 dash Apricot Brandy. Stir.

White Lady. ¼ Lemon juice; ¼ Cointreau; ½ Dry Gin. Shake well and strain into cocktail glass.

Yale. ½ Gin; ½ Italian Vermouth: a splash of seltzer; a squeeze of lemon peel on top.

COENEN or KOENEN

One of the smaller wine-producing localities of the lower Saar Valley, not far from Trier; its white wines are often rather sharp but they can be very nice when of a particular fine vintage.

COGNAC

The name of an old French city on the River Charente; also the name of the Brandy distilled from white wine made in a strictly delimitated area, of which Cognac is the centre. The soil of the vineyards nearer to Cognac is the richest in lime and it is from their wines that the finest Cognac is distilled; the very best of all from what is called the Grande Champagne vineyards, the next best from those of the Petite Champagne, and the next from those of the Borderies. There are a great many more vineyards to the west, north and east of Cognac which produce white wines from which much more Brandy is distilled, genuine Cognac but not of the same fine quality. The best Cognac is the best blend of brandies from those various Cognac vineyards. Time is also an important factor; not even pure Grande Champagne Cognac shows its worth as it leaves the still; it must be given time to grow and mellow in cask; once it is bottled the best thing to do is to drink it and enjoy it.

COINTREAU

One of the best-known French distillers of Liqueurs. Their best-known Liqueur is an Orange Curaçao sold in a distinctive square-shaped bottle under the name of *Triple Sec Cointreau*; it is colourless and has a pleasing orange flavour. The shape of the bottle and the label are always the same, but the alcoholic strength of the liqueur itself varies appreciably according to the country in which it is sold.

COLLARES

Beverage wines, mostly red, from the hillside vineyards of Cintra, near Lisbon.

COLOGNY

Swiss white wine of the *ordinaire* class from the vineyards of Cologny, in the Canton of Geneva.

COLOMBIER-MONEPLOU, Château du

Bourgeois growth of the Médoc; Pauillac (Claret).

COLONIE, Cru de la

The name under which is marketed the second best Claret from the vineyards of Château Malescot - Saint - Exupéry (Margaux).

COLOUR

The colour of wines and spirits is a matter of taste and, as such, a matter of importance; it is also a matter of fashion. Up to the first decade of the twentieth century, the demand, in England, was mostly for 'Old Gold' and 'Old Brown' Sherries, Vintage Port as black as night, deep amber Hocks and brown Brandy. But public taste gradually changed, and now demands 'paper-white' Hocks, pink or *rosé* red wines, tawny Ports, and the palest of pale Sherries and Brandies. All spirits being colourless as they leave the still, distillers, compounders and rectifiers have all the colours of the rainbow to play with, and give spirits, liqueurs and cordials any and every shade of colour likely to prove attractive, remembering that few people use their senses of taste and smell, and that whatever pleases the eye is almost certain to be a winner.

COMÈTE-LABARDE, La

Bourgeois growth of the Médoc; Labarde (Claret).

COMMANDERIA

A sweet wine which has long been regarded as the best dessert wine from the island of Cyprus.

COMMANDERIE, Château de la
Bourgeois growth of the Médoc; Saint-Estèphe (Claret). There is another Château of the same name in the Lalande-de-Pomerol Commune (Claret).

COMO
Greek fortified wine from the island of Syra.

CONDRIEU
Small town, some twenty miles south of Lyons, in the Rhône Département, on the right bank of the Rhône. Its vineyards produce a fair quantity of white wines of good quality and one of superlative excellence, Château Grillet.

CONEGLIANO
Large village north of Venice; its many vineyards produce some good white wines such as the Verdiso, which is dry, and the Prosecco, which is sweet; the red *Conegliano* wines are of the *ordinaire* class.

CONGIUS
A former Roman wine measure equal to an eighth of the Amphora, 0·70 gallon (British) or 3·18 litres.

CONSEILLANTE, Château la
First growth of Pomerol (Claret).

CONSTANT-BAGES-MONPELOU, Château
Bourgeois growth of the Médoc; Pauillac (Claret).

CONSTANTIA
The oldest and most famous of the wine-producing Estates of South Africa. Its vineyards were planted by Simon van der Stell, the Dutch Governor of the Cape, in the seventeenth century, and grapes are still being grown and wine is still being made at Groot Constantia, now State-owned, which is the original Estate; as well as at Klein Constantia and High Constantia, two privately owned adjoining properties. Early in the nineteenth century, when the Cape had been acquired from the Dutch by the English, a sweet dessert wine, made exclusively from small muscadelle grapes from the vineyards of Groot Constantia, was one of the most expensive and fashionable wines, not only in the British Isles but in Holland and also in France.

CONSUMO
The Portuguese name of table wines of the *ordinaire* class.

CONTHEY, Château
One of the better white wines of the Valais (Switzerland).

COOLERS
An American name for a number of 'long' drinks, always served in a tall glass with a lump of ice in it. Some of the more popular forms of *Coolers* are:

Ardsley. 1 jigger Tom Gin to a pint of ginger Ale, and decorated with a bunch of fresh mint.

Billy Taylor. 1 jigger Gin to a pint of Soda water and the juice of half a lime.

Blackstone. 1 jigger Jamaica Rum to a pint of Soda water; the rind of one lemon.

Bull Dog. 1 jigger Dry Gin to 1 pint Ginger Ale; the juice and rind of one Orange.

Bull Pup. 1 jigger Dry Gin to 1 pint of Ginger Ale; the juice of half a lemon.

Country Club. ½ jigger Grenadine syrup; ½ jigger French Vermouth to a pint of Soda Water.

Floradora. ½ jigger Dry Gin and ½ jigger Raspberry syrup to 1 pint Ginger Ale; also the juice of half a lime.

Khatura. ½ jigger French Vermouth; ½ jigger Italian Vermouth; ½ jigger Gin; 1 pint of Soda Water and 2 dashes of Angostura Bitters.

Mint. 1 bunch of fresh mint leaves lightly bruised in a pint of iced Ginger Ale.

Narragansett. 1 jigger Bourbon Whisky to 1 pint of Ginger Ale; the juice and rind of one orange.

Orange Blossom. 2 jiggers Orange juice; 1 jigger Gin; 1 small spoonful sugar; fill the glass with Seltzer water.

Robert E. Lee. 1 jigger Scotch Whisky; juice of half a lime; 2 dashes Absinthe; 1 pint dry Ginger Ale. Mix and stir with ice.

Sabbath. ½ jigger Brandy; ½ jigger Vermouth; the juice of half a lime; to 1 pint of Soda Water; decorate with fresh sprigs of mint.

Sea Side. 1 jigger Grenadine syrup to 1 pint Soda; juice of one lime.

White. ½ a jigger of Scotch Whisky to a bottle of Ginger Ale; the juice of half an orange, and a dash of Angostura Bitters.

CORBIN-ET-JEAN-FAURE, Château
A first growth of Saint-Emilion (Claret).

CORBIN-MICHOTTE, Château
A first growth of Saint-Emilion (Claret).

CORDIALS
Sweetened and variously flavoured spirits which owe their name to their real or supposed stimulating action upon the heart. Cordials are compounded, whereas spirits are distilled.

CORKED
Often and quite wrongly used in place of 'corky', a wine tainted by a defective cork; 'corked', of course, means a bottled wine before it is uncorked. Fr. *Bouché.*

CORKS
Bottle stoppers made of cork bark, the only substance known which will keep wine in a bottle without shutting off the oxygen of the air completely and without giving the wine any taste or smell.

CORKY
A wine spoilt beyond repair by a mouldy or otherwise objectionable smell and taste due to a defective cork. Fr. *Bouchonné.*

CORNAS
Commune on the right bank of the Rhône near Saint-Péray; its vineyards produce some fairly stout but by no means coarse red table wines of the red Hermitage type.

CORPS
French for 'body', which, when applied to wine, means rather stouter than most.

CORSÉ
French for 'full-bodied', referring to a wine of rather high alcoholic strength and full body, but well-balanced withal.

CORSICA
The largest of the French islands in the Mediterranean. Its vineyards produce an abundance of table wines, red, white and *rosés*, many of them most acceptable in Corsica itself, but none of them possessing really fine quality.

CORTAILLOD
The best of the few red table wines of the Canton of Neuchâtel (Switzerland).

CORTESE
The palest of the few white table wines of Piedmont, named after the Cortese white grape from which it is made.

CORTON, Le
Tête de Cuvée of Aloxe-Corton, Côte d'Or (Red Burgundy).

CORVO DI CASTELDACCIA
A golden and rather heady Sicilian wine of fine quality. There is also a red *Corvo* which is an *ordinaire* table wine.

COS D'ESTOURNEL, Château
A second *Cru Classé* of the Médoc; Saint-Estèphe (Claret).

COS LABORY
Fifth *Cru Classé* of the Médoc; Saint-Estèphe (Claret).

CÔTE DE BEAUNE
The vineyards of the southern half of the Côte d'Or, from Aloxe-Corton to Santenay.

CÔTE DE NUITS
The vineyards of the northern half of the Côte d'Or from Marsannay-la-Côte to Comblanchien.

CÔTE D'OR
A French Département which may be called the golden heart of the vinelands of Burgundy. Its chief city is Dijon, but Beaune and Nuits-Saint-Georges are more vinously famous. The vineyards of the Côte de Nuits produce the finest red wines of Burgundy; those of the Côte de Beaune are responsible for a greater quantity of red Burgundy of fine quality and a much greater quantity of white Burgundy, some of which are acknowledged as the finest of all French white wines.

CÔTE RÔTIE
The name of the hill above the little town of Ampuis, on the right bank of the Rhône, south of Lyons. Also the name of the red wines made from the vineyards of the Côte Rôtie; these are divided into two parts known as Côte Brune and Côte Blonde, both producing red wine of high quality, but the Côte Brune wine is regarded as the better of the two.

CÔTEAUX DE LA LOIRE, Vins des
White wines from the hillside vineyards upon both banks of the Loire in the Maine-et-Loire Département, formerly Anjou. *La Coulée de Sarrant, La Roche aux Moines,* and *Château de Savennières* are among the more attractive of these light and fruity Loire wines.

CÔTEAUX DU LAYON, Vins des
The white wines, many of them quite charming table wines, from the hillside vineyards of both banks of the river Layon during the latter part of its course, before it flows into the Loire. The best-known Côteaux du Layon wine is the *Quarts de Chaume.*

CÔTES, Vins de
Wines from hillside vineyards, as opposed to *Vins de Plaine,* which are never so good.

CÔTES DU RHÔNE
A name allowed to any wine which comes from vineyards of the Rhône Valley from Ampuis, below Lyons, to Tavel, opposite Avignon. There are more and better red than white *Côtes du Rhône* wines, but all the best wines bear the name of their native vineyard, i.e. *Côte Rôtie, Hermitage, Cornas, Châteauneuf-du-Pape, Tavel,* etc.

COUFFRAN, Château
Bourgeois growth of the Médoc; Saint-Seurin de Cadourne (Claret).

COUHINS, Château
Bourgeois Supérieur growth of the Graves de Bordeaux; Villenave d'Ornon (Claret).

COULÉE DE SARRANT
One of the most charming light and naturally sweet white wines of Anjou (Côteaux de la Loire).

COUPE
French for Cup.

COUPÉ
French for Cut, in the sense of a wine blended with another; also means watered wine.

COUPERIE, Château
Second growth of Saint-Emilion (Claret).

COURONNE, Château la
Bourgeois Supérieur growth of the Médoc; Pauillac (Claret).

COUTELIN-MERVILLE, Cru
Bourgeois growth of the Médoc; Saint-Estèphe (Claret).

COUTET, Château
There are two Châteaux of this name in the Gironde, one is a first growth of Saint-Emilion (Claret), and the other a first *Cru Classé* of Sauternes; Barsac (white wine).

COUVENT, Clos du
First growth of Saint-Emilion (Claret).

CRAMANT
First growth of the Côte des Blancs, near Avize (Champagne).

CRÉMANT
French for creaming, meaning just a little lively, not fully sparkling; not even *pétillant*, or half sparkling.

CRÈME
When applied to liqueurs, mostly French ones, *Crème* denotes a more than usual degree of sweetness; it is followed by the name of the fruit or plant responsible for its informing flavour, such as:

Crème d'Ananas. A sweet liqueur the informing flavour of which is that of pineapples.

Crème de Bananes. A sweet liqueur the informing flavour of which is that of bananas.

Crème de Cacao. A sweet liqueur the informing flavour of which is that of cocoa and vanilla. The name *Chouao* on the label of this liqueur is that of the Chouao district of Venezuela, which is renowned for the excellence of its cocoa.

Crème de Cassis. A sweet liqueur the informing flavour of which is that of black currants.

Crème de Fraises. A sweet liqueur the informing flavour of which is that of strawberries.

Crème de Framboises. A sweet liqueur the informing flavour of which is that of raspberries.

Crème de Menthe. A sweet liqueur the informing flavour of which is that of mint. It is one of the most popular of all liqueurs, and there are many different brands of it, many of them coloured green, but a few of them pure white.

Crème de Moka. A sweet liqueur flavoured with coffee.

Crème de Noyau. A sweet liqueur the informing flavour of which is that of the crushed kernels of stone fruit, mostly cherries.

Crème de Vanille. A sweet liqueur the informing flavour of which is that of vanilla.

Crème de Violette. A sweet liqueur the informing flavour of which is that of violets.

Crème Yvette. A sweet liqueur, violet in colour, which was distilled in Connecticut, U.S.A.

There are also *Crèmes de Cumin, de Prunelle, de Roses, de Thé*, etc.

CROCK, Château le
Bourgeois growth of the Médoc; Saint-Estèphe (Claret).

CROIX, Château la
There are two Châteaux La Croix in the Gironde; one is a first growth of Pomerol and the other a *Bourgeois* growth of the Entre-deux-Mers (Claret).

CROIX-BLANCHE, La
One of the few white wines of the Ludon Commune (Haut-Médoc).

CROIX-DE-GAY, La
A first growth of Pomerol (Claret).

CROIX-DE-MERLET, Domaine de la
Bourgeois growth of the Blayais (Claret).

CROIX-ROUGE, La
Palus growth of the Ludon Commune
(Claret).

CROIZET-BAGES
See *Château Calvé-Croizet-Bages.*

CROQUE-MICHOTTE, Château
First growth of the Graves de Saint-
Emilion (Claret).

CRÖV or KRÖV-KÖVERING
One of the important villages of the
Mittel Mosel near Bernkastel; its vineyards produce some very attractive white
wines.

CROZES
An important Commune of the Rhône
valley in the Drôme Département, near
the Hermitage Hill; its vineyards produce
both red and white wines, more and
better reds than whites.

CRUSCAUT, Château
Bourgeois growth of the Médoc; Saint-
Laurent (Claret).

CRUSSAL
One of the better table white wines from
the Rhône Valley, from vineyards near
Saint-Péray.

CRUST
A fairly hard sediment, chiefly tartrates
which red wines cast off as they age in
bottle; crust should adhere to the glass
of the bottle when the wine is decanted
with care.

CRUSTAS
An American name, the origin of which
is obscure, for an elaborate cocktail.
  Gin Crusta. Put into a small tumbler
30 drops of gum, 10 drops of Angostura
Bitters, a wine-glass of London Gin, and

10 drops of Curaçao; fill one-third with
ice; shake well, and strain into a coloured
wine-glass; pare half a lemon in one piece
and place the paring round the rim, after
damping with juice of lemon, and frost-
ing by dipping the edge of the glass in
sugar.

CRUSTING PORT
A vintage-type, full-bodied red Port,
bottled early and given time to mature
in bottle. When the wine is bottled and
'binned' for the first time, a splash of
whitewash over the punt of the bottle
makes it easy to tell ever after how the
bottle was first laid down, hence where
the 'crust', as well as any loose sediment,
will be in the course of time. Whenever
the wine may be moved from one cellar
to another, it must always be binned
again with the splash uppermost; also
when the wine is eventually decanted.

CRUZEAU, Château
Bourgeois growth Sables de Saint-
Emilion (Claret).

CSOPAKI FURMINT
One of the better white table wines of
Hungary: it is made from Furmint grapes
grown in some of the Csopak vineyards
of the Balaton district.

CUJAC, Château de
Bourgeois growth of the Médoc; Saint-
Aubin (both Red and White Bordeaux).

CUMIÈRES
One of the good growths of the Marne
Valley (Champagne).

CUPS
Summer drinks prepared in large jugs
and made up of any kind of wine watered
down by ice, soda, or seltzer, with the
addition of some spirit—usually Brandy
or Gin—one or two or even more sweet
liqueurs, that bring strength and flavour
to the *Cup.* Sprigs of mint or borage and
some cucumber rind, as well as grapes,

strawberries and pieces of other fruit, are added to make the *Cup* more attractive.

Badminton Cup. Peel half a middle-sized cucumber, and put it into a silver cup or bowl with 4 oz. icing sugar, juice of a lemon, a little nutmeg, half a glass of Curaçao, and a bottle of Claret; when the sugar is thoroughly dissolved, pour in a bottle of soda-water, ice, and it is ready for use. A couple of sprigs of borage is an improvement when obtainable.

Balaclava. Throw into a large bowl the thinly-pared rind of half a lemon, add 2 tablespoonfuls of icing sugar, the juice of 2 lemons, and the half of a small cucumber cut into thin slices with the peel on. Mix well; then add two bottles of Soda-water, two bottles of Claret and one of Champagne; stir well together; add a small piece of balm, put in a small block of ice, and serve.

Bull's Eye. One pint sparkling Cider. 1 pint Ginger Ale; 1 jigger Brandy.

Burgundy Cup. The same as Claret Cup, using red Burgundy in place of Claret. Good Burgundy, however, is too dear and too good for a Cup, whilst cheap Burgundy is usually not worth buying.

Champagne Cup. To a bottle of Champagne add a glass of Brandy and two slices of sweet orange, a piece of lemon-peel, a sprig of verbena or borage, and very thin peeling of a small cucumber. Let stand half an hour, add plenty of clear ice and serve.

Cider Cup. Put into a bowl 1 quart of sweet Cider, 1 bottle of Soda-water, 1 wine-glass of Sherry, half a wine-glass of Brandy, the juice of half a lemon and the rind of a quarter; add sugar and nutmeg to taste, and a dash of extract of pineapple; a sprig of verbena and 2 sprigs of borage may be added. Strain and ice well.

Claret Cup. To each bottle of ordinary Claret add a bottle of Soda-water, a glass of Sherry or Curaçao, the peel of a lemon, cut very thin, with powdered sugar according to taste. Let the whole stand an hour or two before serving, and then add some clear ice.

Dry Champagne in place of Soda-water is an improvement.

Copus Cup. Heat 2 quarts of Ale; add 4 wine-glasses of Brandy, 3 wine-glasses of noyau, 1 lb. of lump sugar, and the juice of 1 lemon. Toast a slice of bread, stick a slice of lemon on it with a dozen cloves, over which grate some nutmeg, and serve hot.

Hock Cup. To a bottle of Hock add 3 wine-glasses of Sherry, 1 lemon sliced, and some balm or borage. Let it stand 2 hours; sweeten to taste and add a bottle of seltzer-water.

Loving Cup. Rub the rind of 2 oranges on loaf sugar, and put the sugar into a cup or bowl; add ½ pint of Brandy, the juice of 1 lemon, ⅓ pint of orange juice, and 1 pint of water; add more sugar if required and ice well.

Velvet Cup. A pint of iced Champagne and a pint of Stout poured together in a large jug.

CURAÇAO

The most popular of all Dutch liqueurs. It was first made in Amsterdam from green oranges from Curaçao, brandy and sugar. There are now many different brands of Curaçaos made in Holland, France, England and elsewhere. They all differ according to the quality and strength of the various spirits used, but in all of them the informing flavour is that of the orange.

CURÉ-BON-LA-MADELEINE

First growth of Saint-Emilion (Claret).

CUSSAC

One of the minor Communes of the Haut-Médoc: its wines are entitled to be sold under the better-known name of the adjoining Commune of Saint-Julien.

CUVE
French for Vat.

CUVÉE
French for Vatting, or a blend of wines. In Champagne, *La Cuvée*, or *Le Vin de Cuvée*, refers to the wine of the first pressing, which is a great deal better than the wines of the next pressings, called *Tailles*, and of the last squeeze, called *Rebèche*.

CYGNE, Cru du
The name under which is marketed the white wine of Château de Laurenzane, a Graves de Bordeaux; Commune de Gradignan.

CYPRUS
The vineyards of Cyprus cover about 160,000 acres and produce nearly five million gallons of wine, as well as five thousand tons of raisins. The best-known wine of Cyprus is known as *Commanderia*.

CZECHOSLOVAKIA
Pilsen and Pilsener beer are first liquid assets of Czechoslovakia, but there are also vineyards, chiefly in Ruthenia and Slovakia, which produce a fair quantity of *ordinaire* wines.

DAISIES
The name given to iced long drinks or *Coolers* of a somewhat superior kind, usually served in goblets and decorated with various fruits, flowers or leaves. The more popular *Daisies* are:

Brandy Daisy. 1 jigger Brandy, ½ jigger raspberry syrup; the juice of half a lemon and half a lime.

Gin Daisy. 1 jigger Gin: ½ jigger raspberry syrup; the juice of half a lemon.

Highland Daisy. ⅔ jigger Scotch Whisky; 1 jigger syrup, the juice of half a lemon, half a lime and half an orange.

Rum Daisy. 1 jigger Rum; ½ jigger raspberry syrup; the juice of half a lemon.

Star Daisy. ½ jigger Gin, ½ jigger Applejack; ¼ jigger Grenadine; the juice of half a lime.

DACKENHEIMER
White wine of moderate quality from the Palatinate, Dürkheim district (Hock).

DALMATIA
That part of Yugoslavia facing the Eastern Adriatic; it is chiefly noted for its Cherry Liqueur, or *Maraschino*.

DALSHEIMER
White wine of moderate quality from Rhinehesse, Worms district.

DAME-JEANNE
French for Demijohn (q.v.).

DAMERY
One of the good growths of the Marne Valley (Champagne).

DAMPIERRE
Commune of Maine-et-Loire (Anjou) noted for its *Vins rosés*.

DAMSON GIN
A popular English cordial.

DANZIGER GOLDWASSER
A colourless liqueur originally made at Danzig, with plain spirit as its basis, flavoured with orange rind and various herbs: its chief feature is a number of small gold-leaf specks, which are tasteless and harmless; they float about when the *Goldwasser* is shaken and poured out.

D'ARCHE, Château
Second *Cru Classé* of Sauternes. There is also a *Château d'Arche*, a *Bourgeois* growth of the Haut-Médoc; Ludon (Claret); also a *Cru Darche* in the Commune of St. Pierre du Mons (white wine).

DAUGAY, Château
Second growth of Saint-Emilion (Claret).

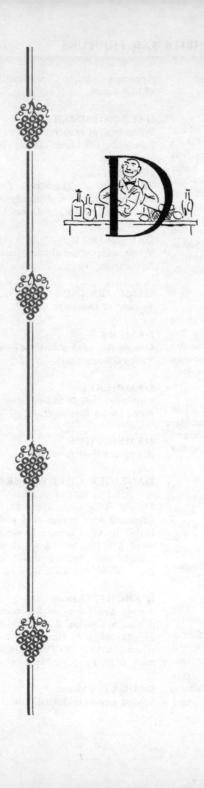

DAUZAC, Château
Fifth *Cru Classé* of the Médoc; Labarde (Claret).

DEBRÖI HÁRSLEVELÜ
One of the better white table wines of Hungary, from the vineyards of Debrö.

DECANT, To
Whether a wine should be decanted or not is a matter of opinion. A white wine, young or old, may equally well be served either straight from its bottle or from a beautiful crystal decanter, but it *looks* better in the decanter. An old bottled red wine, with much or even a little loose sediment, is best when served after it has been carefully decanted so that none of the sediment which may be in the bottle passes into the decanter, and the wine will be absolutely bright when passed round the table.

DÉGORGEMENT
The Champagne process of getting rid of all the sediment resulting from the second fermentation of the wine after it has been bottled.

DE HILDE, Château
Bourgeois growth of the Graves de Bordeaux; Bègles Commune (Claret).

DEIDESHEIM
First growth of the Palatinate (Mittelhaardt) (Hock).

DEKELEIA
Red and white table wines of no particular merit from vineyards in the vicinity of Marathon (Greece).

DEMI, Un
French for a double *Bock*, or half a litre (0·88 British pint, or 0·528 American quart). *Une Demie* stands for half a bottle, 0·40 litre (Champagne) and 0·375 (Bordeaux).

DEMIJOHN
A bulging, narrow-neck glass container, holding from 3 to 10 gallons, usually cased in 'wicker' for protection, and with two wicker handles.

DEMI-SEC
French for 'half-dry', which is used as a rule for Champagne which is quite sweet.

DEMOISELLE
A Normandy name for a tot of applejack.

DÉPÔT
French for the deposit or sediment which wine casts off during fermentation and long after, in the process of maturing.

DERNAU
Village of the Ahr Valley; its vineyards produce red wine of no particular merit.

DÉSERT, Châteaux
Bourgeois growth of the Graves de Bordeaux; Léognan (Claret).

DESMIRAIL, Château
Third *Cru Classé* of the Médoc; Margaux (Claret).

DESPLATS, Château
Palus growth of the Médoc; Macau (Claret).

DETZEM
Village near Trier in the Moselle Valley: its vineyards produce some white wine from fair to middling in quality.

DÉZALEY
One of the best white wines of the Vaud Canton (Switzerland).

DHRONER
One of the better white wines of the Mittel Mosel, Bernkastel district.

DIEDESFELD
A village of the Landau district (Palatin-

ate); its vineyards produce a fair amount of undistinguished wines.

DIENHEIM
Important wine-producing parish of Rhinehesse; Oppenheim district (Hock).

DIETLINGEN
Parish of Karlsruhe district (Baden); its vineyards produce both red and white wines of the *ordinaire* class.

DILLON, Château
Bourgeois growth of the Médoc; Blanquefort (Claret, mostly; a little white wine).

DIRMSTEIN
Parish of the Palatinate: Frankenthal district. Its vineyards produce both red and white wines of the *ordinaire* class.

D'ISSAN, Château
Third-class growth of the Médoc; Cantenac (Claret).

DISTILLATION
The art of separating the alcohol contained in any alcoholic liquid by the application of heat. The art of distillation is based on the fact that alcohol is vaporized at a lower temperature than water, 78° instead of 100°. Wine, barley mash, molasses or any other liquid containing a certain proportion of alcohol will be vaporized at a temperature varying between 78° and 100°, according to the proportion of water to alcohol, as follows:

Percentage of Alcohol	Percentage of Water	Boiling Point
100	0	78·0°
90	10	78·8°
80	20	79·7°
70	30	80·9°
60	40	81·9°
50	50	83·1°
40	60	84·1°
30	70	88·3°
20	80	92·6°
10	90	99·6°
0	100	100·0°

The receptacle in which the liquid to be distilled is placed is called a still. Heat being applied, some alcohol-cum-water leaves the still in the form of vapour which is led away from the heated still through a tube or pipe until it reverts to the original liquid form, owing to lower temperature. By separating the tube or channel through which the vapour has to travel, before it is condensed, into a series of compartments, and by regulating the temperature of each compartment from 100°, the boiling point of water, down to 78°, the boiling point of alcohol, the whole of the alcohol in any alcoholic liquid could be separated from the rest. But the object of distillation, as applied to potable spirits, is not to extract the whole of the alcohol contained in wine, barley mash or the sugar cane, but to reduce the water contents of such alcoholic liquids, so that they shall contain a greater proportion of alcohol, a smaller proportion of water and the largest possible proportion of the most suitable 'by-products' or impurities present in the original liquid from which each kind of spirit is distilled. The distinctiveness of potable spirits is due to the nature and proportion of such impurities, in the first place. In the second, to methods of rectification and to later additions.

DITTELSHEIM
Parish of Rhinehesse; Worms district: its vineyards produce mostly white wines, none of outstanding excellence.

DIZY-MAGENTA
Good Champagne growth in the Marne Valley, above Ay and below Hautvillers.

DOISY-DAËNE, Château
Second growth of Sauternes: Haut-Barsac (white wine).

DOISY-DUBROCA, Château
Second growth of Sauternes; Haut-Barsac (white wine). It was formerly known as Château Doisy-Gravas.

DOISY-VÉDRINES, Château
Second growth of Sauternes; Haut-Barsac (white wine).

DÔLE DE SION
Swiss red table wine: it is made in the Sion district from Pinot noir grapes, called Dôle in the Valais Canton of Switzerland.

DOMDECHANEY
The best-known vineyard of Hochheim, at the southern limit of the Rhinegau (Hock).

DOMINIQUE, La
First growth Graves de Saint-Emilion (Claret).

DORSHEIM
Village of the Nahe Valley; Bingerbrück (Hock).

DOUMENS, Château
Bourgeois growth of the Médoc; Margaux (Claret).

DOURO
The most famous river of the Iberian Peninsula from a wine point of view. It rises in the north of Spain and flows into the Atlantic shortly after passing between Oporto, on the right, and Villa Nova de Gaya, on the left. During its run in a general east-to-west direction through Portugal, the River Douro may be divided into the Upper Douro, from the Spanish frontier to Regoa, and the Lower Douro, from Regoa to Oporto. The best wines of the Douro are those from the vineyards of the schistous hills of the Upper Douro; the Lower Douro hills are chiefly granite, and the wines which are obtained from their vineyards are more suitable for beverage wines than for the making of Port.

DOUSICO
An unsweetened brand of Greek aniseed of high alcoholic strength.

DRACHENBLUT
A white wine of moderate quality from the Drachenfelt vineyards, the northern-most vineyards of the Rhine (Hock).

DRAKENSTEIN
One of the best white wine districts of the Cape Peninsula, South Africa.

DRAMBUIE
A Scotch liqueur with a world-wide reputation: it is made at Leith with whisky and sugar as its basis.

DREILING
An Austrian wine measure equal to 38·3 gallons.

DROMERSHEIM
A village of Rhinehesse; Bingen district. Its vineyards produce white wines of moderate quality (Hock).

DRY
An adjective with more than one meaning when applied to wine.

Champagne described as Dry is a wine not excessively sweet, but one which, as a rule, has been sweetened more or less according to age: the younger and more acid it is, the more sweetening has to be added to make the wine palatable.

White Graves and other white beverage wines described as Dry White Wines are not really dry; they are, however, dry compared with Sauternes and other naturally sweet wines.

Sauternes, Ports and other wines are intended by nature or designed to be sweet, that is to say, full of natural grape-sugar sweetness; if they are described as dry, it is that they have lost or have never had one of their chief assets.

Clarets and other red beverage wines

are dry by comparison with fortified wines, but they should retain their 'fruit', and be free from tartness. When they lose their smoothness, they are described as 'going' or 'gone' dry, and they have lost much of their charm.

DUBONNET
One of the most popular of all French *apéritifs*.

DUCRU-BEAUCAILLOU, Château
Second *Cru Classé* of the Médoc; Saint-Julien (Claret).

DUCRU-RAVEZ, Château
Palus growth of the Médoc; Macau (Claret).

DUHART-MILON, Château
Fourth *Cru Classé* of the Médoc; Pauillac (Claret).

DULAMON, Château
Bourgeois growth of the Médoc; Blanquefort (Claret).

DUR
French for harsh or rasping; usually used for wines with an excess of tannin.

DURBACH
A parish of Baden, Offenburg district. Its best vineyards are those of *Schloss Staufenberg*.

DURFORT-VIVENS, Château
Second *Cru Classé* of the Médoc; Margaux (Claret).

DÜRKHEIMER
One of the better white wines of the Palatinate; Bad-Dürkheim area (Hock).

DUTRUCH-GRAND-POUJEAUX, Château
Bourgeois growth of the Médoc; Moulis (Claret).

DUTTWEILER
A minor growth of the Palatinate; Neustadt a.d. Haardt area (Hock).

EAST INDIA
A description often used in connection with Madeira and Sherry in the days of sailing ships and previous to the cutting of the Suez Canal. Casks of Madeira, chiefly, and also of Sherry, were then frequently used as ballast in ships going to the East Indies via the Cape of Good Hope and back, no freight or a nominal amount being charged. The long and slow rocking of the wine during the double journey aged and improved it. Now, however, owing to the vibration, the excessive heat in the hold, the more limited, hence more valuable, space available in steamers, the East India Madeiras and Sherries are merely a memory of more leisurely days.

EAU-de-VIE
French for 'Water of Life', the first name given to Brandy. When not qualified, *Eau-de-Vie* means Brandy, or distilled wine. Other spirits are known as *Eau-de-vie-de grains, Eau-de-vie de fruits, Eau-de-vie de Cidre, Eau-de-vie de Marc*, etc.

EBERBACH, KLOSTER
The site of a Cistercian Abbey built in the twelfth century, some two and a half miles from Hattenheim (Rhinegau): its vineyards produce one of the greatest Hocks, *Steinberg*.

EBERNIGEN
A Baden village of the Freiburg district; its vineyards produce both red and white wines of no particular distinction.

EBULUM
To a hogshead of strong lusty Ale add an over-flowing bushel of the berries of Elder and a half pound of the berries of juniper, both thoroughly crushed. Put the berries to the Ale when you put in the

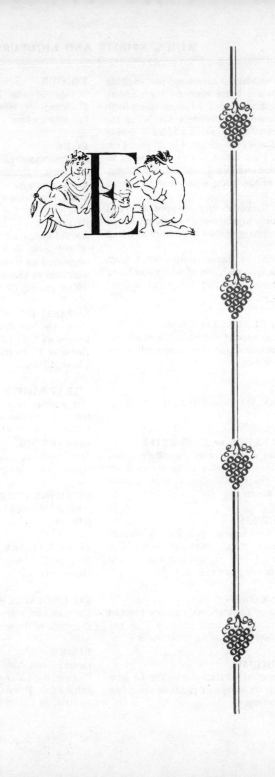

Hops and let the compound boil until the berries are burst apart by the scalding water, developing the Liquor thenceforth as you would with simple Ale. When the fermentation has ceased, add the following ingredients: ½ lb. ginger, ½ oz. cloves, ½ oz. mace, 1 oz. nutmegs, 1 oz. cinnamon, all pounded and mixed together, ½ lb. citron, ½ lb. eringo root, ½ lb. candied orange peel.

Cut the sweets very thin; put these and the spices together into a cloth bag which you will hang in the Cask before you stop it.

When the liquor is fine, serve it in glasses, into each one of which you have, previously laid two lumps of refined sugar.—C.E.M.

ECHÉZEAUX, Les Grands
The best wine of Flagey-Echézeaux (Côte de Nuits) and one of the finest red wines of Burgundy.

ECHT
German for 'unsugared', referring to wine.

EDELFÄULE or EDELREIFE
German equivalent of *Pourriture noble*, an over-ripe stage of white grapes from which the finer naturally sweet dessert wines are made.

EDELWEISS
An Italian liqueur, pale gold in colour, flavoured with aromatic herbs and sweetened with crystallized sugar on a twig standing in the bottle.

EDENKOBEN
Village of the Palatinate in the Landau district; its vineyards produce both red and white wines of no great merit.

EDESHEIM
Village of the Palatinate in the Landau district; its vineyards produce some fair white wines.

EDIGER
Village of the Moselle Valley, near Cochem; its vineyards produce some fair white wines.

EGER
A city, some 120 miles north-west of Budapest, surrounded by extensive vineyards which produce some of the best Hungarian table wines.

EGGNOG
An old-fashioned 'pick-me-up', made up of hot milk with an egg beaten in it, sweetened to taste, braced also to taste with rum or brandy or both, and usually with a grating of nutmeg.

ÉGLISE, L'
There are four first growths of Pomerol known as *Clos l'Église, Cru de l'Église, Domaine de l'Église*, and *Clos l'Église-Clinet* (Claret).

EGRAPPAGE
The process of tearing away the grapes from their stalks before the pressing.

EGRAPPOIR
The revolving colander cylinder which separates the ripe grapes from their stalks.

EGRI BIKAVER
Red table wine from Eger vineyards (Hungary).

EGRI KADARKA
Red table wine from Eger vineyards (Hungary).

EIGENGEWÄCHS
German for 'own growth', followed by the name of the grower.

EIMER
German and Austrian wine measure. In Prussia, the *eimer* corresponds to 15·121 gallons; in Bavaria, to 14·117; and in Austria, to 12·448 gallons.

EITELSBACH

Village of the Ruwer Valley, not very far from Trier. Its best-known vineyard is one that originally belonged to the Carthusians: Karthäuserhofberg.

ELLER

Village of the Moselle Valley, near Cochem; its vineyards produce some fair white wines.

ELLERSTADT

Townlet of the Palatinate; Bad-Dürkheim district. Its vineyards produce both red and white wines of the *ordinaire* class.

ELLMENDINGEN

Village of the Karlsruhe district (Baden); its vineyards produce both red and white wines of the *ordinaire* class.

ELSHEIM

Village of Rhinesse, in the Bingen district; its vineyards produce some fair white wines.

ELTVILLE

Township of the Rhinegau where some important German wine shippers have their offices and cellars. The vineyards of Eltville produce some very fine white wines (Hock).

EMILIA

Important wine-producing Province of Italy: most wines of Emilia are undistinguished, but the red *Sangiovese* and the white *Trabbiano* enjoy a measure of local esteem.

ENCLOS-POMEROL, L'

Second growth of Pomerol (Claret).

ENDINGEN

Village of the Kaiserstuhl (Baden); its vineyards produce both red and white wines of the *ordinaire* class.

ENFANT-JÉSUS

A very fine red Burgundy from one part of *Les Grèves* vineyard, Beaune.

ENGADDI

A small town in the valley of the Jordan, on the road to Bethlehem (Palestine). The vine still grows there as it did about a thousand years before Christ, when Solomon wrote the 'Song of Songs' and praised the vines of Engaddi:

'Botrus Cypri dilectus meus mihi, in vineis Engaddi.' (I, 14.)
(A cluster of Cyprus my love is to me, in the vineyards of Engaddi. *Vulgate.*)

What is the most remarkable feature of this line is that it shows that even in the days of King Solomon the vine of Cyprus, the Malvasia grape, was highly prized and had been introduced into Palestine as it was to be introduced into Italy by the Romans, into the island of Madeira by the Portuguese, in the fifteenth century, and by the Dutch, at the Cape, in the seventeenth century.

ENKIRCH

Important village of the Middle Moselle Valley, Zell district; its vineyards produce some very fine white wines.

ENTRE-DEUX-MERS

That part of the Gironde Département between the Rivers Garonne and Dordogne: the vineyards of Entre-deux-Mers produce a great deal of wine, mostly white, none of them possessing real distinction.

ÉPERNAY

The most important town of Champagne after Rheims and Châlons-sur-Marne.

EPESSES

A quality white wine of the Canton de Vaud (Switzerland).

ÉPINEUIL
Village of the Yonne Département (Burgundy), near Tonnerre: its vineyards produce some common red wines and better white ones.

EPPAN
Small town of south Tyrol; its vineyards produce both red and white wines from fair to middling in quality.

ERBACH
Village next to Hattenheim (Rhinegau): its vineyards produce some very fine white wines (Hocks).

ERDEN
Village of the Moselle Valley, near Bernkastel: its vineyards produce some very fine white wines.

ERLACH
Village of the Bernese Alps, the vineyards of which produce one of the few good red wines of Switzerland.

ERLAU
One of the more important wine-producing districts of Hungary (Borsod County).

ERLENBACH
A minor wine-producing parish of the Neckar Valley (Württemberg); its vineyards produce both red and white wines of the *ordinaire* class, as well as *Schillerwein*.

ERMITAGE, Coteau de l'
The usual French spelling of *Hermitage* (q.v.).

ERMITAGE, Domaine de l'
Palus growth of Ludon; Haut-Médoc (Claret).

ERPOLZHEIM
Village of the Palatinate, Dürkheim district: its vineyards produce both red and white wines of the *ordinaire* class.

ESCHERNDORF
Village of Franconia, the vineyards of which produce some fair white wines.

ESSINGEN
Village of the Palatinate, Landau district: its vineyards produce white wines of moderate quality.

ESSLINGEN
Small town of the Neckar Valley, Württemberg: its vineyards produce some red wine but mostly Schillerwein. It was at Esslingen that the first sparkling German wine was made, in 1826.

EST-EST-EST
An Italian Muscatel white wine from Montefiascone.

ESTUFAS
The hot chambers in which the young wines are lodged and 'cooked' for a while at Madeira.

ÉTAMPÉ
French for 'branded'.

ÉTOILE DE CANTENAC
Palus growth of Cantenac; Haut-Médoc (Claret).

ÉTOILE-POURRET, Cru de l'
First growth of Saint-Emilion (Claret).

ETTENHEIM
Village of the Offenburg district, Brisgau: its wines are of the *ordinaire* class.

EUCALYPTINE
An Italian digestive Liqueur made by the Trappist Fathers of the Via Quattro Fontane, in Rome; it is free from the smell of Eucalyptus leaves, being flavoured with Eucalyptus blossoms.

EVANGILE, L'
First growth of Pomerol (Claret).

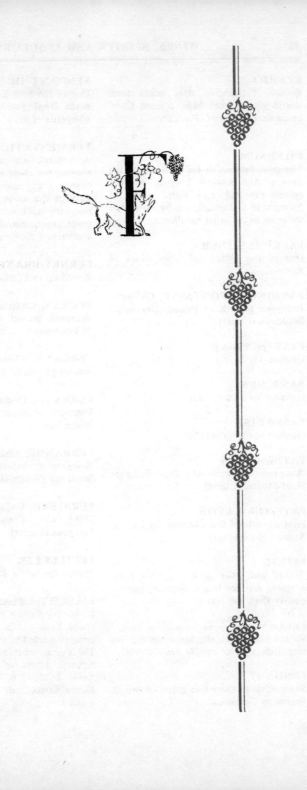

EZERJÓ
Golden, full-bodied wine made from Ezerjó grapes from Mór, a small Commune near Budapest (Hungary).

FALERNUM
The most famous of Italian wines in the days of the Roman Empire, but the present-day red and white wines of Falerno, in Campania, are by no means wines of exceptional excellence.

FALKENSTEINER
One of the better red table wines of Austria.

FANNING-LAFONTAINE, Château
Bourgeois growth of Pessac, Graves de Bordeaux (Claret).

FASS (*pl.* Fässer)
German for cask.

FASSCHEN
German for a small cask.

FASSWEISE
German for 'on draught'.

FATIN, Château
Bourgeois growth of Saint-Estèphe: Haut-Médoc (Claret).

FAYE-SUR-LAYON
First growth of the Coteaux du Layon, Anjou (white wines).

FEINTS
'Heads' and 'Tails', or first and last parts of spirits distilled in a pot-still: of poorer quality than the rest.

FELLBACH
Village near Stuttgart, Württemberg: its vineyards produce mostly *Schillerwein.*

FENDANT
Swiss name of the white grape known in France as *Chasselas.*

FENDANT DE SION
One of the best Swiss white wines: it is made from Fendant grapes from the vineyards of Sion in the Valais.

FERMENTATION
A natural, almost inevitable, phenomenon, the chief feature of which is to change grape-juice, or *must*, into wine through the molecular re-adjustment of the carbon, hydrogen and oxygen of grape-sugar, mainly into ethyl alcohol and carbon dioxide.

FERNET-BRANCA
A well-known Italian brand of apéritif.

FERRAN, Château
Bourgeois growth of Martillac: Graves de Bordeaux (Claret and White Graves).

FERRAND, Château de
Second growth of Saint-Emilion (Claret).

FERRAND, Domaine de
Entre-deux-Mers growth: both Claret and White Bordeaux.

FERRANDE, Château
Bourgeois growth of Castres: Graves de Bordeaux (White Graves).

FERRIÈRE, Château
Third *Cru Classé* of the Médoc: Margaux (Claret).

FEUILLETTE
French for half a *Barrique.*

FIASCO (*pl.* Fiaschi)
Italian for flask, a glass bottle with a flat, round base and a long neck, the body being protected by a coat of matted straw. The Tuscan or standard *fiasco* holds two reputed quarts of wine; the Modena *fiasco* holds 3·667 pints. There is a *Mezzo fiasco*, 'half a flask', which holds a quart.

FIEUZAL, Château
Bourgeois growth of Léognan; Graves de Bordeaux (both Claret and White Graves).

FIGEAC, Château
First growth Graves de Saint-Emilion (Claret).

FILHOT, Château
Second growth Sauternes (white wine).

FILZENER
The white wine of Filzen vineyards, in the Valley of the Upper Moselle, close to where the Saar joins the Moselle.

FINE (*pronounced Feene*)
French for Liqueur Brandy.

FINE CHAMPAGNE
French for a Cognac Brandy which should be from the Grande Champagne, Petite Champagne or Borderies vineyards but it must have the guarantee of a reputable Cognac firm as distiller or shipper.

FINE MAISON
The staple Brandy of the house (hotel or restaurant), seldom very fine but usually a fair Cognac brandy.

FININGS
Finings act as a very small mesh net cast over new wine, a net which settles down slowly to the bottom of the cask, provided there is no draught nor trepidation, and carries with it every particle of mucilage or sediment in suspension in the wine. The chief finings are white of eggs for red wines, isinglass for white wines, and gelatin; also milk, fresh blood and a number of patent powders. But whatever the finings used, they must be thoroughly *whisked* (beaten up) before being poured into the wine, and the wine must be thoroughly *roused* (shaken) immediately after the finings have been added.

FINO
The most intensely clean on nose and palate of all Sherries; the real *Fino* is dry without any bitterness, and delicate without being thin.

FIOR D'ALPI
Italian liqueur, aromatic and very sweet, which is bottled with a 'Christmas tree' standing inside, or a twig covered with crystallized sugar.

FIRKIN
The fourth part of a barrel of beer, i.e. nine gallons.

FIXES or TWISTS
These are iced summer drinks compounded in many different ways.
  Gin Fix. Put into a small tumbler a tablespoonful of icing sugar, half a wine-glass of water, the juice and peel of a quarter of a lemon, and one wine-glassful of Gin; fill the tumbler two-thirds with shaved ice, shake well, and decorate with berries in season; insert one straw, or use a straining spoon on top of glass.
                                        —F.D.S.D.

FIXIN
One of the smaller wine-producing Communes of the Côte d'Or, producing some red Burgundy of very fair quality. Its best wine is that of *Le Clos de la Perrière*; its best known that of *Le Clos du Chapître*.

FIZZ
A common name for any beverage which is effervescent, more particularly Champagne.

FIZZES
American 'long' drinks made up of various kinds of spirits and some sugar or syrup, well shaken with plenty of ice, then strained and served in tall glasses which are then filled with a syphon: a pinch of carbonate of soda is sometimes used instead of a syphon to ensure effervescence.

Bayard Fizz. The juice of 1½ lemons; 1 barspoon sugar; 1 jigger Dry Gin; 1 dash Maraschino; 1 dash raspberry syrup. Shake, strain and fill glass with syphon.—L.T.C.R.

Brandy Fizz. The juice of 1 lemon; 1 barspoon sugar; 1 jigger French Brandy; 2 dashes yellow Chartreuse; shake and strain, and fill glass with syphon.—L.T.C.R.

Daisy Fizz. The juice of half a lemon; juice of half a lime; ½ jigger orange juice; ⅔ jigger Brandy. Shake, strain and fill glass with syphon.—L.T.C.R.

Galvez Fizz. The juice of 1 lemon; 1 barspoon sugar; 4 dashes raspberry syrup; 1 jigger Dry Gin; 1 white of egg; 1 dash orange flower water; 1 jigger cream. Shake well; strain into lemonade glass and fill with syphon.—L.T.C.R.

Gin Fizz. Put into a tumbler the juice of half a lemon and one wineglass of Gin; fill with shaved ice, shake well, strain, add a teaspoonful of icing sugar, in which place a pinch of carbonate of soda, stir well, and drink while effervescing.
—F.D.S.D.

Golden Fizz. Put into a tumbler the juice of half a lemon, one wineglass of Gin; fill up to three parts with shaved ice, then break the yolk of an egg into the tumbler, shake well, strain, add a teaspoonful of icing sugar, in which place a pinch of carbonate of soda, stir well, and drink while effervescing.—F.D.S.D.

Ramos Fizz. 1 heaping teaspoonful confectioner's sugar; 2 teaspoons lemon juice; ¼ teaspoonful orange flower water; 1 egg white; 1 oz. dry Gin; 2½ oz. milk; cracked ice. Shake 5–10 minutes and strain into 8-oz. glass.—A.C.

Sloe Gin Fizz. ½ jigger of lemon juice; 1 teaspoonful of powdered sugar; 1 jigger Sloe Gin. Shake thoroughly with cracked ice, strain and fill with charged water.—H.J.G.

FLAGEY-ECHÉZEAUX
The last but one of the villages of the Côte de Nuits, coming from Dijon: its vineyards produce some red wines of superlative excellence (Burgundy).

FLEURENNES, Château
Bourgeois growth of Blanquefort; Haut-Médoc (Claret).

FLEURIE
One of the more important wine-producing Communes of Beaujolais, in the Rhône Département (Burgundy).

FLIPS
Winter drinks made up of hot ale, wine or spirits, sweetened to taste, with an egg beaten in and some nutmeg grated on top at the time of serving.

FLOR
Spanish for the *Mycoderma vini* yeast which spreads on top of newly-made wines whilst the slow fermentation is proceeding.

FONBADET, Château
Bourgeois growth of Pauillac; Haut-Médoc (Claret).

FONGRAVET, Château
Bourgeois growth of Blanquefort; Haut-Médoc (Claret).

FONPETITE, Château
Bourgeois growth of Saint-Estèphe; Haut-Médoc (Claret).

FONPLÉGADE, Château
First growth of Saint-Emilion (Claret).

FONRÉAUD, Château
Bourgeois growth of Listrac; Haut-Médoc (Claret).

FONROQUE, Château
First growth of Saint-Emilion (Claret).

FONTANET, Château
Bourgeois growth of Le Taillan; Haut-Médoc (Claret).

FONTBONNE-AGASSAC,
Domaine de
Bourgeois growth of Ludon; Haut-Médoc (Claret).

FONTESTEAU, Château
Bourgeois growth of Saint-Sauveur et Cissac; Haut-Médoc (Claret).

FORBIDDEN FRUIT
An American liqueur with a citrus fruit basis; it is sold in an ornate globular bottle.

FORST
First growth of the Palatinate (Hock).

FOUDRE
French for the largest casks used as vats to store wine.

FOURCAS-DUPRÉ, Château
Bourgeois growth of Listrac; Haut-Médoc (Claret).

FOURCAS-HOSTEIN, Château
Bourgeois growth of Listrac; Haut-Médoc (Claret).

FOURCHAUME
First growth of Chablis (Burgundy).

FOURTET, Clos
First growth of Saint-Emilion (Claret).

FRAISIA
French liqueur, red in colour, with a strawberry taste.

FRAMBOISE
French colourless spirit distilled from fermented raspberry juice in Alsace.

FRANC DE GOÛT
French for 'clean' in reference to the bouquet and taste of a wine free from any suspicion of undesirable smell or taste.

FRANCONIA
An important wine-producing district of Germany of which Würzburg is the chief city and mart: it produces more and better white wines than red.

FRANKENWINE
German for 'wine of Franconia', also known as *Steinwein.*

FRAPPÉ
French for 'iced'.

FRASCATI
One of the showplaces of the Roman Hills: its vineyards produce a white wine of repute.

FRASCO
Spanish and Portuguese for 'flask'.

FREEZOMINT
A popular brand of French *Crème de Menthe.*

FREIBURG-IM-BRISGAU
The chief wine-mart of Upper Baden (Germany).

FREINSHEIM
A village of the Palatinate in the Bad-Dürkheim district: its vineyards produce some fair white wines (Hock).

FREISA
One of the better red wines of Piedmont (Italy).

FRENCH HOEK
One of the oldest vine-growing settlements of the Cape Peninsula at the eastern end of the Paarl Valley (South Africa).

FRIEDELSHEIM
Village of the Palatinate, Bad-Dürkheim district; its vineyards produce some fair white wines.

FRIESENHEIM
Village of Baden, Offenburg district; its vineyards produce some white wines, from fair to middling in quality.

FRIULARO
An Italian black grape grown in the Veneto Province; also the name of a common red table wine made from this grape.

FRONSAC
An important Canton of the Gironde Département; its vineyards produce red wines of no great distinction, the best of them being those of the *Côtes de Fronsac* (Claret).

FRONTIGNAN
Sweet dessert wine made from white Muscat grapes in the Frontignan vineyards of the Languedoc. *Frontignan* is tawny in colour and acquires a *rancio* flavour after some years in bottle, which was highly appreciated in England in the early years of Queen Victoria's reign.

FUDER
German cask equal to 6 Ohms which is used for blending and storing wine. Its contents vary from 211 gallons for Moselle wines, to 388 gallons in Württemberg.

FUISSÉ
Small Commune of Saône-et-Loire: its vineyard adjoins those of Pouilly and their wine is usually sold as Pouilly Fuissé (White Burgundy).

FUMADELLE
Palus growth of Soussans; Haut-Médoc (Claret).

FÜNFKIRCHEN
Townlet of the Komitat Baranya, in Hungary; its vineyards produce both table wines and dessert grapes.

FURIANI
A white, sweet, dessert wine of Corsica.

FURMINT
A 'quality' white grape from which Tokay wines are made.

GAILLAC
The most important wine-producing area of the Tarn Département. The vineyards of Gaillac produce in abundance a variety of table wines, red, white, and *rosés*, as well as sparkling wines.

GAINFARN
One of the better wine-producing areas of Southern Austria: its best wine is the red *Oberkirchen*.

GALAMUS
A tawny dessert wine, with a *rancio* flavour, from Roussillon.

GALLAIS, Château
Bourgeois growth of Ordonnac et Podensac; Médoc (Claret).

GALLON
Standard British and American wine measure which was the same until 1826, when the present imperial gallon of 277·274 cubic inches was introduced. In the U.S.A. the gallon still is the old English gallon of 231 cubic inches. The imperial gallon is divided into 4 quarts or 8 pints and is equivalent to 4·543 litres.

GAMAY
One of the most extensively cultivated species of black grapes, more particularly in Burgundy. In the Côte d'Or, red wines from Gamay grapes are not allowed to be sold as *Bourgonne*, but in the Saône-et-Loire and Rhône Départements Gamay grapes produce the attractive red wines of Mâconnais and Beaujolais.

GARRAFA
Portuguese for Bottle.

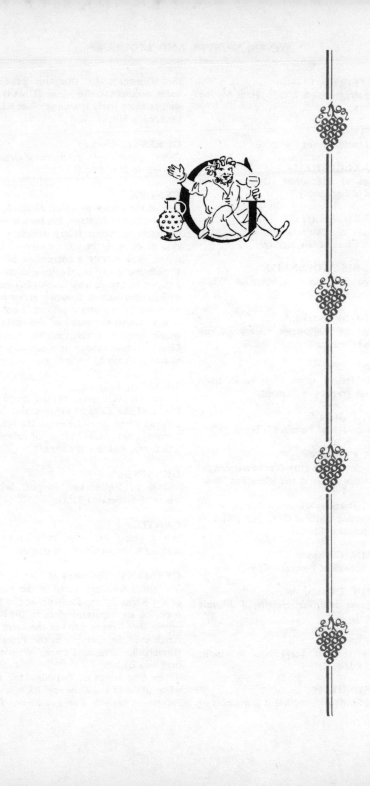

GASTEBOIS, Château
Bourgeois growth of Moulis; Haut-Médoc (Claret).

GATTINARA
A red table wine of Piedmont.

GAU-ALGESHEIM
Village of Rhinehesse; Bingen. White wines of fair quality.

GAU-BICKELHEIM
Village of Rhinehesse; Oppenheim. White wines of fair quality.

GAU-BISCHOFSNEIM
Village of Rhinehesse; Mayence. White wines of fair quality.

GAU-ODERNHEIM
Village of Rhinehesse; Alzey. White wines of fair quality.

GAVI
White Italian table wine made from Cortese grapes in Piedmont.

GAY, Château le
First growth of Pomerol (Claret).

GAY, Château du
Entre-deux-Mers growth producing equal quantities of Claret and white Bordeaux.

GAY, Domaine du
Bourgeois growth of Gradignan; Graves de Bordeaux (Claret).

GAZIN, Château
First growth of Pomerol (Claret).

GAZIN, Domaine de
Bourgeois supérieur growth of Blayais (Claret).

GEIERSLAY
One of the best vineyards of Wintrich, Middle Moselle.

GEISENHEIM
One of the more important townships of the Rhinegau. Its vineyards produce some excellent white wines (Hocks) as well as some lively sparkling white wines (Sparkling Hock).

GENESTE, Château
Palus growth of Villenave d'Ornon; Graves de Bordeaux (Claret).

GENEVA
One of the names by which *Hollands*, or Gin distilled in Holland, has been known for many years past. It has nothing whatever to do with the city or lake of that name; it is merely a corruption of the French name of Gin, *Genièvre*, meaning Juniper, Gin being a plain spirit flavoured with juniper berries. *Geneva* is either pure white or faintly straw coloured; colour is not due to the wood of the casks in which Geneva is kept, but to caramel. Geneva is sold as soon as distilled: it has nothing to gain by being kept.

GENEVA, Lake of
There are vineyards on the northern banks of the Lake of Geneva and they produce some fair white wines, the better-known ones being those of *Bernex, Dardagny, Russin* and *Saligny*.

GENSINGEN
Village of Rhinehesse; Bingen. White wines of moderate quality.

GENTIL
White grape cultivated in Alsace for making white wines of fair quality.

GERMANY, The wines of
Viticulture was introduced in the valley of the Rhine by the Romans, and it has occupied an important place in the economic life of many parts of the German Reich ever since, chiefly in the Prussian Rhineland, Bavaria, Hessen, Württemberg and Baden.

The best wines of Germany are the white wines of the *Rhinegau, Rhinehesse, Palatinate, Moselle, Saar* and *Ruwer*. The white wines of *Franconia* come next. There are no red wines made in Germany of the same excellence as the best white wines of the country, but there are a few Rhine red wines which enjoy a high degree of popularity in Germany.

GEROPICA
Boiled grape-juice or grape syrup used to sweeten wines.

GEVREY-CHAMBERTIN
One of the more important parishes of the Côte de Nuits; its vineyards produce some remarkably fine red Burgundies, none finer than *Chambertin* and *Clos de Bèze*.

GEWÄCHS
German for 'the growth of', followed by the name of the person or concern owning the vineyard which produced the wine in the bottle.

GEWURZTRAMINER
One of the white grapes grown in Alsace, Austria and Germany for the making of fine quality wines.

GILL
English liquid measure equivalent to 1·42 decilitre.

GIMMELDINGEN
Township of the Palatinate, Neustadt; white wines of moderate quality.

GIN
A spirit distilled from grain and flavoured with juniper berries. Its name is the abbreviation of its French name *Genièvre*, meaning juniper. *Gin* has been distilled in England to a far greater extent than any other spirit, ever since the eighteenth century. There are two main sorts of English *Gins*, *Dry Gin* or *London Gin*, and *Old Tom* or *Plymouth Gin*. There are, of course, differences between *London Gins* and *Plymouth Gins* from different distilleries, but the first are always dry and the second sweetened. All are white as they come from the still, and none of them are matured, in the same sense as Brandy is matured in cask, but there are straw-coloured gins which are coloured with caramel. English *Gins* are quite distinct from Dutch *Gins*, which are sold under the names of *Geneva*, *Hollands* or *Schiedam*.

Gin is the purest of all spirits, being distilled at a higher strength than other spirits. This is particularly so in the U.S.A., where the basis of *Gin* is practically neutral alcohol, that is a spirit out of which everything has been distilled; this means that it matters little from what material the *Gin* is originally distilled. It is entirely flavourless, as well as colourless, and is flavoured, coloured at will and brought down in strength by the addition of distilled water. *Gin* is not particularly welcome to the palate, but it is most helpful to the bladder. It is largely used in the mixing of *Cocktails*, *Collins*, *Slings* and other drinks, long and short.

Gin and Bitters. One of the simplest and one of the most popular forms of *Cocktails*. It is also known as *Pink Gin*.

Gin and Ginger Ale. A palate-paralysing and bladder-stimulating mixture, refreshing on a hot day, when well iced.

Gin and Tansy. This is an old-fashioned and excellent tonic. It is prepared by steeping a bunch of tansy in a bottle of Hollands Gin, which will extract the essence.

Gin Cocktail. 3 dashes of plain syrup; 2 or 3 dashes of bitters; 1 wine-glass of Hollands or Gin; 1 or 2 dashes of orange Curaçao. Squeeze lemon peel. Fill one-third full of ice, and shake well, and strain in a small tumbler.

Gin Crusta. Peel of half a lemon in long string; place in glass; add ½ glass of fine ice; 1 dash Bitters; juice of half a lemon;

dash of Maraschino; 100 per cent dry Gin. And serve.

Gin Daisy. The juice of half a lemon; ¼ teaspoonful powdered sugar; 6 dashes Grenadine; 1 glass Gin. Use long tumbler. Half fill with cracked ice, stir until glass is frosted. Fill with syphon Soda-water; put 4 sprigs of green mint on top and decorate with slices of fruit in season.

Gin Fix. One tablespoonful of sugar; ¼ a wine-glass of water; quarter of a lemon; 1 wine-glass of Gin. Fill two-thirds full of ice, stir with a spoon and ornament the top with fruits in season.

Gin Fizz. One teaspoonful sugar; juice of 1 lemon; 1 dash cream; 100 per cent Gin. Fill glass with fine ice. Shake, strain, fill glass with fizz water, stir and serve.

Gin High-Ball. One piece of ice in glass; 100 per cent Dry Gin. Fill glass with fizz water, stir and serve.

Gin Julep. One tablespoonful sugar; 3 sprigs mint; ¼ glass of fine ice; 100 per cent Dry Gin. Stir well, trim with fruits in season and serve.

Gin Punch. Half pint of old Gin; 1 gill of Maraschino; the juice of 3 lemons; the rind of half a lemon; 1 quart bottle of German seltzer water. Ice well and sweeten to taste.

Gin Rickey. On of the most refreshing of summer long drinks. *Recipe:* Put some ice (2 cubes) in a tumbler, then the juice of half a ripe lime and some of the rind as well; add 2 oz. Dry Gin and fill with soda or seltzer water. Stir and drink slowly. This cooling drink was first served to Colonel Joe Rickey at 'Shoemaker's', a famous Washington drinking place, in the 'nineties.

Gin Sangaree. It is prepared in the same way as the *Brandy Sangaree*, substituting Gin for Brandy.

Gin Sling. It is made in the same way as the *Gin Toddy* (q.v.), adding a little grated nutmeg on top before serving.

Gin Sling (*Hot*). One lump of sugar dissolved in hot water; 100 per cent Hollands Gin. Fill with hot water. Stir well, grate nutmeg on top and add slice of lemon.

Gin Smash. Half a tablespoonful of white sugar; 1 tablespoonful water; 1 wine-glass of Gin. Fill two-thirds full of chipped ice. Use 2 sprigs of mint, the same as in the recipe for a *Mint Julep*. Lay 2 small pieces of orange on top, and ornament with berries in season.

Gin Sour. Half a teaspoonful of sugar; 100 per cent Dry Gin; juice of 1 lemon; ¼ a glass of cracked ice. Shake, strain, add a slice of orange and serve.

Gin Toddy. One teaspoonful of sugar; ¼ a wine-glass of water; 1 wine-glass of Gin; 1 small lump of ice. Stir with a spoon.

GINGER ALE

One of the most popular forms of *Minerals*. It is made with a few drops of essence of ginger, or capsicum extract, and a few drops of colouring matter; also some sugar or glucose, put into a bottle, which is then filled up with carbonated water. Occasionally a little mucilaginous matter variously known technically as *Froth*, *Heading*, etc., is added to give the *Ginger Ale* a 'better head' and the drinker thereof a greater thrill.

GINGER BEER

An effervescing beverage made by fermenting ginger, cream of tartar, and sugar with yeast and water, and bottling before the fermentation is completed. The carbonic acid generated within the fluid gives, after a few days or weeks, an aerated drink; but this variety of Ginger Beer is also an alcoholic drink, for the fermentation which is set up by the yeast in a part of the sugar gives rise to a little alcohol, as well as to carbonic acid. Two per cent of alcohol is the strict legal limit.

GINGER WINE

A British Wine or liquor, generally made with water, sugar, lemon rinds, ginger, yeast, raisins, and frequently fortified with added spirit and a little capsicine.

GIRO DI SARDEGNA
The most ambitious of the many ordinary wines made in the Island of Sardinia. It is a red dessert wine, quite sweet and fairly high in alcoholic strength.

GIRONDAS
One of the best red wines of the Côtes du Rhône.

GIRONDE
The waterway formed by the junction of the Rivers Garonne and Dordogne, below Bordeaux. It gives its name to the Gironde Département, of which Bordeaux is the chief city.

GIRONVILLE, Château
Bourgeois supérieur growth of Macau; Haut-Médoc (Claret).

GISCOURS, Château
Third *Cru Classé* of the Médoc; Labarde (Claret).

GIVRY
Small town of the Côte Chalonnaise; its vineyards produce some very fair red wines (Burgundy).

GLANA, Château du
Bourgeois supérieur growth of Saint-Julien; Haut-Médoc (Claret).'

GLASSES
Fine glasses materially add to the enjoyment of fine wines. Wine never tastes well in (a) coloured glasses, because one is unable to enjoy the beautiful ruby or gold of the wine; (b) thick glasses; (c) small glasses, because there must be a fair volume of wine for the bouquet to show off; (d) glasses filled to the brim. Glasses which have been dried with a dirty cloth, and glasses which have been left for any length of time bowl down-

wards, will spoil any and every wine by their foul or musty smell.

The size and shape of drinking glasses vary considerably, and the smaller the glass the farther the bottle will go. The 'reputed' quart, or ordinary wine bottle, should hold one-sixth of a gallon, or 26⅔ liquid ounces.

It is generally advisable for the purpose of estimating how many glasses of a given size can be got out of a bottle to treat the quantity as 26 ounces only, as all bottles are not always one-sixth of a gallon. It also allows for any wastage, bottoms, etc. On this basis the following are the results:

Size of Glass (ounces)	No. of Glasses per bottle
$\frac{1}{2}$	52
$\frac{3}{4}$	$34\frac{2}{3}$
1	26
$1\frac{1}{4}$	$20\frac{4}{5}$
$1\frac{1}{2}$	$17\frac{1}{3}$
$1\frac{3}{4}$	$14\frac{6}{7}$
2	13
$2\frac{1}{4}$	$11\frac{5}{9}$
$2\frac{1}{2}$	$10\frac{2}{5}$
$2\frac{3}{4}$	$9\frac{5}{11}$
3	$8\frac{2}{3}$
$3\frac{1}{4}$	8
$3\frac{1}{2}$	$7\frac{3}{7}$
$3\frac{3}{4}$	$6\frac{14}{15}$
4	$6\frac{1}{2}$
$4\frac{1}{4}$	$6\frac{2}{17}$
$4\frac{1}{2}$	$5\frac{7}{9}$
$4\frac{3}{4}$	$5\frac{9}{19}$
5	$5\frac{1}{5}$

A *Pony* is a *small* glass and it often means a *very small* glass.

GLETSCHER or GLACIER WINE
Swiss white wine made from the highest vineyards of the Valais.

GOLDWASSER
A spirit which was originally made at Dantzig and continued to be made there exclusively for a long time. It is now distilled in other places as well. It is a highly rectified spirit, flavoured with aniseed, cinnamon, and a number of

herbs and spices; it is colourless and as a rule of very high strength, but its outstanding feature is that it contains a large number of very small pieces of gold leaf or yellow and gold-like pieces, which settle at the bottom of the bottle but float about like tiny golden snowflakes when the Liqueur is being served.

GONNHEIM
Village of the Palatinate, Bad-Dürkheim district; red and white wines of moderate quality.

GOMBAUDE-GUILLOT, Château
First growth of Pomerol (Claret).

GOÛT
French for Taste; as applied to wine, *Goût* is used in such expressions as the following:

Goût américain, denotes a fairly sweet wine, chiefly Champagne;

Goût anglais, denotes a dry wine, chiefly Champagne;

Goût de bois, meaning woody, tainted by too long a stay in cask;

Bon goût, pleasant to the taste;

Goût de bouchon, corky;

Goût d'évent, flat, stale, dumb, dead;

Goût de ferment, still fermenting, not ready to drink;

Goût français, denotes a very sweet Champagne;

Franc de goût, perfectly clean on the nose and palate;

Mauvais goût, wrong, not fit to drink;

Goût de moisi, musty, foul;

Goût de paille, wet straw stink, foul;

Goût de pierre à fusil, a flinty and not unpleasant after-taste;

Goût de piqué, pricked, on the way to the vinegar tub;

Goût de rancio, bottle-stink; some people enjoy it, others dislike it;

Goût de taille, rasping (*taille* being the last pressing of the grapes);

Goût de terroir, a somewhat assertive quality, usually highly appreciated locally, where the wine is made, but not so much to the taste of the unbiased.

GRAACH
Township of the Middle Moselle, the vineyards of which produce some excellent white wine.

GRAND-BARRAIL-LAMARZELLE-FIGEAC, Château
First growth of Graves de Saint-Emilion (Claret).

GRAND CLOS
First growth of Bourgueil (red Touraine wine).

GRAND CORBIN, Château
First growth of Graves de Saint-Emilion (Claret).

GRAND-CORBIN-DAVID, Château
First growth Graves de Saint-Emilion (Claret).

GRAND-CORBIN-DESPAGNE, Château
First growth Graves de Saint-Emilion (Claret).

GRAND-DUROC-MILON, Château
Bourgeois supérieur growth of Pauillac; Haut-Médoc (Claret).

GRAND-FAURIE, Domaine de
First growth Saint-Emilion (Claret).

GRAND-LA-LAGUNE, Château
Third *Cru Classé* of the Médoc; Ludon (Claret).

GRANDMAISON, Domaine de
Bourgeois growth of Léognan; Graves de Bordeaux (Red and White Graves).

GRAND MARNIER
Popular French liqueur with an orange flavour and a Cognac brandy basis; it is made in two styles: *Cordon Rouge*, which is drier, and *Cordon Jaune*, which is both sweeter and of lower alcoholic strength.

GRAND MAYNE, Château
Second growth Saint-Emilion (Claret).

GRAND-PONTET, Château
First growth of Saint-Emilion (Claret).

GRAND-PUY-DUCASSE, Château
Fifth *Cru Classé* of the Médoc; Pauillac (Claret).

GRAND-PUY-LACOSTE, Château
Fifth *Cru Classé* of the Médoc; Paulliac (Claret).

GRAND-SAINT-JULIEN, Château du
The white wine of Château Lagrange, Saint-Julien (White Bordeaux). There is also a *Cru Grand-Saint-Julien*, a *Bourgeois* growth of Saint-Julien, Haut-Médoc (Claret).

GRAND-SAINT-LAMBERT, Château
Bourgeois growth of Pauillac; Haut Médoc (Claret).

GRAND-SOUSSANS, Château du
Bourgeois growth of Soussans; Haut-Médoc (Claret).

GRANDE-CÔTE, La
First growth Saint-Emilion (Claret).

GRANDES-MURAILLES
First growth Saint-Emilion (Claret).

GRANDES-VIGNES, Clos des
First growth Pomerol (Claret).

GRANDS-ECHÉZEAUX, Les
Tête de Cuvée of Flagey-Echézeaux (Red Burgundy).

GRANJO
A Portuguese white wine of the Sauternes type from the estates of the late Marquis de Soveral, Portuguese Ambassador to the Court of St. James's and personal friend of King Edward VII.

GRAPES
The fruit of the Vine.

(a) A bunch of grapes: Latin, *Botrus*; Italian, *Grappolo*; Spanish, *Racimo*; Portuguese, *Cacho*; French, *Grappe*, *Raisins*.

(b) The stalk of a bunch of grapes; Latin, *Scapus*; Italian, *Raspo*; Spanish, *Raspa*; Portuguese, *Engaco*; French, *Rafle*.

(c) The grape berries; Latin; *Uva*, Italian, *Uva*; Spanish, *Uva*; Portuguese, *Uva*; French, *Raisins*.

(d) What is left of the grapes after they have been pressed and their juice drawn, i.e. Husks; Latin, *Vinacea*; Italian, *Vinaccio*; Spanish, *Orujo*; Portuguese, *Bagaco* ; French, *Marc*.

(e) Grape-stones or pips; Latin, *Vinaceum*; Italian, *Vinacciuolo*; Spanish, *Granuja*; Portuguese, *Bagulho, Grainha*; French, *Pépins*.

GRAPPA
A crude Italian spirit distilled from the husks—the skins, pips and stalks of the grapes—after they have been pressed and the wine made.

GRAVES
The wine of Graves, when not otherwise qualified, refer to the wines from one of the most important wine-producing districts of the Gironde, a district which begins just outside Bordeaux, extends about five and a half miles to the west and some thirteen miles to the south. The Graves district produces both red and white wines, the red wines being of higher quality than the white, although the white are better known than the red under the name of Graves. There are thirty-five parishes or 'Communes' within

the Graves district. Their average yield is half a million gallons of very fine red wine, a million and a half of fair wines and a quarter of a million gallons red wines of moderate quality. The Communes of Graves which produce the best wines are those of *Pessac, Léognan, Martillac, Villenave d'Ornon* and *Mérignac.*

After *Château Haut-Brion,* the best-known Châteaux of the Graves district are: *La Mission - Haut - Brion, Pape-Clément, Bellegrave, Phénix-Haut-Brion,* all in the Commune of Pessac. *Haut-Bailly, Malartic-Lagravière, Domaine de Chavalier, Haut-Brion-Larrivet, Carbonnieux, Haut-Gardère,* all in the Commune of Léognan. *Smith-Haut-Lafitte, de Lagarde, Ferrand* and *Latour* in the Commune of *Martillac. Carbonnieux* and *Pontac-Monplaisir* in the Commune of Villenave d'Ornon. *Bon-Air, La Tour-du-Pape* and *Pique-Caillou,* in the Commune of *Mérignac. La-Tour-Haut-Brion,* in the Commune of Talence.

GRAVES DE SAINT-EMILION
The name given to a small district of the Saint-Emilion vinelands, the soil of which differs from that of other Saint-Emilion vineyards, being more gravelly. The finest wine of the *Graves de Saint-Emilion* is that of *Château Cheval Blanc.* Other famous Estates of this district are: *Château* and *Domaine Figeac, Châteaux La Tour-Figeac, La Tour-du-Pin-Figeac, Lamarzelle, La Dominique, Grand-Barrail - Lamarzelle - Figeac* and *Ripeau.* Also *Château Chauvin.*

GRECO DI GERACE
An agreeably dry white wine made from Greco grapes grown in the vineyards of Gerace, in Calabria (Italy).

GREECE
Considerable quantities of wine have been made in Greece for a far longer time than in any other part of the world, China excepted. Much wine is still being produced in Greece, but none of outstanding merit. The largest wine-producing districts of Greece, in order of importance, are: *Messinia, Attica, Achaia, Arcadia* and *Argolido-Korinthos.* The best Greek wines are the sweet wines of *Samos, Patras* and *Cephalonia.* The best-known are the *Mavrodaphne* and the *Agios Georgios,* a sweet dessert wine, dark red like vintage Port.

GREEK WINE
Wine from Greek vineyards. The Romans used to give the name of Greek or Greekish wine to an Italian wine which was sweet and potent.

> *Achilles.* I'll heat his blood with Greekish wine tonight.
> *Troilus and Cressida,*
> Act V, Scene ii.

GRENACHE
A sweetish red or tawny dessert wine from the Pyrénées (Roussillon), made chiefly in the *Banyuls* district from Grenache grapes.

GRENADINE
A *sirop* or liquid form of sugar, bright red in colour, entirely free from any trace of alcohol. It is used as a sweetening agent in *Cocktails* or with *Bitters.*

GRIGNOLINO
A red wine of no great distinction but none the less greatly prized locally; it is made in various parts of Piedmont from Grignolino grapes.

GRILLET, Château
The finest white table wine of the Rhône Valley: it is made from Viognier grapes grown in the Commune of Condrieu.

GRINZINGER
Red and white table wines from the vineyards of Grinzing, near Vienna.

GRUAUD-LAROSE, Château
Second *Cru Classé* of the Médoc; Saint-Julien (Claret).

GRÜNHÄUSER
One of the finest white wines of the Ruwer Valley (Trier district). The best vineyard of *Mertesdorf-Grünhaus* is *Herrenberg*, and its wine is sold under the name of *Maximin Grünhäuser Herrenberg*. Another good vineyard is *Lorenzberg*.

GRUMELLO
Italian red table wine from Valtellina vineyards (*Lombardy*).

GUEBWILLER
Township of Upper Alsace; its vineyards produce some very fine white wines.

GUIGNOLET
French Cherry Brandy from Angers.

GUIRAUD, Château
First-class growth of Sauternes.

GUMPOLDSKIRCHNER
Austrian red table wine from vineyards of the Vienna district; their white wine is usually sold as *Gumpoldskirchner Steinwein*.

GUNDERSHEIM
White wine of moderate quality from Rhinehesse, Worms district.

GUNTERSBLUM
White wine of fair quality from Rhinehesse, Oppenheim district.

GYÖNGYOS
Hungarian table wines, red and white; also sparkling wine.

HAARDT
Township of the Palatinate, Dürkheim district. White wines of fair quality.

HAGNAU
Township of Baden. White wines of moderate quality.

HAINFELD
Village of the Palatinate, Landau district. White wines of moderate quality.

HALBROT
Swiss *ordinaire*, light red table wines made from both black and white grapes; the equivalent of the German *Schillerwein*.

HALLAU
Swiss village of the Schaffhausen district: its wines are considered the best of the red table wines made in the eastern Cantons of Switzerland.

HALLGARTEN
Township of the Rhinegau. Fine to great white wines (Hock).

HALMHEIM
Village of Rhinehesse, Oppenheim district. White wines of moderate quality.

HAMBACH
Village of the Palatinate, Neustadt district. Fair white wines.

HARO
Township of Northern Spain, Ebro Valley, 60 miles from Burgoa. Good quality Rioja wines.

HARXHEIM
Village of the Palatinate, Mayence district. White wines of moderate quality.

HATTENHEIM
Township of the Rhinegau. Fine to great white wines (Hock).

HAUT-BAGES, Château
Fifth-class growth of the Médoc; Pauillac (Claret).

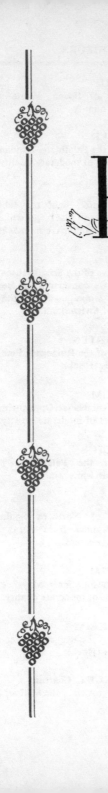

HAUT-BAILLY
First growth Léognan; Graves de Bordeaux (Claret).

HAUT-BARSAC
White wine from the vineyards of that part of the Commune of Barsac which is farthest away from the Garonne.

HAUT-BERGEY, Château
Bourgeois growth of Léognan; Graves de Bordeaux (Claret).

HAUT-BRION, Château
First *Cru Classé* of the Médoc, although in the Commune of Pessac, Graves de Bordeaux. Its ancient fame rests upon the excellence of its red wines, but there is also a small quantity of quite fair white wine made now at Château Haut-Brion.

HAUT-BRION LA MISSION, Château
First growth of Pessac; Graves de Bordeaux (Claret).

HAUT-BRION LARRIVET, Cru
First growth Léognan; Graves de Bordeaux (Claret).

HAUT-CAMENSAC, Cru
The name of the white wine from the vineyards of Château Camensac (Haut-Médoc).

HAUT-GARDÈRE, Château
First growth of Léognan; Graves de Bordeaux (white wine).

HAUT-MADÈRE, Château
Bourgeois growth of Villenave d'Ornon; Graves de Bordeaux (Claret and a little white wine).

HAUT-MÉDOC
The part of the Gironde Département from Blanquefort to Saint-Seurin-de-Cadourne along the left bank of the Garonne and Gironde rivers. The vineyards of the Haut-Médoc produce a much greater quantity of truly great red table wines than the vineyards of all other parts of France or of the world.

HAUT-PEYRAGUEY, Clos
First *Cru Classé* of Sauternes; Bommes.

HAUT-POURRET, Château
Second growth of Saint-Emilion (Claret).

HAUT-SAUTERNES
A commercial appellation which does not correspond to any geographical or administrative division of the Sauternes vinelands. It is usually given to a sweetish white wine, from middling to fair in quality, which may be a blend of Sauternes wines from different vineyards and vintages.

HAUT-SIMARD, Château
First growth of Saint-Emilion (Claret).

HAUT-BARDE, Château
Bourgeois growth of Villenave d'Ornon; Graves de Bordeaux (Claret).

HAUTERIVE, Château
Bourgeois growth of Saint-Germain d'Esteuil; Médoc (Claret and White Bordeaux).

HAUTVILLERS
First growth Champagne; Marne Valley (Champagne).

HECTOLITRE
French wine measure equal to 100 litres or 22 gallons.

HEDDESHEIM
Village of the Nahe Valley; Kreuznach district. White wines of moderate quality.

HEILBRONN
Township of the Neckar Valley, Württemberg. Both red and white wines of moderate quality.

HELLEICH or HELLMASS

German for new wine when it has 'fallen bright', as opposed to *Trübeich or Trübmass*, meaning new wine still in its original turbid state.

HERMITAGE

The red and white wines which are entitled to the name *Hermitage* are those from the vineyards which cover three sides of the hill rising sharply from the little town of Tain, on the left bank of the river Rhône, some distance south of Lyons and north of Avignon, opposite Tournon. Among the best vineyards of the Coteau de l'Hermitage are *La Sizer*, *La Chapelle*, *Les Bessards* (red wines), and *Les Recoulles*, *Les Murets* and *Chante-Alouette* (white wines).

HERKHEIM

Township of the Palatinate, Bad-Dürkheim district. Both white and red wines of moderate quality.

HESSLOCH

Village of Rhinehesse, Worms district. White wines of moderate quality.

HEURIGE

The name of the new wine served in the Cafés of Grinzing, near Vienna, at vintage time.

HIGHBALL

A 'long' drink of diluted spirits, usually whisky, served with cracked ice in a large, heavy tumbler, sometimes with a little glass stick for stirring.

When not otherwise qualified, a *Highball* is understood to be Whisky, ice and syphon. There are *Bourbon*, *Brandy*, *Gin*, *Rye Highballs* made in a similar way with these different spirits. There are also less orthodox *Highballs* such as: the

Bermuda Highball: ⅓ Brandy, ⅓ Gin, ⅓ French Vermouth.

Cascade Highball: ½ Italian Vermouth, ½ Crème de Cassis.

Pompier Highball: ½ French Vermouth, ½ Crème de Cassis.

HILDE, Château de

Bourgeois growth of Bégles; Graves de Bordeaux (Claret).

HIPPOCRAS

One of the most popular forms of aromatized and spiced wines during the Middle Ages and even long after. There is every reason to believe that the basis of Hippocras was sour or pricked wine, of which there must have been an embarrassingly large quantity at a time when wine was kept on ullage, in casks, or in ill-stoppered bottles, before the use of cork for stoppers. Such wine being heavily sweetened with honey and flavoured with herbs and spices was then filtered through a woollen bag, known as Hippocrates sleeve, hence the name *Hippocras*, often written *Ipocras* or *Ypocras*.

HIPPOCRAS, WHITE

Take a gallon of white Lisbon-wine, 2 pounds of Sugar, 2 ounces of Cinnamon, 4 corns of whole Black Pepper, a little Mace and 2 Lemons; cut the Lemons into quarters. Let these stand to infuse some time in the wine, and afterwards pass all through a straining Bag, which is to be hanged up, and a vessel set under it to receive the Liquor; you should keep the Bags open by the means of two sticks set across. The Hippocras ought to be strained three or four times, and if it does not pass freely, you may add a wineglass of Milk, which will soon facilitate its passing. If you would have it scented with Musk or Amber, wrap up a grain of it beaten with Sugar in cotton, and stick it at the end of the straining Bag.
—c.c.c.c.

HOCHHEIM

At the extreme limit (south) of the Rhinegau, not far from Wiesbaden, on the river Main, close to where it joins the Rhine. The wines of Hochheim are believed to be responsible for the name 'Hock', which replaced, in England, the old appellation of 'Rhenish' for all Rhine wines. Best vineyards of Hochheim: *Domdechaney, Kirchenstûck, Stein, Falkenberg, Daubhaus, Hölle.*

HOCK

Although no actual evidence has as yet come to light to place beyond all doubt the fact that the name Hock is derived from Hochheim, a village surrounded by vineyards, upon the right bank of the River Main, close to where it flows into the Rhine, such is the generally accepted origin of the name Hock, a name which has completely replaced, in England, the older name 'Rhenish'. Under the designation 'Hock' are included the wines of the Rhinegau, Rhinehesse, Palatinate, Nahe Valley and Franconia. Hocks are bottled in red bottles, brown or brick red, whilst Moselles are bottled in green or blue-green bottles.

HOGSHEAD

Wine cask, the actual contents of which are not defined by law; according to the custom of the Trade, however, a hogshead is accepted as containing 1½ *tierce* or 52·486 imperial gallons (22 dozen).

HOLLANDS

The name of a very distinctive type of *Gin*, made in Holland. Originally the Dutch used to crush the juniper berries and ferment their juice, which they distilled after. Now *Hollands* is distilled from a mash of barley malt mixed with ground juniper (or equivalent flavouring agent), and it is distilled at a much lower strength than *London Gin* or *American Gin*, so that it has a flavour of its own, greatly valued by those who are accustomed to it, but too pronounced for *Hollands* to be used in the mixing of Cocktails and other drinks, where its assertiveness would not be welcome.

HOMER

The Father of Poetry was a true son of Bacchus, so much so that Horace dared call him 'vinosus Homerus' (Epist. xix. Lib. I, v. 6). Homer describes many wines in both the Iliad and Odyssey, as 'sweet', 'honey-sweet', 'sweet to the tongue', 'life-giving', 'mirth-provoking', 'worthy of the gods', 'beverage divine', etc.

HORACE (68–8 B.C.)

The bouquet of wine permeates practically the whole of Horace's poetry. The 19th Ode of the Second Book of Odes, *In Bacchum*, which begins with 'Bacchum in remotis', is assuredly one of his finest; and so is the 25th Ode of the Third Book, *Ad Bacchum*, which begins thus:

Quo me Bacche, rapis tui Plenum?

Better known, however, is the 37th Ode of the First Book, calling upon the Romans to rejoice at the news of Cleopatra's death:

Nunc est bibendum!
(Now is the time to drink!)

In many of his Odes, Horace sings the praises of the various Latin and Greek wines, chiefly the wines of Cæcuba and Falernum, Chios and Lesbos.

The wine of Cæcuba appears to have been the favourite wine of Horace:

Festo quid potius die
Neptuni faciam? Prome reconditum,
Lyde, strenua Cæcubum,
Od. XXVIII, Lib. III, vv. 1–3.

(What is there for me to do on this. Neptune's feast? Lydee, quickly let us have your best Cæcuban wine.)

Horace admitted that the wines of Lesbos were the most fashionable of all Greek wines, but he preferred the wines of Chios:

Quo Chium pretio cadum
Mercemur. . . .
Od. XIX, Lib. III, v. 5.

But he liked the wines of Italy better than those of the Greek Archipelago: thus, addressing the serving boy, he asks that his glass be filled with wines of Chios or of Lesbos, then, thinking better of it, he adds: 'Give me rather some Cæcuba wine which tones up the heart'.

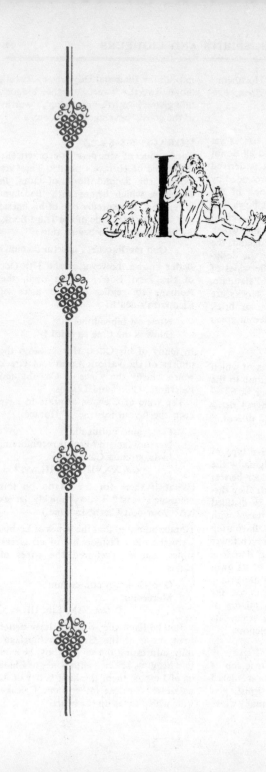

HÖRSTEIN
White table wine from the Freigeríct vineyards of Franconia.

HOSPICES DE BEAUNE
A home for the aged and poor, founded in the fifteenth century, at Beaune, in Burgundy. Its chief income has been for centuries past, and still is, the sale of the wines from the vineyards bequeathed from time to time to the Hospices. The wines of the Hospices are sold by auction every year. Genuine *Hospices de Beaune* wines, and of a good vintage, should always bear the name of the Cuvée, that is to say the name of the donor of the vineyard from which the wine offered for sale was made, as well as the name of the Commune where such vineyards are situated. Thus:

RED WINES

Cuvées				Communes
Bétault	-	-	-	- Beaune
Billardet	-	-	-	- Pommard
Blondeau	-	-	-	- Volnay
Boillot	-	-	-	- Auxey-Duresses
Brunet	-	-	-	- Beaune
Charlotte Dumay			-	- Corton
Clos des Avaux			-	- Beaune
Cyrot	-	-	-	- Savigny
Dames de la Charité			-	- Pommard
Dames Hospitalières				- Beaune
Docteur Peste	-		-	- Corton
Du Bay-Peste	-		-	- Savigny/Vergelesses
Estienne	-	-	-	- Beaune
Forneret	-	-	-	- Savigny/Vergelesses
Fouquerand	-	-	-	- Savigny/Vergelesses
Gauvain	-	-	-	- Meursault/Santenots
Guigone de Salins		-		- Beaune
Henri Gélicot	-		-	- Meursault
Jacques Lebelin			-	- Monthélie
Jehan de Massol			-	- Meursault/Santenots
Nocolas Rollin	-		-	- Beaune
Rousseau-Deslandes				- Beaune

WHITE WINES

Albert Grivault		-		- Meursault/Charmes
Baudot	-	-	-	- Meursault
De Bahézre de Lanlay				- Meursault/Charmes
Goureau	-	-	-	- Meursault
Jehean Humblot		-		- Meursault
Loppin	-	-	-	- Meursault

HRAD
The best wine of Bzenec, one of the more important wine-producing parishes of Czechoslovakia.

HUCKLE-MY-BUFF
Sussex slang for beer, eggs and brandy mixed. (*Cooper's Sussex Glossary*.) Farmer and Henley's *Dictionary of Slang* calls *Huckle-my-but*, 'beer, egg and brandy made hot'.

HUNGARY
Besides *Tokay*, the finest Hungarian wine, Hungary produces a great variety of red and white table wines, as well as many liqueurs and spirits. The more popular table wines are: *Red: Egri Bikaver, Egri Kadarka. White: Apczer.*

Among the dessert wines other than *Tokay*, the best known are the white *Debroë Hárslevelü.*

HYDROMEL
Primarily honey diluted in water, with herbs and spices added according to taste and available supplies.

HYMETTUS, Mount
One of the best-known wine-producing areas of Attica (Greece).

IHRINGEN
The largest wine-producing parish of the Kaiserstuhl ridge, in Brisgau (Baden). Mostly white wines of fair quality.

ILBESHEIM
A small wine-producing parish of the Palatinate, Landau district: some fair white wines.

ÎLES DE LA GIRONDE
The principal vineyards of the islands in the course of the River Gironde are: *Île Bouchard*, opposite Blaye; *Île Fumadelle*, Commune of Soussans; *Île Margaux*, Commune of Margaux; *Île du Nord*, *Île Nouvelle*, also called *Île sans-pain; Île Patiras; Île Verte.*

ILLATS
A wine-producing parish of the Graves de Bordeaux, south of Podensac and Cérons, west of Barsac and Pujols: mostly

white wines from middling to fair in quality.

IMMI or POT
Swiss wine measure equal to a tenth of the *Viertel*, or 0·35 gallon.

IMPÉRIALE
The name given to an outsize glass bottle, made in France, of green glass, for bottling fine Clarets which are intended for long keeping. An *Impériale* should hold at least eight bottles of wine, allowing for the sediment; eight and a half bottles are commonly decanted from an *Impériale*, and occasionally up to nearly nine bottles.

INFERNO
One of the better red table wines of the Valtellina (Lombardy).

IPHOFEN
A township of Franconia, Scheinfeld district: some fair white wines.

IRISH WHISKEY
A grain spirit distilled from malted barley, mostly, and in pot stills in preference to patent stills. The chief difference between Irish and Scotch whiskys is one of flavour; it is due to the fact that, in Ireland, the malt is dried in a kiln which has a solid floor, so that the smoke from the fuel used does not come in contact with the grain, whereas, in Scotland, the malt is 'smoke-cured'.

IROULÉGUY
A rather heady red table wine from the Basque country, south of Bayonne: it possesses a distinctive character of its own and is very highly appreciated locally.

ISCHIA
A small island in the Bay of Naples: its vineyards produce some white wines middling to fair in quality, which are usually sold under the better-known name of Capri.

ISSAN, Château d'
A third *Cru Classé* of the Médoc; Cantenac (Claret).

ITALY
Italy is, after France, the largest wine-producing country in the world. The following tables give the names of the Italian wine-producing provinces with the average quantity of wine made in each of them to show their importance bibulously.

Districts	Wine Production Hectolitres
Piemonte - - - -	5,064,260
Liguria - - - -	742,000
Lombardia - - -	2,877,060
Venezia Tridentina - -	872,350
Veneto - - - -	2,711,180
Venezia Giulia e Zara -	679,520
Æmilia - - - -	4,060,630
Toscana - - - -	4,543,680
Marche - - - -	2,709,920
Umbria - - - -	1,082,150
Lazio - - - -	2,085,070
Abruzzi e Molise - -	1,950,080
Campania - - - -	5,888,900
Puglie - - - -	4,548,870
Lucania - - - -	550,910
Calabria - - - -	786,630
Sicilia - - - -	4,358,110
Sardegna - - -	686,503
Total	46,197,670

Red and white, also some *rosés*, table wines, mostly of the *ordinaire* class, constitute the bulk of the Italian wine production, but there is also a fairly important quantity of table wines made of a sufficiently high standard of quality to be exported and to compete with quality table wines from other lands in the markets of the world.

IZARRA
A Basque liqueur with an Armagnac brandy basis and flavoured with wild flowers from the Pyrénées. It is made in two colours, yellow, which is the sweeter

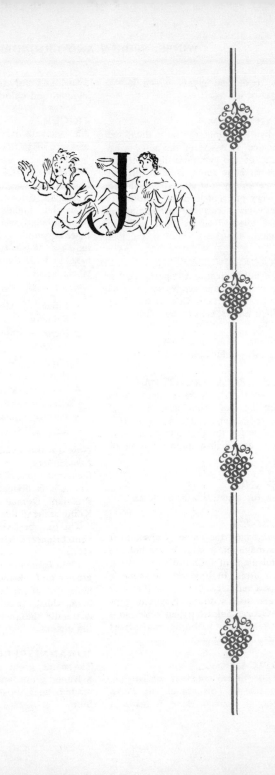

of the two, and green, which is the stronger of the two.

JAMAICA RUM
Rum distilled from molasses in the island of Jamaica. It is one of the best-known and one of the commercially most important of cane rums. It is distilled at a comparatively low strength so that it has a very pungent 'rummy' flavour. Its colour varies, with the proportion of caramel used, from a light gold to mahogany.

JARNAC
A small but ancient and important town of the Cognac country, where some of the more important Cognac distillers have their homes, cellars and offices.

JEAN DU MAYNE, Château
First growth Saint-Emilion (Claret).

JEREZ DE LA FRONTERA
The hub of the Sherry trade. An old Arab fortified city of Andalucia, north of Cadiz, it is surrounded by vineyards responsible for the best Sherry, a name which is an English approximation of *Jerez*.

JEREZANO
Spanish for a native wine of Jerez.

JEROBOAM
In Champagne the name is given to a double magnum, a large bottle holding the equivalent of four ordinary bottles, or 3·20 litres. In England the name is used for a very large bottle, one that may be larger than a double magnum. Professor George Saintsbury, in *Notes on a Cellar Book*, gives six bottles as the right contents of a Jeroboam.

JEROPIGA
Grape juice boiled to a syrup consistency: it is made in Portugal as the *Pedro Ximenez*, or *Vino de color*; is made in Spain and for the same purpose, to sweeten and colour other wines.

JIGGER
An American barman's name for a small measure of spirits: 1½ liquid oz.

JOHANNISBERG
One of the most famous growths of the Rhinegau, between Winkel and Geisenheim, but higher up the hill, with a beautiful view over the Rhine and Rhinehesse beyond. The best wines of Johannisberg are the best of the *Schloss Johannisberg*, and these are sold under different labels according to a carefully graded scale of excellence, as follows:

1 Fürst v. Metternichscher *Cabinet* Spätlese.
2 Fürst v. Metternichscher *Cabinet* Auslese.
3 Fürst v. Metternichscher *Original Abfüllung* Auslese.
4 Fürst v. Metternichscher *Original Abfüllung* (not Auslese).
5 *Schloss Johannisberg*, Wachstum Fürst v. Metternich.

Next to the *Schloss* comes the *Klaus Johannisberg*, a growth always bearing the name of one of the proprietors among whom it is divided, such as the Royal Prussian Domains, Graf Schönborn, Kommerzierat Krayer Erden, etc.

The next best vineyards are known as Erntebringer, Kochsberg, Schlossberg and Hölle.

Plain *Johannisberg*, with the name of a grower and whether 'Auslese' or not, is never one of the best wines of Johannisberg, whilst the name *Dorf Johannisberg* is usually that of the cheapest wine of the district.

JOHANNISBERG (Valais)
The name given in the Valais to the Sylvaner grape and to the white wine made from it, mostly in the vineyards of Sion.

JOIGNY

One of the oldest towns of the Yonne Département (Lower Burgundy), the vineyards of which produce much red and white wines of no outstanding merit. The best–known wine of Joigny is the *Vin gris* of the Côte St. Jacques, a wine which one occasionally sees listed in some Paris restaurants.

JULEP

Formerly a great country favourite, in England; it is often said to have been introduced by Captain Marryatt, but it is not so, as Milton's lines clearly prove:

. . . 'Behold this cordial Julep here,
That foams and dances in his crystal bounds,
With spirits of balm and fragrant syrups mix'd'.

Applejack Julep. 3 fresh mint sprigs, ½ teaspoon powdered sugar, 1 jigger *Applejack*. Crush leaves from 1 mint sprig in glass, cover with sugar, stir, and let sugar dissolve. Add *Applejack* and fill glass with finely cracked ice. Stir until glass is frosted. Decorate with remaining mint sprigs.

Brandy Julep. Fill the glasses or jug with finely cracked or shaved ice. For each person allow one Port glass of Cognac. Bruise several sprigs of mint with half a teaspoonful of sugar for each person, and strain into the glass or jug. Add a dash of rum for each glass, dress with fruit and a few sprigs of mint which have been moistened and dipped in sugar. Serve with straws.

Mint Julep. Crush one lump of sugar at the bottom of a tall glass. Add half a dozen small sprigs of mint, which should first be lightly twisted between the fingers to break the skin of the leaves. Cover with whisky and allow to stand for ten minutes. Then pour in balance of whisky (to make a long drink a full whisky glass should be used), fill the glass with finely crushed ice and stir rapidly with a spoon until the outside of the glass is frosted.

Served garnished with mint sprigs. The best Maryland Juleps are made with old rye. *Frederic Arnold Kummer, Baltimore.*

Ben Clark Mint Julep. Crush in bottom of each glass 5 large crisp mint leaves, with a dash of sugar syrup. Let stand 15 minutes, if possible, to steep, after adding a generous shot of good bourbon whisky. Pack tight into each glass shaved ice, dried in towel. Stir gently until glass is frosted. Decorate with mint sprig and serve, wrapping bottom of glass in paper napkin to catch sweat.

Rum Julep. Dissolve three tablespoonfuls of soft sugar in a little water and add a few sprigs of mint. Let this soak until the flavour of the mint is extracted, and then strain this juice into a tumbler. Add a brandy glass of rum, one or two cherries, a slice of tangerine and any other small fruits that are in season. Fill up the glass with finely crushed ice and serve with straws.

JULIÉNAS

One of the Beaujolais wine-producing Communes which is responsible for some of the best red wines of the Rhône Département. One of its best vineyards is that of Château des Capitans.

JURA

Many good wines are made from grapes grown upon the lower slopes of the Jura Mountains facing the Burgundian plains, but those which have attained the greatest measure of fame are those of Arbois, L'Etoile, and Poligny, towards the east, and, further west, the wine made near Lons-le-Saulnier and known as *Château-Chalon.*

JURANÇON

A luscious, orange-coloured 'dessert' wine made from over-ripe grapes from vineyards near Pau. A very rare wine, hardly ever obtainable commercially, as there is so little made.

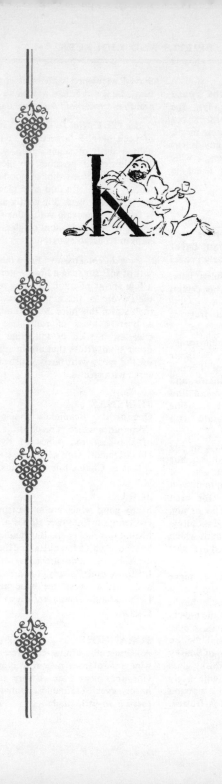

KABINETT WEIN
German for 'Special Reserve' or 'Private Bin'.

KAISERSTUHL
A volcanic ridge in Brisgau (Baden), with twenty-one parishes the vineyards of which produce the best wines of Baden, mostly white.

KALAVRYTA
One of the red wines of Morea (Greece).

KALLSTADT
One of the more important townships of the Bad-Dürkheim district (Palatinate); its vineyards produce both red and white wines, some of the white being wines of fine quality.

KALTERERSEEWEIN
One of the best red wines of the Tyrol, from lakeside vineyards.

KAN
Dutch for *Litre* (0·88 gallon).

KANNE (*pl.* **Kannen**)
German for *Litre* (0·88 gallon).

KARTHÄUSER HOFBERG
The best wine of Eitelsbach, in the Ruwer Valley (Moselle).

KAYSERBERG
One of the good white wine-producing townships of Alsace.

KECSKEMÉT
One of the wine-producing localities of Hungary which is noted for its white wines.

KÉKNYELÜ
One of the better white wines of the Badacsony Hills (Hungary).

KELLER
German for cellar.

**KELLERABFÜLLUNG and
KELLERABZUG**
German for 'cellar bottled', the equivalent of the French 'Château bottled'.

KEPHESIA
The district of Attica, the vineyards of which produce the best wines of Greece.

KIEDRICH
One of the smaller townships of the Rhinegau, near Eltville; its vineyards produce some very fair white wines (Hock).

KILDERKIN
Small casks, of which there are two sizes, one for beer (18 gallons) and another for wine (15 gallons).

KINHEIM
One of the smaller wine-producing townships upon the left bank of the Moselle; some fair white wines.

KIRCHHOFEN
One of the best white wines of Freibourg-im-Brisgau (Baden).

KIRRWEILER
One of the less important localities of the Landau district (Palatinate); red and white wines from middling to fair in quality.

KIRSCH, KIRSCHWASSER
A very popular spirit distilled chiefly in Germany, Alsace and Switzerland from the fermented juice of small, black and very juicy cherries which grow in a wild state in the Black Forest, the Vosges and other mountains. The *Schwartzwalder Kirschwasser* (Black Forest Cherry Brandy) has a world-wide reputation for excellence; so has the *Kirsch* of Alsace. *Kirsch* is always pure white: it is matured in demijohns, not in wooden casks from which it would extract some colouring matter.

KIRWAN, Château
Third *Cru Classé* of the Médoc (Claret).

KLEVNER
The name of a white grape grown in Alsace and from which a white wine is made, which is sold under the same name, usually coupled with the name of the vineyard where it came from, or that of the owner thereof.

KNIPPERLÉ
The name of a white grape grown in Alsace for the making of white wines, which are sold under the same name usually coupled with the name either of the vineyard where the wine came from, or that of the owner thereof.

KOBERN or COBERN
A small township of the Lower Moselle, near Coblence; white wines from middling to fair in quality.

KOCHEM or COCHEM
One of the more important townships of the Lower Moselle; white wines from fair to fine in quality.

KOENEN
One of the smaller wine-producing localities of the Lower Saar valley, near Trier; some fair white wines (Moselles).

KÖNIGSBACH
One of the best growths of the Palatinate (Neustadt); very fine white wines (Hock).

KRESCENZ
German for 'the growth of . . .' followed by the name of the vineyard owner.

KREUZNACH, Bad
The most important wine-producing centre and wine-mart of the Nahe Valley; white wines from middling to fair and fine.

KRÖV-KÖVENIG
A small township of the Middle Moselle, Bernkastel district; white wines from fair to fine in quality.

KRÖVER
The wine of Kröv-Kövenig vineyards.

KUMMEL
One of the most popular of all liqueurs, with definite digestive properties. It has been made in Holland since 1575, in Riga, and Berlin. *Kummel* has as its basis some highly distilled or almost neutral spirit, sometimes distilled from grain, sometimes from potatoes, rarely if ever from wine. It is flavoured with caraway seeds and cumin, to which it owes its digestive qualities. It is more or less sweetened, according to the formulæ used for different brands, but is always pure white.

KVASS
A very refreshing Russian beverage which is made in many Russian households about once a week:

'With 8 quarts water take 1½ lb. malt, 1 lb. rye flour, 1¼ lb. sugar, ¼ of a lb. mint leaves, ¼ pepper pod, and ¼ cake of yeast. Mix the malt and flour with boiling water and make a thick dough. Put into barely warm oven, and leave for the night. Next day dilute dough with 8 quarts boiling water and pour into a wooden tub. Let stand for 12 hours, then pass through a cloth. Pour 1 quart into an enamel saucepan, put on fire, add 1½ lb. sugar and an infusion made with the mint leaves (resembling weak tea). Boil once, then take off fire, cool until just warm, and add the yeast previously diluted with 1 cup of this same warm liquid. Let stand in warm place until it begins to ferment; then pour into the rest of the kvass in the wooden tub, and let stand until bubbles appear. Prepare clean bottles, putting 1 Malaga raisin into each; pour in the kvass, cork the bottles, tie the corks with string to the necks of the bottles, and keep in warm place for a day or two. Then put in a cold cellar.'

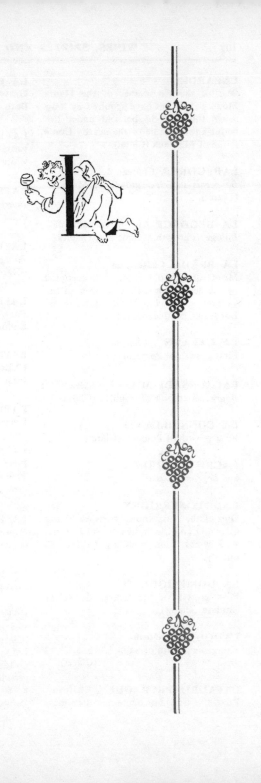

LABARDE
One of the Communes of the Haut-Médoc: its wines have acquired by long usage the right to be sold under the better-known name of the nearby Commune of Margaux (Claret).

LABÉGORCE, Château de
Bourgeois supérieur growth of Margaux (Claret).

LA BÉGORCE-ZÉDÉ, Domaine de
Bourgeois growth of Soussans (Claret).

LA BRÈDE, Château de
Montesquieu's old home, still occupied by his descendants. Its vineyards, in the Commune de La Brède, Graves de Bordeaux, produce some fair white wines.

LA CABANNE, Château
First growth of Pomerol (Claret).

LACAUSSADE-MILON, Château
Bourgeois growth of Pauillac (Claret).

LA CONSEILLANTE
First growth of Pomerol (Claret).

LACRIMA CHRISTI
See *Lagrima Christi.*

LADOIX-SERRIGNY
One of the least known parishes of the Côte d'Or, a little to the north of Beaune. Red wines from middling to fair in quality.

LA DOMINIQUE
First growth of the Graves de Saint-Emilion (Claret).

LADOUYS, Château
Bourgeois growth of Saint-Estèphe
(Claret).

LAFAURIE-PEYRAGUEY, Château
First *Cru Classé* of Sauternes; Bommes.

LA FERRADE, Château
Graves de Bordeaux; Villenave d'Ornon. Both Claret and white wine of fair quality.

LAFFITTE, Château
Entre-deux-Mers; Yvrac. Both red and white wines of the *ordinaire* class.

LAFFITTE-CANTEGRIC, Château
Bourgeois growth of the Médoc; Listrac (Claret).

LAFITTE, Château
Bourgeois growth of the Médoc; Bégadan (Claret).

LAFITTE-CANTELOUP, Château
Bourgeois supérieur growth of the Médoc; Ludon (Claret).

LAFITE or LAFITE-ROTHSCHILD, Château
First *Cru Classé* of the Médoc (Claret).

LAFITE, Cru
Entre-deux-Mers; Camblanes (Claret).

LA FLEUR, Château
First growth of Saint-Emilion (Claret). There is also a Château Lafleur, a first growth of Pomerol (Claret).

LA FLEUR-MILON, Château
Bourgeois growth of the Médoc; Pauillac (Claret).

LA FLEUR-PÉTRUS, Château
First growth of Pomerol (Claret).

LAFON, Château
Bourgeois growth of the Médoc; Listrac (Claret). There are three other Châteaux Lafon; one in the Graves de Bordeaux, Gradignan (Claret); one a *Bourgeois* growth of the Blayais (Claret); and one a second *Cru Classé* of Sauternes (Sauternes).

LAFONTA, Château
Île Nouvelle, Gironde; its vineyards are capable of producing 450 tuns of Claret and 50 tuns of white wine.

LA GAFFELIÉRE-NAUDES, Château
First growth of Saint-Emilion (Claret).

LAGAR
Spanish and Portuguese name of the square stone trough in which the ripe grapes are piled at vintage time to be crushed underfoot.

LAGARDE, Domaine de
Bourgeois growth of the Graves de Bordeaux; Martillac (Claret).

LA GAUDE
A small township of Provence; Var. Its vineyards produce some fair red wines.

LA GRANDE CÔTE
First growth of Saint-Emilion (Claret).

LAGRANGE, Château
Third *Cru Classé* of the Médoc; Saint-Julien (Claret). There is also a *Cru Lagrange*, a first growth of Pomerol (Claret) and a *Domaine de Lagrange*, at Lussac, Saint-Emilonnais (Claret).

LAGRIMA CHRISTI
The name of a golden, rather sweet and very delicate wine made from grapes grown on the lower slopes of Vesuvius. There is also a little red *Lagrima Christi* made, but it is not nearly as attractive as the white.

LAHONTAN, Château
Bourgeois growth of the Graves de Bordeaux; Villenave d'Ornon. Mostly Claret of fair quality; a little *ordinaire* white wine.

LA HOURINGUE, Château
Bourgeois growth of the Médoc; Macau (Claret).

LA LAGUNE, Château
Third *Cru Classé* of the Médoc; Ludon (Claret). Now known as *Château Grand La Lagune*.

LALANDE, Château
Bourgeois supérieur growth of the Médoc; Saint-Estèphe (Claret). There are also two *Châteaux Lalande, Bourgeois* growths of the Médoc, at Listrac and at Bégadan (Claret).

LA LOUVIÈRE, Château
Graves de Bordeaux; Léognan (Claret and some white wine).

LA MADELEINE, Château
First growth of Saint-Emilion (Claret).

LA MAQUELINE, Cru
Palus growth of the Médoc; Macau (Claret).

LAMARQUE
A Commune of the Médoc 36 kilometres north-west of Bordeaux; its wines have acquired by long usage the right to be sold under the better-known name of the adjoining Commune of Listrac.

LAMARZELLE FIGEAC
First growth Graves de Saint-Emilion (Claret).

LAMBRUSCO
One of the best red wines of the Province of Emilia (Italy).

LAMB'S WOOL
'To 1 quart of strong hot ale add the pulp of 6 roasted apples, together with a small quantity of grated nutmeg and ginger, with a sufficient quantity of raw sugar to sweeten it; stir the mixture assiduously, and let it be served hot.'
'What would one have given to sit

with Pepys on a night, as he sat on November 9, 1666, at "Cards till two in the morning drinking Lamb's Wool".' That was two months after the Great Fire of London.

LA MISSION HAUT-BRION
First growth of the Graves de Bordeaux; Pessac (Claret)

LAMOTHE, Château
One of the second growths of Sauternes; it is divided between two owners and its total average is 14 tuns white wine. There are also no less than seven other Châteaux Lamothe in the Gironde, producing both red and white wines, mostly red, none of which possesses any particular merit.

LANDAU
An important wine-producing locality of the Palatinate. Its vineyards produce some fair white wines.

LANESSAN, Château
Bourgeois growth of the Médoc; Cussac (Claret).

LANGENLONSHEIM
Small township of the Nahe Valley, near Kreuznach; white wines of fair quality (Hock).

LANGOA-BARTON, Château
Third *Cru Classé* of the Médoc; Saint-Julien (Médoc).

LANGOIRAN
One of the Communes of the Gironde, 26 kilometres south-south-east of Bordeaux, the name of which is used, like that of Sauternes, for the wine-producing district, including its own vineyards and those of seven nearby Communes: Langoiran, Baurech, Haux, Lestiac, Le Tourne, Paillet and Tabanac. This district is responsible for the production of a large quantity of red wines, not of outstanding excellence, as well as a larger quantity still of white wines, of fair to middling quality, for which the demand is keener. The vineyards of the Langoiran district are on the right bank of the Garonne, opposite those of the Graves district.

LANGON
A small town on the left bank of the Garonne, the market town of the Sauternes District.

LANGUEDOC
One of the southernmost wine-producing Provinces of France. It is, since the French Revolution, divided into several Départements, including the Gard, Aude and Hérault, the three 'Midi' Départements responsible for enormous quantities of common wines every year. There are a few good Languedoc wines, chiefly of the Dessert Wine type.

LAROSE, Château
There are several wine-producing estates in the Gironde bearing this name, mostly hyphenated with the name or names of present or past owners. Much the best wine is that of the *Château Gruaud-Larose*, a second *Cru Classé* Commune of Saint-Julien; then that of the *Châteaux Larose-Perganson* and *Larose-Trintandon*, two *Bourgeois* growths of the Commune of Saint-Laurent (Médoc). The least distinguished of all is the wine of plain *Château Larose* in the Commune of Baurech, Entre-deux-Mers.

LASCOMBES, Château
Second *Cru Classé* of the Médoc; Margaux (Claret).

LA SERRE, Château
First growth of Saint-Emilion (Claret).

LAS PALMAS
The chief wine-exporting centre of the Canary Islands: it was responsible, in Shakespeare's time, for such names as Palm Sack and Palm Wine, as alternative

appellations for the more usual Canary Sack.

LA TÂCHE

One of the finest vineyards of the Côte d'Or; *Vosne-Romanée* (Red Burgundy). *La Tâche* is owned by the Domaines de la Romanée Conti.

LATOUR, Château

First *Cru Classé* of the Médoc; Pauillac (Claret). There are seven other Châteaux in the Gironde Département called Latour, La Tour and de la Tour, but none of them produces any wine comparable to that of the one and only *Grand Cru Château Latour*, Pauillac.

LA TOUR-BLANCHE, Château

First *Cru Classé* of Sauternes; Bommes (white wine).

LA TOUR-CARNET, Château

Fourth *Cru Classé* of the Médoc; Saint-Laurent (Claret).

LA TOUR-DE-MARBUZET, Château de

Bourgeois growth of the Médoc; Saint-Estèphe (Claret).

LA TOUR-DE-MONS, Château

Bourgeois growth of the Médoc; Soussans (Claret).

LA TOUR-FIGEAC, Château

First growth of Saint-Emilion (Claret).

LATOUR-HAUT-BRION, Château

Graves de Bordeaux; Talence (Claret).

LATOUR-PIBRAN, Château

Bourgeois growth of the Médoc; Pauillac (Claret).

LA TOUR POMEROL, Château

First growth Pomerol (Claret).

LA TOUR-POURRET, Château

Second growth Saint-Emilion (Claret).

LA TOUR-RAUZAN

Bourgeois growth of the Médoc; Saint-Sauveur (Claret).

LAUBENHEIM

Village of the Nahe Valley; Kreuznach. Its vineyards produce some white wines middling to fair in quality. There is another Laubenheim, the first town on the road from Mainz to Worms, in Rhinehesse; its vineyards produce a fair quantity of white wines of moderate quality.

LAUJAC, Château

Bourgeois growth of the Médoc; Bégadan (Claret).

LAURENZANE, Château

An important estate of the Graves de Bordeaux; Gradignan (Claret).

LAVAUX

The semi-circle of terraced vineyards from Lausanne to Vevey (Canton de Vaud) at the eastern end of the Lake of Geneva, which produce some of the finest white wines of Switzerland.

LAYON, Coteaux du

Some of the best white wines of the Maine-et-Loire Département (Anjou). The best wines of the Coteaux du Layon are those from the vineyards of the right bank of the Layon: *Quarts de Chaume, Faye, Beaulieu* and *Bonnezeaux*.

LEAGUER

A South African wine measure equal to 26¼ gallons.

LEANYKA

A light table wine from the Eger and other wine-producing districts of Hungary. There are two types of Leanyka wines, the *Leanyka Szaraz* which is an absolutely dry wine, and the *Leanyka Edes*, which is fairly sweet.

LE BOSCQ, Château
Bourgeois growth of the Médoc; Saint-Estèphe (Claret).

LE BURCK, Château
Entre-deux-Mers; Ambès (Claret).

LE CADET, Château
First growth Saint-Emilion (Claret).

LE COUVENT, Clos
First growth Saint-Emilion (Claret).

LE CROCK, Château
Bourgeois growth of the Médoc; Saint-Estèphe (Claret).

LE DÉSERT, Château
Graves de Bordeaux; Léognan (Claret).

LE GAY, Château
First growth Pomerol (Claret).

LEISTADT
Village of the Palatinate; Dürkheim: its vineyards produce both red and white wines of moderate quality.

LEITACHER
The white wine of Bozen, in the Tyrol, up to 1919 when Bozen became Bolzano and Leitacher, Santa-Giustina-Leitach.

LEIWEN
A parish of the Middle Moselle which adjoins Trittenheim and produces some very fair white wines (Moselle).

LE MESNIL
First growth of the Côte des Blanes, between Avize and Oger (Champagne).

LÉOGNAN
One of the finest of the wine-producing Communes of the Graves district, 13 kilometres south of Bordeaux. Its best wines are those of *Château Haut-Bailly*,

Gazin, Rigailhou, Malartic-Lagravière and *Boismartin; Domaine de Chevalier* and *Cru Larrivet-Haut-Brion* (Claret only); and *Châteaux Carbonnieux, Olivier, Le Désert, Le Pape, Fieuzal, Haut-Gardère* and *La Louvière* (both Claret and White Wines).

LÉOVILLE-BARTON, Château
Second *Cru Classé* of the Médoc; Saint-Julien (Claret).

LÉOVILLE-LAS-CASES, Château
Second *Cru Classé* of the Médoc; Saint-Julien (Claret).

LÉOVILLE-POYFERRÈ, Château
Second *Cru Classé* of the Médoc; Saint-Julien (Claret).

LE PAPE, Château
Graves de Bordeaux; Léognan. (Claret and a little white wine).

LE PIAN
One of the lesser wine-producing Communes of the Médoc, the wines of which have acquired by long usage the right to be sold under the name of the adjoining and better-known Commune of Ludon.

LE PRIEURÉ, Château
Fourth *Cru Classé*; Cantenac (Claret). Renamed *Le Prieuré-Lichine*, in 1953.

LESBIAN WINE
The wine of the Greek island of Lesbos. It was highly valued by the Greeks of old as a dessert wine, but it does not appear to have enjoyed the same measure of fame in ancient Rome as did the Chian wine. Horace calls Lesbian wine 'innocent':
  'Hic innocentis pocula Lesbii
    Duces sub umbra'.
                (Carm. I. xvii. 21)
and he places Chian and Lesbian wines on par:
  'Capaciores affer huc, puer, sycphos,
    Et Chia vina, aut Lesbia'.
         (Od. ix. Lib. v. 11.33/34)

Pliny places the wines of Chios and Thasos as superior to those of Lesbos.

LESSONA
A red table wine from Novara (Piedmont).

LESTAGE, Château
Bourgeois growth of the Médoc; Listrac (Claret).

LE TAILLAN, Château
Bourgeois growth of the Médoc; Le Taillan (Claret).

LE TERTRE, Château
Fifth *Cru Classé* of the Médoc; Arsac (Claret).

L'ÉTOILE
Commune of the Jura, near Lons-le-Saulnier; its vineyards produce both table and sparkling wines.

L'ÉVANGILE
First growth of Pomerol (Claret).

LIBOURNE
An ancient city upon the right bank of the Dordogne where it is joined by the river L'Isle, and the chief wine-mart for the wines of Saint-Emilion, Pomerol and Fronsac.

LIEBFRAUENSTIFT (Rhinehesse)
The only reliable white wine of Worms. The best is sold as *Liebfrauenstift Klostergarten*.

LIEBFRAUMILCH (Rhinehesse)
Formerly the white wine of Worms vineyards; now merely the name of a Hock of fair quality but not from any particular vineyard. The wine of the Liebfrauenkirche vineyards, near Worms, is sold under the name of *Liebfrauenstift*.

LIESER
One of the smaller villages of the Middle Moselle; its vineyards produce white wines from fair to fine in quality.

LILLET
A medicated wine used as an aperitif in France. It is made in the Gironde Département.

LIMOUX
A small town, near Carcassonne, in the Aude Département, noted for a curious white wine known as *Blanquette de Limoux*, which is highly praised by some but not at all appreciated by others. There are also some red wines of Limoux: they are supposed to resemble *Beaujolais* wines.

LIQUEUR
A French name which has several meanings: (*a*) it is chiefly used for flavoured and sweetened spirits. All liqueurs have sugar and alcohol in common, although in varying proportions. They differ owing to the nature of the alcohol used in their manufacture, and to the number of aromatic substances used to flavour them, as well as to others used to colour them, unless, as is the case with a few liqueurs, they are left colourless, as all spirits are when they leave the still. Liqueurs may be divided according to the spirit which is their basis—brandy, gin, rum, whisky or a neutral spirit distilled from potatoes or sawdust. They may be further subdivided according to whether their chief flavour is derived from fruit, flowers, roots, leaves or seeds, or a combination of a number of these. But there are many liqueurs, among the oldest and more famous ones such as *Chartreuse* and *Bénédictine*, which are sold under a name or brand giving no indication whatever as to the nature of the spirit used as a basis and the substances used as flavouring agents.

Liqueur is also used for (*b*) a spirit of quality and age which is to be enjoyed 'neat', i.e. not watered down; such are Liqueur Brandy and Liqueur Whisky; and (*c*) a very sweet syrup used for sweetening wine: such are *Liqueur de tirage* and *Liqueur d'expédition*, the confection of candy added to Champagne at the time of bottling (*tirage*) and when ready for sale (*expédition*).

LIQUOR
A term which in usual parlance includes all forms of alcoholic beverages, but in the 'Liquor Trade' itself, more particularly in the distilling industry, 'Liquor' means distilled water used for breaking down spirits.

LISBON WINES
Red and white wines, dry and dessert wines, are made on both banks of the Tagus above and below Lisbon. The fortified wines are chiefly known merely as Lisbon wines; they are a cheap edition of Port. The best Lisbon wines are the golden *Bucellas*; the most popular, the red *Collares*; the cheapest, the *Torres Vedras* red wine and the *Termo* white wine; whilst the most famous, once upon a time, and now little more than a mere memory, the *Carcavellos*.

LISTRAC
One of the important wine-producing Communes of the Médoc. The Commune of Listrac cannot boast any of the first five classed growths, but it produces some good red wines and a greater quantity of more ordinary ones; also a little white wine. Some of the wines made in the adjoining Communes of Moulis, Lamarque, Arcins and Castelnau have acquired by long usage the right to be sold under the better-known name of *Listrac*.

LITRE
French standard liquid measure of 100 centilitres or 0·22 gallon.

LIVERSAN, Château
Bourgeois growth of the Médoc; Saint-Sauveur (Claret).

LIVRAN, Château
Bourgeois growth of the Médoc; Saint-Germain d'Esteuil (Claret and white Bordeaux).

LOGROÑO
One of the more important wine-marts for the Rioja wines: Ebro Valley (Spain).

LOMBARDY
The largest and the most important wine-producing Province of Northern Italy. Its more popular wines are those of Broni, Canneto Pavese, San Gemignano and Valtellina.

LONGUICH
One of the less important wine-producing parishes of the Upper Moselle (Trier district). White wines from middling to fair quality (Moselle).

LONS-LE-SAULNIER
A French town which is the principal wine-mart for *Château Chalon, L'Étoile* and other Jura wines.

LORCH and LORCHHAUSEN
The northern limit of the Rhinegau; white wines from middling to fair in quality (Hock).

LORRAINE
One of the wine-producing provinces of eastern France, the wines of which are mostly light and somewhat sharp. They are highly appreciated locally, but nowhere else. The best are those of the Moselle Valley. There are red and white Lorraine wines; also *Vins Gris*, a dirty pink in colour, not attractive to look at but quite refreshing on a hot summer's day. The best white wines are those of *Gueutrange* and *Dornot*; the best red those of *Thiaucourt, Pagny* and *Gueutrange*; one of the best *Vins Gris* is that of *Bruley*.

LOUDENNE, Château
Bourgeois growth of the Médoc, St. Yzans (Claret).

LOUPIAC
One of the Communes of the Gironde, 40 kilometres south-south-east of Bordeaux, on the right bank of the River Garonne. Its vineyards produce some fair beverage red wines but more and better white wines, similar to those of the adjoining Commune of Sainte-Croix-du-Mont.

LOUVIÈRE, Château La
One of the better growths of the Graves de Bordeaux; Léognan (Claret and White Wine).

LUDES
One of the first growths of the Montagne de Reims (Champagne).

LUDON
An important wine-producing Commune of the Haut-Médoc; its finest wine is *Château Grand La Lagune*, a third *Cru Classé*. The Clarets from vineyards in the nearby Communes of Macau, Blanquefort, Parempuyre, St. Aubin, Le Taillan and Le Pian have acquired by long usage the right to sell their wines under the better-known name of *Ludon*.

LUNEL
One of the most attractive of the French unfortified, sweet dessert wines; it comes from the vineyards of Lunel, in the Languedoc, on the French side of the Pyrenees. It is tawny in colour and has a delicate bouquet.

LUXEMBOURG
The vineyards of Luxembourg grace the banks of the Moselle, mostly the left bank, from Schengen, where the Moselle leaves France, to Wasserbilig, where it enters Germany and is joined by the River Sauer or Sure. The Luxembourg 'Moselle' wines are pleasing, light white wines, mostly still and some sparkling.

LYNCH-BAGES, Château
Fifth *Cru Classé* of the Médoc; Pauillac (Claret).

LYNCH-MOUSSAS, Château
Fifth *Cru Classé* of the Médoc; Pauillac (Claret).

MACAU
An important wine-producing Commune of the Haut-Médoc: its finest Estate is Château Cantemerle, a fifth *Cru Classé* of the Médoc (Claret).

MACAU, Château de
Bourgeois growth of the Bourg district on the right bank of the Gironde (Claret and White Wine).

MAC-CARTHY, Château
Bourgeois growth of the Médoc; Saint-Estèphe (Claret).

MACHARNUDO
A wine-producing area immediately to the west of Jerez famous for the excellence of its 'Fino' sherries.

MÂCON
The metropolis of the Mâconnais and an important mart of the wines of Lower Burgundy.

MÂCONNAIS
An important wine-producing district of Lower Burgundy, south of the Côte Chalonnaise and north of Lyons. It includes the Cantons of Saint-Gengoux, Lugny, Mâcon, Tournus and Cluny.

MADEIRA
Madeira is a wine made not from any kind of grape grown in the island of Madeira but only from certain suitable grapes. Madeira is a fortified wine which owes its excellence to the grapes from

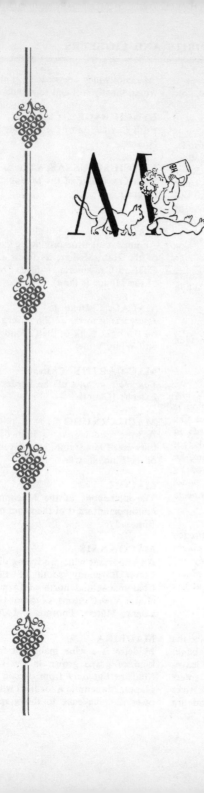

which it is made, to the way in which it is made and to the climate of the island of Madeira, where it is made. Time is an all-important factor in the making of Madeira, a fact which means that it is impossible for true Madeira—the only kind of Madeira worth drinking—to be very cheap. Madeira is not necessarily a sweet wine: *Sercial* Madeira has a distinctly dry finish; *Bual* Madeira is rich, and *Malmsey* Madeira is the sweetest of all. Standard gauge of a Madeira pipe, 92 gallons. Average yield, 44 dozens.

The wines of Madeira were not known in England in the time of Henry IV, but they were known to Shakespeare:

Poins. . . . Jack, how agrees the devil and thee about thy soul, that thou soldest him on Good Friday last for a cup of Madeira and a cold capon's leg?

First Part *Henry IV.*
Act I, Scene ii.

The following figures, which were issued by the Madeira Branch of the British Chamber of Commerce in Portugal, give some indication of the wine production of the island of Madeira and of the proportion of the island's wines retained for home consumption:

	Production Litres	Exports Litres
1931	..	12,815,059	4,672,803
1932	..	8,590,928	3,296,771
1933	..	10,151,459	3,238,925
1934	..	9,219,835	3,886,955
1935	..	9,007,173	3,974,658

MADÈRE
The French name for both the wines of the island of Madeira and imitations made mostly at Sète.

MADÈRE, Château de
One of the Estates of the Podensac Commune of the Graves district (Claret.)

MADÉRISÉ
The polite French word to use to describe the bottle stink of a wine which has been kept too long.

MADIRAN
The best red wine of Bigorre (Basque country). The best Madiran wine is that from the vineyards of Anguis and Tichanères.

MADRE, VINO
New wine boiled to syrup consistency and used, in Italy, to sweeten dessert wines as *Geropiga* is made and used in Portugal.

MAGDELAINE, Château
First growth of Saint-Emilion (Claret).

MAGDELEINE, Clos La
First growth of Saint-Emilion (Claret).

MAGNUM
A wine bottle holding two reputed quarts, or one third of a gallon.

MAIKAMMER-ALSTERWEILER
One of the less important growths of the Palatinate, Landau district (Hock).

MAILBERGER
One of the better white wine growths of Austria.

MAILLY
A first growth of the Montagne de Reims (Champagne).

MAIN
A tributary of the Rhine. There are many vineyards in almost the whole of the Valley of the Main from Franconia to Hochheim, where the Main joins the Rhine.

MAINZ or MAYENCE
One of the most interesting of the ancient ecclesiastical cities of Germany, and an

important wine mart for the wines of Rhinehesse and the Palatinate.

MAJORCA
A large Spanish island off the coast of Catalonia: its many vineyards produce a great deal of *ordinaire* wines and a small quantity of fine dessert Malmsey wine.

MALAGA
Malaga is one of the best sweet wines made in Spain. It comes from the Province of Eastern Andalucia and is shipped from the port of Malaga. It is a blend of new wine and old wine, known as *Vino Tierno* or *Vino Maestro*, and a dark, sweet wine known as *Vino de Color*. The best wine of Malaga is made from the Muscatelle grapes and known as *Lagrima* in Spain: it is made in very much the same manner as Tokay.

MALANGIN, Château
A second growth of the Saint-Emilionais; Parsac (Claret).

MALARTIC-LAGRAVIÈRE, Château
Graves de Bordeaux; Pessac (Claret).

MALBEC, Château
Entre-deux-Mers; Sainte Eulalie (Claret and White Wine).

MALESCASSE, Château
Bourgeois growth of the Médoc; Lamarque (Claret).

MALESCOT, Cru
Entre-deux-Mers; Montferrand (Claret).

MALESCOT-SAINT-EXUPÉRY, Château
A third *Cru Classé* of the Médoc; Margaux (Claret).

MALLE, Château de
A second *Cru Classé* of Sauternes; Preignac (Sauternes).

MALMESBURY
One of the more important wine-producing areas of the Cape Province (South Africa).

MALMSEY
A sweet dessert wine made from the Malvasia or Malvoisie grape grown under particularly favourable conditions such as exist in the islands of Cyprus, Madeira, Majorca and the Canaries.

MALVASIA
The name of a species of white grapes and of the sweet wine made therefrom. Both the Malvasia grape and the wine originated in Crete and the islands of the Aegean Sea. Malvasia grapes were introduced in the fifteenth century in Madeira, and, later on, in Portugal, Spain, the Canaries and Azores, and sweet dessert wines known as Malvasia (*anglice* Malmsey) have since been made from Malvasia and other grapes in many wine-producing lands.

MALVASIA DI LIPARI
A sweet dessert wine from the Lipari islands (Italy).

MALVASIA DI PANTELLERIA
Sweet dessert wine made from Malvasia grapes grown in the small island of Pantelleria.

MALVOISIE
A sweet, tawny, unfortified dessert wine made from Malvoisie grapes from vineyards on the French side of the Eastern Pyrenees (Roussillon).

MANDARINE
A French liqueur, the informing flavour of which is that of tangerines.

MANZANILLA
A very pale and dry type of Sherry from the vineyards of San Lucar, to the west of Jerez. It has a peculiar and attractive

flavour of its own, which is easy to recognize but impossible to define.

MARASCHINO
A liqueur distilled from marasca cherries, in Dalmatia. It used to be shipped to all parts of the world from Zara, now called Zadar, in very distinctive straw-covered bottles. The popularity of this excellent liqueur is responsible for the many imitations of it offered for sale by distillers of different countries where the Dalmation cherry is not obtainable.

MARBUZET, Château de
Bourgeois growth of the Médoc; Saint-Estèphe (Claret).

MARC
A spirit distilled from the husks of grapes or the pulp of apples after the wine or cider has been made. Usually distilled at a very high strength, it requires many years to become tolerably palatable.

MARCHE
One of the least important of the wine-producing Provinces of Italy: its only wine above the *très ordinaire* class is a dry white wine called *Castelli di Gesi*.

MARCOBRUNNEN or MARKO-BRUNNEN
One of the more famous growths of the Rhinegau, in the parish of Erbach where it joins that of Hattenheim (Hock).

MAREUIL-sur-AY
A first growth of the Marne Valley (Champagne).

MARGAUX, Château
One of the four first *Crus Classés* of the Médoc; Margaux (Claret).

MARIENTHAL
A village of the Ahr Valley, the vineyards

of which produce one of the few good red table wines of Germany.

MARING-NOVIAND a.d. LIESER
One of the less known white wine-producing areas of the Mittel Mosel; Bernkastel (Moselle).

MARKELSHEIM
A locality of the Mergentheim district of Württemberg; white wines from middling to fair in quality.

MARNIQUE
The only Australian liqueur for which there has been a demand in the British Isles; its basis is Australian brandy and Australian tangerines.

MARNOZ
A white table wine of the Jura which enjoys a fair (local) reputation.

MARQUIS-D'ALESME-BECKER, Château
A third *Cru Classé* of the Médoc; Margaux (Claret).

MARQUIS-de-TERME, Château
A fourth *Cru Classé* of the Médoc; Margaux (Claret).

MARSALA
The best and best-known dessert wine of Italy; it is made from grapes grown in Sicily, between Palermo and Messina, north and south of Marsala. Standard gauge of a Marsala pipe, 93 gallons. Average yield, 45 dozens.

MARSANNAY-LA-CÔTE
One of the less important Communes of the Côte d'Or immediately south-west of Dijon (red Burgundy).

MARTILLAC
One of the more important wine-producing Communes of the Graves de Bordeaux.

MARTINENS, Château
Bourgeois growth of the Médoc; Cantenac (Claret).

MARTINI COCKTAILS
The straight Martini, oldest and simplest form of this very popular cocktail, is just half Gin and half French Vermouth well mixed together. Then there is the Dry Martini, with two-thirds of dry Gin to one of French Vermouth, and a dash of orange bitters. If a Very Dry Martini should be called for, the proportion of the Gin is increased to three-quarters or four-fifths and that of the French Vermouth is correspondingly reduced to one quarter or one fifth. When Italian Vermouth is used to sweeten the Martini, it is no longer a Martini but is called a Bronx.

MARTINSTHAL
The new name of the village of Neudorf, in the Rhinegau, near Rauenthal but farther from the Rhine: some fair white wines (Hock).

MASDEU
Red, fortified wines of Roussillon, very popular in England in early Victorian days. Also written *Masdu* and *Masdieu*.

MATRAS, Château
Second growth of Saint-Emilion (Claret).

MAURY
One of the wine-producing Communes of the Aude Département (Languedoc). Both red and white table wines of fair quality.

MAUVES
One of the smaller wine-producing Communes of the Ardèche Département; Côtes du Rhône. Red wines of the *ordinaire* class.

MAUVEZIN, Château
Bourgeois growth of the Médoc; Moulis (Claret).

MAVRODAPHNE
One of the best known of the modern Greek wines: it is a red wine, fortified, rather sweet and satisfying, usually served in quite small glasses. It is made from the grape of the same name.

MAYSCHOSS
A village of the Ahr Valley; its vineyards produce none but red table wines from middling to fair in quality.

MEAD
A mildly alcoholic beverage of great antiquity which was fermented from honeyed water, and flavoured with various strongly scented herbs.

'*Mead*. There are different kinds of this wine; but those generally made are two, namely, sack-mead, and cowslip-mead. Sack-mead is made thus: to each gallon of water put four pounds of honey, and boil it three-quarters of an hour, taking care to skim it well. To each gallon add half an ounce of hops, boil it half an hour longer, and let it stand till the next day. Then put it into the cask, and to thirteen gallons of liquor add a quart of brandy or sack. Close it tight till the fermentation is over, and then stop it up very close. It must stand a year before you bottle it.'

MEDDERSHEIM
One of the lesser growths of the Palatinate; Neustadt district. White wines of fair quality.

MÈDOC
A strip of land barely 50 miles long and 6 miles wide, along the left bank of the Gironde, responsible for the output of about half the quantity of really fine red wines produced in the world. There are 70 parishes, or 'Communes', in the Médoc where vineyards are cultivated. The 60 best estates, or 'Châteaux', of the Médoc were classed by order of merit, as regards the excellence of the wines they produce, as far back as 1855, and this classification

still holds good. They are all situated in what is called the Haut-Médoc, that part of the Médoc which stretches from Blanquefort to Saint-Seurin-de-Cadourne. The part of the Médoc nearest the Bay of Biscay, from Saint-Germain-d'Esteuil to Soulac and Talais, was known as Bas-Médoc until World War II, but it is now called 'Médoc'.

OFFICIAL CLASSIFICATION OF THE GROWTHS OF THE MEDOC

First Growths

Lafite	-	-	-	Pauillac
Margaux	-	-	-	Margaux
Latour	-	-	-	Pauillac
Haut-Brion	-	-		Pessae

Second Growths

Mouton-Rothschild	-	-	Pauillac
Rausan-Ségla	-	-	Margaux
Rauzan-Gassies	-	-	,,
Léoville-Lascases	-	- Saint-Julien
Léoville-Poyferré	-	-	,,
Léoville-Barton	-	-	,,
Durfort-Vivens	-	-	Margaux
Lascombes	-	-	,,
Gruaud-Larose	-	- Saint-Julien
Brane-Cantenac	-	-	Cantenac
Pichon-Longueville	-	-	Pauillac
Pichon-Lalande	-	-	,,
Ducru-Beaucaillou	-	- Saint-Julien
Cos d'Estournel	-	-	Saint-Estèphe
Montrose	-	-	-	,,

Third Growths

Kirwan	-	-	-	Cantenac
D'Issan	-	-	-	,,
Lagrange	-	-	- Saint-Julien
Langoa	-	-	-	,,
Giscours	-	-	-	Labarde
Malescot St. Exupéry	-	-	Margaux
Brown-Cantenac	-	-	Cantenac
Palmer	-	-	-	Margaux
La Lagune	-	-	-	Ludon
Desmirail	-	-	-	Margaux
Calon-Ségur	-	-	Saint-Estèphe
Ferrière	-	-	-	Margaux
Marquis-d'Alesme-Bekker	-	,,

Fourth Growths

St. Pierre-Bontemps and St. Pierre-Sevaistre	-	- Saint-Julien
Branaire-Ducru	-	-	-	,,
Talbot d'Aux	-	-	-	,,
Duhart-Milon	-	-	-	Pauillac
Poujet	-	-	-	Cantenac
Rochet	-	-	-	Saint-Estèphe
Beychevelle	-	-	- Saint-Julien
Le Prieuré	-	-	-	Cantenac
Marquis de Terme	-	-	Margaux

Fifth Growths

Pontet-Canet	-	-	-	Pauillac
Batailley	-	-	-	,,
Grand Puy-Lacoste	-	-	,,
Grand-Puy-Ducasse	-	-	,,
Lynch-Bages	-	-	-	,,
Lynch-Moussas	-	-	-	,,
Dauzac	-	-	-	Labarde
Mouton-d'Armailhacq	-	Pauillac
Du Terte	-	-	-	Arsac
Haut-Bages	-	-	-	Pauillac
Pédesclaux	-	-	-	,,
Belgrave	-	-	-	Saint-Laurent
Camensac	-	-	-	,,
Cos-Labory	-	-	Saint-Estèphe
Clerc-Milon	-	-	-	Pauillac
Croizet-Bages	-	-	-	,,
Cantemerle	-	-	-	Macau

The classed growths of the Médoc, on an average, produce about three-quarters of a million gallons of fine red wines every year. Besides those sixty classed growths, there are, in the Médoc, a large number of other wine-producing estates graded as 'Bourgeois Supérieurs', 'Bourgeois', 'Artisans' and 'Paysans'; these produce an average of some seven million gallons of very fair red wines every year. In low lands, close to the Gironde, and in islands in the Gironde, vines are also grown, and they are responsible for the production of about a million gallons of red wines every year, bringing up the total average output of the Médoc to nearly nine million gallons of wine, mostly red.

MÉDOC, Château
Bourgeois growth of the Médoc; Saint-Julien (Claret).

MEERSBURGER
The best white table wine from the vineyards upon the northern shore of the Bodensee (Baden).

MEGASPILEON
The best-known red table wine from the vineyards of Kalavryta, in Morea (Greece).

MEHRING
A village of the Moselle Valley; its vineyards produce a fair quantity of *ordinaire* white wines (Moselle).

MEISENHEIM
A wine-producing locality of the Nahe Valley; white wines from middling to fair quality (Hock).

MELNIK
A wine-producing area of the Labe Valley, in Czechoslovakia; red and white wines of fair quality.

MENDOZA
The oldest and most extensive wine-producing centre of the Argentine Republic, at the foot of the Andes.

MERCUREY
One of the best and most extensive vineyards of the Côte Chalonnaise, in Burgundy. Most of the *Mercurey* wines are red, and they are also of better quality that the few white wines of that district.

MERCUROL
A village of the Rhône Valley, a little to the south-west of the Hermitage Coteau; its vineyards produce both red and white wines, the whites being of finer quality than the reds.

MÉRIGNAC
One of the less important wine-producing

Communes of the Graves de Bordeaux area.

MERTESDORF-GRÜNHAUS
Parish of the Ruwer Valley at no great distance from Trier: its vineyards produce some white wines of superlative excellence (Moselle).

MESCAL
A potent spirit distilled in Mexico and South America from the *Maguey*, or American aloe.

MESSINIA
The largest wine-producing district of Greece.

METHEGLIN
The anglicised form of the Welsh name for Hydromel, Medey-gin, a honey drink.

METHUSELAH
A giant bottle, used for show more than for maturing wine: it holds eight reputed quarts or 6·40 litres, equal to 225,350 fluid ounces. The name is also used in connection with wine to convey the idea of great age.

METTENHEIM
Parish of Rhinehesse, Worms district: its vineyards produce some fair white wines (Hock).

MEUNG-sur-LOIRE
A village of the Orléans country; its vineyards still produce some fair red table wines which enjoyed a greater reputation in olden times than they do now.

MEURSAULT
The most important township of the Côte de Beaune, after Beaune. Its vineyards produce a great deal of wines, more and better white Burgundies than red.

MEXICO
One of the oldest wine-producing countries of the Americas, but its vineyards are not considerable; their average yield is about 3,000 tons of wine-making grapes per annum.

MEYNEY, Château
Bourgeois growth of the Médoc; Saint-Estèphe (Claret).

MIDI
The *Vins du Midi* are the table wines from the Gard, Hérault and Aude Départements of southern France; their vineyards produce considerable quantities of wine, mostly red, and most of them from *ordinaire* to *très ordinaire* in quality.

MIGRAINE
One of the best red wines of the Auxerre district in Lower Burgundy. (There is not a headache in it.)

MILDEW
One of the blights of the vines, a fungoid growth which affects its leaves and grapes in warm and over-wet seasons.

MILLE-SECOUSSES, Château
One of the more important growths of the Bourg district, on the right bank of the Gironde (Claret).

MILLEFIORI
An Italian liqueur, very sweet, flavoured with many wild flowers of the Alps.

MILLÉSIME
French for 'date of the vintage'.

MILLÉSIMÉ, Vin
French for a wine bearing the date of its vintage, i.e. a Vintage wine.

MILLET, Château
Bourgeois growth of the Graves de Bordeaux, Portets; mostly claret; also a small quantity of white wine.

MINERVOIS
A district of the Aude Département (Languedoc) chiefly famous for its *rosés* wines.

MINHEIM
One of the smaller Moselle villages, in the Wittlich district; its vineyards produce some white wines from middling to fair.

MINORCA
One of the Balearic islands; its vineyards produce some middling to fair wines, the best-known being the white *Alba Flora.*

MIRABELLE
An Alsatian spirit distilled from the small golden plums of that name, which grow in many parts of France but nowhere better than in Alsace. Mirabelle is pure white and sometimes slightly sweetened. Like *Kirsch* and all *Eaux-de-vie Blanches, Mirabelle* is matured in glass.

MISTELLE
A white wine of no particular quality, made chiefly from the vineyards on both the French and Spanish sides of the Pyrenees, by the addition of a comparatively small quantity of brandy to partially fermented grape juice soon after the vintage. It is sometimes sold as a cheap dessert wine, but it is mostly used for making Vermouth or as a basis for aperitif wines.

MITTELHAARDT
That part of the Bavarian Palatinate between Neustadt and Bad-Dürkheim which produces some of the best wines of the Palatinate.

MITTELHEIM
A small town of the Rhinegau, between Oestrich and Hallgarten; white wines from middling to fair quality.

MIXED DRINKS
The following *Mixed Drinks* are described

under their own name in the alphabetical order:

Apéritifs	Flips
Cobblers	Highballs
Cocktails	Juleps
Coolers	Punches
Cordials	Sangarecs
Crustas	Shrubs
Cups	Slings
Daisies	Smashes
Eggnogs	Sours
Fixes	Toddies
Fizzes	Tom Collins

MOELLEUX
French for a soft, 'velvety' wine.

MONADET-MARGAUX, Château
Not a Château, but the name given to the second best wine of Château Ferrière (Claret).

MONASTINE
A French liqueur, lemon yellow in colour, and somewhat similar in flavour to the Yellow Chartreuse; it is distilled at the Abbaye Saint-Gratien.

MONBAZILLAC
A rich, golden wine from three Communes of the Dordogne Département: *Monbazillac, Colombier* and *Pomport*.

MONCHHOF
One of the white wines of the Burgenland (Austria).

MONICA
One of the sweet fortified dessert wines of Sardinia (Italy).

MONTAGNA
One of the red wines of the Valtellina (Italy).

MONTAGNE
One of the less important wine-producing Communes of the Saint-Emilionnais (Gironde).

MONTAGNE, Château
Bourgeois growth of the Saint-Emilionnais. Average annual production, 80 tuns of Claret.

MONTAGNE, Château La
Preignac; second growth of Sauternes. Average annual production, 100 tuns of white wine.

MONTAGNY
One of the best white wines of the Côte Chalonnaise (white Burgundy).

MONTAGU
One of the best wine-producing districts of the Cape, South Africa.

MONTBRUN, Château
Bourgeois growth of the Médoc, Cantenac (Claret). There is also some white wine which is sold as *Château Montbrun Goutte d'Or.*

MONTE AGUILAR
A pleasant digestive liqueur made in Jamaica with a basis of Rum.

MONTEFERRATO
Both red and white table wines from the vineyards of Casals, near Turin (Barolo), are sold as Monteferrato.

MONTEFIASCONE
One of the better white table wines of the Latium (Italy).

MONTE-NAPOLEONE
A red wine of the Canneto Pavese type, rather sweet, from Lombardy vineyards (Italy).

MONTEPULCIANO
One of the better red table wines of Tuscany (Italy).

MONTGIRAUD, Château de
Bourgeois growth of the Médoc; Blanquefort (Claret).

MONTHÉLIE

One of the Communes of the Côte d'Or (Côte de Beaune), which produce some red wines of very fair quality: its best vineyards are *Le Cas-Rougeot, Les Champs Fulliot* and *Le Château-Gaillard.*

MONTIBEUX, Clos de

One of the best white wines of the Valais (Switzerland).

MONTILLA

One of the driest types of Sherry wine, which is not really entitled to the name of Sherry as it is made from grapes grown in the Montilla Mountains, in the region of Cordoba, about a hundred miles from Jerez. Yet it is from this 'outsider' that the true Jerez wine called Amontillado owes its name: it is a wine in the Montilla style, that is dry, light, with a clean and nutty finish.

MONTLOUIS

One of the best red wines of the Loire Valley (Touraine).

MONTMÉLIAN

One of the few really good red wines of French Savoy.

MONTMURAT

The only good red wine of the Cantal Département.

MONTRACHET, Le

The finest white Burgundy, first growth Puligny-Montrachet (Côte d'Or).

MONTRACHETS, Les

Le Chevalier-Montrachet; Le Bâtard-Montrachet; Les Demoiselles-Montrachet; first and second growths *Chassagne-Montrachet,* and *Puligny-Montrachet* (White Burgundy). These are, with *Le Montrachet,* the best of all French white wines other than the sweet wines of Sauternes, which are in a different class altogether.

MONTROSE, Château

Second *Cru Classé* of the Médoc; Saint-Estèphe (Claret).

MONTSOREAU

One of the good white wines of the Saumur district (Anjou).

MONT VULLY

The only district of the Canton of Fribourg (Switzerland) producing both red and white wines with a (local) reputation.

MONZINGEN (Nahe Valley)

Kreuznach district. White wine.

MÒR

A small Commune near Budapest which produces the Ezerjo wine (Hungary).

MORANGE, Château

Palus de Ludon; Médoc. Average annual production, 200 tuns of Claret.

MORBISCH (Austria)

Eisenstadt district. White wine.

MOREY SAINT-DENIS

One of the important Communes of the Côte de Nuits. Its vineyards produce a great deal of fine red Burgundy as well as a small quantity of very fair white wine.

MORGON

Red wine of very fair quality from the vineyards of the Commune of Villie-Morgon, Beaujolais.

MORIN, Château

Bourgeois growth of the Médoc; Saint-Estèphe (Claret).

MOROCCO WINES

Although viticulture in Morocco dates from the twentieth century only, it has progressed at such a rate that the country now produces considerable quantities of both red and white wines as well as much grape-juice exported as such for the making of British wines and similar beverages.

MORZHEIM
A village of the Palatinate, Worms district; its vineyards produce white wines from middling to fair in quality.

MOSCATEL
A generic name for wines made in Spain from muscat grapes; none of them is a dry wine but some of them are sweet to a fulsome degree. The best *Moscatel* of Spain is that which is made from the vineyards of Sitges, a small seaport south of Barcelona: it is fully sweet enough, has an alcoholic strength of from 16 per cent to 18 per cent by weight, and a very distinct muscat flavour. They make a wine of the same style in the Argentine, and it bears the same name.

MOSCATELLO, MOSCATO
The name of a variety of sweet Italian dessert wines made from Muscat grapes. The less sweet of such wines are called *Moscato secco* and the sweeter sorts *Moscato passito*. Some of the better known Moscato wines are the *Moscatello di Montefiascone*, a Latium wine; the *Moscato di Salento*, of Apulia; the *Moscato Fior d'Arancio*, of Calabria; the *Moscato di Noto*, from Syracuse; the *Moscato Zucco*, from Palermo; and the *Moscato di Pantelleria*, from the small island of that name.

MOSELLE
The Moselle is a long twist of a river which rises and has its longest run in France: it then forms the boundary between Luxembourg and Germany and enters Germany at Wasserbillig, only seven miles from the old Roman city of Trier. It then buckles its way in a northerly direction with an easterly inclination for more than 120 miles, as far as Coblenz, where it meets the Rhine. Strangely enough, none of the many vineyards which the Moselle passes by,

both in France and Luxembourg, produces any wine of distinction, certainly none comparable to the wines made from the vineyards which grace both banks of the 'Mittelmosel', in the Bernkastel district, or from the vineyards of the Saar and Ruwer, close to the junction of those two small rivers with the Moselle, the first above and the second below Trier. The best wines of the Moselle are those of the middle course of the river between Trier and Coblenz (Mittel Mosel); they are in alphabetical, not geographical, order: *Avelsbach, Bernkastel, Brauneberg, Cues, Dhron, Enkirch, Erden, Graach, Lieser, Piesport, Traben, Trarbach, Trittenheim, Uerzig, Wehlen, Zell* and *Zeltingen*.

The following wines, from the Saar and Ruwer valleys, are of the same high standard of excellence as the wines of the Middle Moselle, and they are usually sold in England as Moselle wines: *Ayl, Canzen, Eitelsbach, Filzen, Grünhaus, Kanzem, Ockfen, Oberemmel, Saarburg, Scharzhof, Serrig, Waldrach, Wawern* and *Wiltingen*.

Next, as regards the quality of their wines, come the vineyards of the Lower Moselle: *Bruttig, Cochem, Pünderich, Senheim, Valwig* and *Winningen*. Last of all are the wines of the Upper Moselle from *Nittel to Wincheringen*.

MOSTO
Italian, Portuguese and Spanish for *Must*, or grape juice, but sometimes it means new wine.

MOSTO COTTO
Boiled *Must*, used in Italy as a sweetening agent in the making of dessert wine of the Marsala type.

MOULERENS, Château
Bourgeois growth of the Graves de Bordeaux: Gradignan (Claret).

MOULIN-à-VENT
The best and best-known red wine of

Beaujolais (Burgundy), from vineyards partly in the Commune of Chénas and partly in that of Romanèche-Thorins. There are thirty-two named vineyards, the wines of which are entitled to the name of *Moulin-à-Vent Grand Cru*.

MOULIN-à-VENT
Small growth of the Graves de Bordeaux; Portets (Claret).

MOULIN-à-VENT, Château
Bourgeois growth of the Médoc; Moulis (Claret). Also one of the growths of Saint-Pierre-de-Mons producing both red and white wines of moderate quality.

MOULIN-à-VENT, Clos
Palus vineyards by the Gironde in the Blayais district (Claret).

MOULIN-à-VENT, Cru
A small vineyard of the Graves de Bordeaux; Villenave d'Ornon. (Average 4 tuns Claret and 2 tuns white wine.)

MOULIN-BLANC, Château
One of the more important growths of Saint-Germain du Puch; Branne (White Bordeaux).

MOULIN DE CALON
Bourgeois growth of the Médoc; Saint-Estèphe (Claret).

MOULIN-de-SOUBEYRAN
Bourgeois growth of the Médoc; Le Pian (Claret and some white wine).

MOULIN-du-BOURG, Domain du
Bourgeois growth of the Médoc; Listrac (Claret).

MOULIN-du-CADET
First growth of Saint-Emilion (Claret).

MOULIN-RICHE, Château
Bourgeois growth of the Médoc; Saint-Julien (Claret).

MOULIN-SAINT-GEORGES
First growth of Saint-Emilion (Claret).

MOULIS
One of the wine-producing Communes of the Médoc. Some of the wines of Moulis are sold also under the name of the adjoining Commune of Listrac.

MOULIS, Château
Bourgeois growth; Moulis (Médoc). Average annual production, 20 tuns of Claret.

MOUNTAIN
A name by which the sweet red wines from the heights round Malaga were known in England during the eighteenth century and early nineteenth century.

MOUSSEUX
The French for 'sparkling'. *Vins Mousseux* means, according to French law, any and every sparkling wine, except Champagne, the prototype of all sparkling wines and the only one entitled to the name Champagne.

MOUTON D'ARMAILHACQ, Château
One of the fifth *Crus Classés* of the Médoc (Pauillac). The name of *Cru des Carruades d'Armailhacq* is given to the second-best wines (Claret) of this Château.

MOUTON-ROTHSCHILD, Château
The first of the second *Crus Classés* of the Médoc (Pauillac). The wines of this Château of recent vintages have been fully equal to those of the First growths. Before 1853, when it was purchased by Baron Nathaniel de Rothschild, it was known as *Château Brane-Mouton*, and it was known by that name during the greater part of the eighteenth century; before that it was called *Cru de Mouton*. Its average is 150 tuns Claret.

MUDEN
Village of the Moselle Valley; Cochem. Some fair white wines.

MUID
French for Pipe, a cask holding about 59 gallons of wine.

MULHEIM
Village of the Moselle Valley; Bernkastel. White wines of no great distinction.

MULLED WINE
One of the most acceptable—and most ancient—forms of prevention or cure for a cold. Any wine may be used, not necessarily the finest, of course, and red for preference. Plenty of sugar is first of all dissolved in a little hot water, in a pan over a slow fire; then the wine is put in and brought to the boil: it must be moved away from the fire as soon as it reaches boiling point, and served to the patient with a little grated nutmeg on top. This is the 'straight' form of mulled wine, the form which Falstaff, and Shakespeare himself without a doubt, approved of. But there were in Shakespeare's days and there are now people who believe in adding a well-beaten egg to mulled wine, stirring it well in the hot wine *off* the fire.

MULLHEIM
Growth of the Lörrach district, in Baden, near the Black Forest: white wine of *ordinaire* quality.

MUNDELSHEIM
Growth of the Neckar Valley, in Württemberg; mostly red wines.

MUNSTER-BEI-BINGENBRÜCK
One of the wine-producing parishes of the Nahe Valley, in the Kreuznach district. White wines. Best vineyards: *Pittersberg* and *Kapellenberg*.

MUNZINGEN (Baden)
Freiburg district. Mostly red wines.

MURCIA
One of the lesser wine-producing provinces of Spain. The best wine is that of *Yecla*.

MURETS DE SION, Les
A noted 'Fendant' white wine of the Valais (Switzerland).

MUSCADEL
A sweet dessert wine made from Muscat grapes. It was popular in England from early times and it was well known to Shakespeare:

> *Gremio. . . . A health*, quoth he; as if
> He had been aboard,
>   carousing to his mates
> After a storm: quaff'd off
>   the muscadel,
> And threw the sops all in
>   the sexton's face; . . .
>   *The Taming of the Shrew*,
>   Act III, Scene ii,

MUSCADELLE
A small but delicious grape which used to be extensively cultivated at the Cape in the early part of the nineteenth century and made the reputation of the famous Constantia wine.

MUSCADET
The principal white wine of the lower Loire (Nantes district).

MUSCADINE WINE
Another name for Muscatel wine or any wine made from Muscat grapes.

MUSCAT
The generic name of the most highly scented varieties of *Vitis vinifera*, the European parent grape. The Muscat d'Alexandrie is grown on a very large scale in California for wine-making, but in Europe it is mostly grown for table grapes. Wines made from other Muscat grapes are known as plain Muscat, or *Muscat de Frontignan, Muscat de Samos*, etc.; they are sweet, muscat-scented, dessert wines.

MUSCATEL
The name of a sweet fortified wine made in California. Also, in England, that of a cheap, sweet, white, sparkling wine, usually flavoured with elderberry flowers essence.

MUSIGNY, Les
The most famous vineyards of Chambolle-Musigny, Côte d'Or. They produce chiefly red wines of very fine quality; also a little very good white wine. Les Musigny vineyards are cut in two by a road from east to west, the northern half being the larger and is sometimes called *Grand Musigny*, and the smaller half *Petit Musigny*.

MUSKOTÁLY
One of the best white Muscat wines, chiefly from Villány (Hungary).

MUSSBACH
A township of the Palatinate; Neustadt district. Some fair white wines, but more *ordinaire* reds.

MUST
Unfermented grape juice. The freshly pressed juice of wine-making grapes before it has had time to ferment. Latin, *Mustum*: Italian, *Mosto*; Spanish, *Mosto*; Portuguese, *Mosto*; French, *Moût*; German, *Most*.

MUSTY
A foul, fungus smell which wine acquires when in contact with a decaying pipe-stave or bad cork.

MUTCHKIN
Scotch wine measure equal to 0·746 Imperial Pint.

MUTENICE (Czechoslovakia)
By Göding. White wine. Best vineyard: Zarybnicke.

MYCODERMA VINI
Microscopic spores commonly known as yeast, the presence of which in grape-juice and other sweet liquids is to a very large extent responsible for fermentation.

MYRAT, Château
Second Growth of Sauternes; Barsac.

NACKENHEIM
One of the smaller Growths of Rhinehesse, in the Oppenheim district: white wines from fair to fine quality (Hock).

NAHE
A tributary of the Rhine. The vineyards of the Nahe Valley produce both red and white wines, the white being the better of the two. The best vineyards of the Nahe are those of *Bad Kreuznach, Burgsponheim, Heddesheim, Langenlonsheim, Münster, Niederhausen, Norheim, Schloss Böckelheim, Winzenheim.*

NATURE, NATUR, NATURREIN
The French and German words used to convey the idea of a wine which has not been 'sweetened'.

NAVARRA
A part of northern Spain, the vineyards of which produce some red table wines darker in colour and of greater alcoholic strength than most red table wines.

NEBBIOLO
One of the best black grapes grown in the North of Italy for the making of red table wines. Many of the wines made from Nebbiolo grapes are sold as *Nebbiolo* wines, sometimes with the name of their vineyards coupled with it.

NEBUCHADNEZZAR
A giant bottle, made for show purposes, and too unwieldy for use.

NECKAR
A river which runs through parts of Württemberg and Baden, where viticulture has flourished for many centuries.

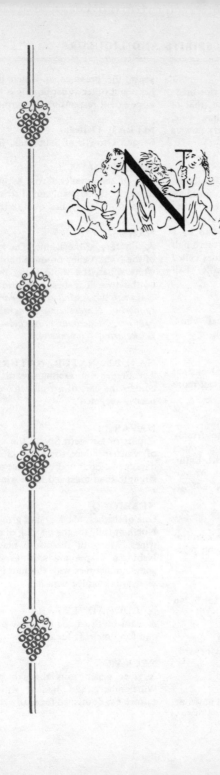

The Neckar Valley wines are mostly red and of no outstanding merit.

NECTAR

'The drink of the gods', in Greek mythology. Milton describes *Nectar* as follows:

'. . . one sip of this
Will bathe the drooping spirits in delight
Beyond the bliss of dreams.'

(*Comus*. 813)

A number of French Liqueurs used to be given the name of *Nectar*, such as *Nectar de Bonaparte, Nectar de Mazagran*, etc.

NEGUS

To every pint of port allow 1 quart of boiling water: ¼ lb. loaf sugar, 1 lemon, grated nutmeg to taste. Put the wine in a jug; rub some lumps of sugar (¼ lb.) on the lemon rind until all the yellow part of the skin is absorbed; then squeeze the juice and strain it; add the sugar and lemon juice to the port wine, with the grated nutmeg; pour on the boiling water, cover the jug, and when the beverage has cooled a little, it will be ready for use.—L. EN.

NEMES KADARKA

One of the best red Hungarian wines, from the *Kadar* district.

NÉNIN, Château

First growth Pomerol (Claret).

NERTHE, Clos de la

First growth Châteauneuf-du-Pape (Rhône).

NERVEUX

French, not for 'nervous' but for 'vitality', as applied to wines which, besides being sound, have body and spirit to spare.

NEUCHÂTEL

One of the smallest wine-producing (red and white wines) Cantons of Switzerland. Its most noted red wine is that of *Cortaillod*.

NEUDORF (Rhinegau)

Between Nieder-Walluf and Frauenstein. White wine. Best vineyards: *Mückenberg* and *Pfaffenberg*.

NEUMAGEN

A small but very old village of the Moselle Valley, Bernkastel district; white wines of fair quality.

NEUSTADT a.d. HAARDT

The centre of an important wine-growing area of the Palatinate: white wines of fair quality.

NEUVILLE

Lake of Bienne, Canton of Berne (Switzerland). Golden and rather full wines. The best wine of Neuville is that of the *Hôpital de Pourtalès*.

NEUWEIER (Baden)

Both red and white wines; the white superior to the red. The best vineyards are those of the *Schloss Neuweier*.

NEW SOUTH WALES

The cradle of Australian viticulture; still one of the three most important wine-producing States of Australia, not so much as regards quantity but the quality of the wines it produces.

NEZMÉLY

One of the best white table wines of Hungary, made from Riesling grapes.

NIEDEREMMEL

Middle Moselle growth, Bernkastel district: white wines from fair to fine quality.

NIEDERHAUSEN
A first growth of the Nahe Valley, Kreuznach district. Some very fine white wines.

NIEDER-INGELHEIM
A good growth of Rhinehesse, Bingen district. White wines from fair to fine quality.

NIEDERLEUKEN
One of the smallest growths of the Saar Valley, Saarburg district; fine white wines.

NIEDERMENNIG
A small village of the Saar Valley, between Oberemmel and Ayl; some very fair white wines.

NIEDERSAULHEIM
A little-known growth of Rhinehesse, Oppenheim district; some fair white wines.

NIERSTEIN
The most important wine-producing parish of Rhinehesse. It produces much white wine, some of which is of very fine quality.

NIP
A quarter bottle.

NITTEL
A little-known growth of the Upper Moselle, Saar district. Some fair white wines.

NOÉ, Cru de
Palus de Macau, Haut-Médoc (Claret).

NOGGIN
Quarter of a pint.

NONNOS
A Greek poet, who lived probably at the end of the fourth century A.D., and whose chief work is an epic in forty-eight books entitled *Dionysiaca*:

Give way, ye warrior, to the wine-grower:
To Mars ye offer a bloody offering,
But to Bacchus the other offers
The sparkling blood of the inebriating grape.
Ye, Ceres, and ye also, Pallas,
Both, indeed, own yourselves beaten.
Olive trees make not men merry,
Nor does golden wheat charm their soul.
Greater am I than either of you;
Without wine where would they be
The pleasures of the table
And the joys of the dance.
Nonnos, Canto XII, vv. 218–225

NORDHEIM
There is a growth of that name on the River Main, in Lower Franconia (white wines); and another in Württemberg, in the Valley of the Neckar (red wine).

NORHEIM
A first growth of the Nahe Valley, Kreuznach district; some fair white wines.

NOUCHET, Château de
Bourgeois growth of the Graves de Bordeaux; Martillac (Claret and a little white wine).

NUITS-SAINT-GEORGES
The chief town of the Côte de Nuits, between Dijon to the north, and Beaune to the south. It produces a large quantity of fine red Burgundies.

NUSSDORF
A little-known growth of the Palatinate, Landau district; mostly *ordinaire* white wines.

OBEREMMEL
A first growth of the Saar Valley, just east of Wiltingen; Saarburg district. Very fine white wines.

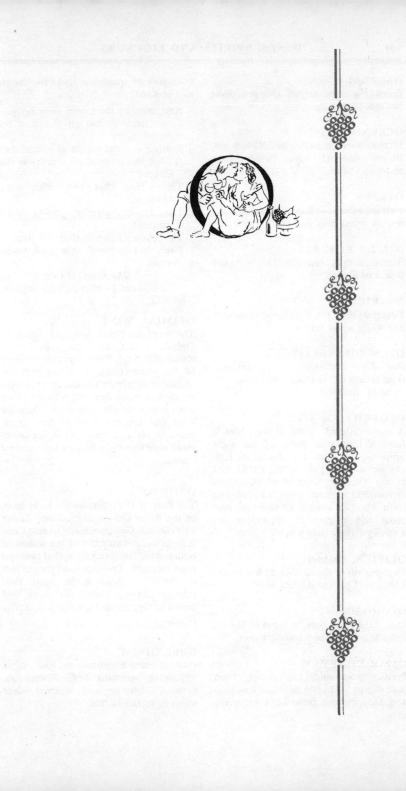

OBERNAI
One of the better-known wine-producing parishes of Alsace.

OCKENHEIM
Little-known growth of Rhinehesse, Bingen district; white wines from middling to fair.

OCKFEN
First growth of the Saar Valley, Saarburg district. Some very fine white wines.

ŒIL DE PERDRIX
'Partridge eye', referring to the tawny colour of a wine.

ŒSTRICH
First growth of the Rhinegau; some very fine white wines (Hock).

OFEN-ADELSBERG
One of the best red wines of Hungary, from Ofen-Pest; it is also sold under the name of *Aldesberg*.

OKOLEHAO or OKE
A spirit distilled in the Hawaii Islands from a fermented mash of the right proportion of sugar-cane molasses, Koji rice lees and the juice of the baked root of the Taro or Kalo plant (*Colocasia antiquorum*) to which water is added. The spirit is bottled at from 80 to 90 per cent proof and is dark in colour; it has a smoky flavour and a fierce action.

OLIVIER, Château
First growth of the Graves de Bordeaux; Léognan (Claret and white wine).

OLOROSO
One of the more popular types of Sherry, fuller than a *Fino* and usually richer.

OMAR KHAYYÁM
Persian poet and astronomer, born probably at Nîshâpûr, between A.D. 1025 and 1050, whose fame rests upon the collection of quatrains (rubá'îs) known as *The Rubá'iyát*.

> And lately by the tavern door agape,
> Came stealing through the dusk an Angel shape
> Bearing a vessel on his shoulder; and He bid me taste of it: and 'twas the Grape!
> The Grape that can, with logic absolute,
> The two-and-seventy jarring sects confute;
> The subtle Alchemist that in a trice Life's leaden metal into gold transmute.
>
> *The Rubá'iyát*, vv. 42–43,
> Edward FitzGerald's translation.

OPIMIAN WINE
The wine that was vintaged when L. Opimius was Consul, the year 633 of Rome (121 B.C.). Pliny says that the heat of the summer was so great that the grapes were literally cooked and the wine which was made from them lasted as no other wine ever did. But not all Opimian wine was actually wine of that extraordinary vintage, the name being sometimes used merely to mean a very ancient vintage.

OPORTO
The Port of Portugal, on the right bank of the River Douro, immediately facing *Vila Nova de Gaia*, originally named *Cale*. It is to the conjunction of the names of both towns, *Porto* and *Cale*, that *Portugal* owes its name. They are together the hub of the Port Wine trade, most Port shippers having their residences and offices at Oporto and their cellars at Vila Nova.

OPPENHEIM
One of the better-known and more important growths of Rhinehesse, between Mayence and Worms; white wines from fair to fine.

ORANGE BITTERS
The most popular form of Bitters used for flavouring Cocktails and other mixed drinks. It is made from the peel of the bitter Seville orange.

ORANGE BRANDY
1 gallon best brandy; rind of 8 Seville oranges and 2 lemons cut very thin, and 2 lb. loaf sugar; put into a stone jar, cork down and shake daily for a few minutes for 3 weeks; then strain off, bottle and cork.

ORDONNAC-ET-POTENSAC
A Commune of the Médoc 62 kilometres north-north-west of Bordeaux, the vineyards of which produce some undistinguished Claret, the best of which being the wine of *Châteaux Gallais* and *Potensac*, two of the *Crus Bourgeois*.

ORGEAT
Blanch and pound ¾ of a pound of sweet almonds and 30 bitter ones, with a tablespoonful of water. Stir in by degrees 2 pints of water and 3 pints of milk, and strain the whole through a cloth. Dissolve ½ a pound of loaf sugar in a pint of water, boil, skim well, and mix with the almond water, adding 2 tablespoonfuls of orange-flower water, and a teacupful of good brandy.

ORDINAIRE
French for any 'ordinary' wines, good enough for the thirst of a man but little else.

ORIGINALABFÜLLUNG
German for 'Bottled by the Grower'.

ORIGINALABZUG
German for 'Bottled by the Grower'.

ORLÉANS
The wines of Orléans, have enjoyed in the past a great reputation which none of the wines of the Loiret Département deserves today. The red wine of Beaugency, from vineyards between Orléans and Blois, was a great favourite at Court during the eighteenth century, and still enjoys a certain measure of popularity locally. The white wines of Tavers and Meung-sur-Loire, more particularly the *Vin des Mauves*, of Meung, are pleasant summer wines in great demand in Orléans restaurants and estaminets.

ORVIETO
One of the most picturesque cities of Umbria perched on a hilltop and surrounded by vineyards, the best wines of which are the white *Orvieto*: there are two varieties of it, the dry or *secco* and the sweet or *abboccato*, which is the finer of the two. Both are straw-coloured and bottled in straw-covered flasks similar to the *Chianti* fiasco.

OSOYE, OSEY or AUSSAY
Various forms of the name of a wine which was popular in England in the time of Chaucer: its nature and origin have never been ascertained satisfactorily.

OSTOFEN
A minor growth of Rhinehesse; Worms district. Some fair white wines.

OUZO
The most popular aperitif of Greece: it is a spirit flavoured with aniseed and is usually served in a tall glass, like *Absinthe*, and mixed with iced water, when it turns milky and opalescent. It is most refreshing served thus.

PAARL VALLEY
One of the oldest and best wine-producing areas of the Cape.

PACETA
One of the red table wines of the Ebro Valley; Rioja (Spain).

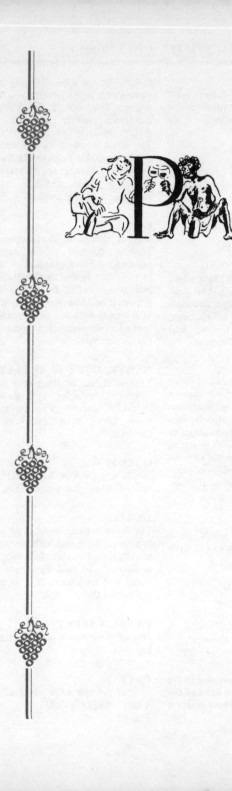

PADARNAC, Château
Bourgeois growth of the Médoc; Pauillac (Claret).

PAJARETE, PAXARETE
A small town of the Jerez district, near Arcos, where there was a famous monastery, now no more; also vineyards still flourishing and noted for their Pedro Ximenez grapes. These grapes are gathered when fully ripe and exposed to the sun for a week or two before being pressed, when they yield a very sweet juice; this is treated with brandy so that it does not ferment and the *Pajarete* or *Paxarete* liqueur wine thus obtained, although it may be drunk as a sweet liqueur, is mostly used for sweetening high-class sweet Sherries. That this wine was popular in England during the latter part of the eighteenth century and the first half of the nineteenth is shown by the number of Wine Labels bearing its name, under various spellings. In the M. V. Brown Collection of Wine and Sauce Labels given to the London Museum in 1915, two labels bear the name *Paxarette*, the one dated 1794, the other 1802; two others in the Ionides Collection of Enamel Wine Labels bear the names *Pacaret* and *Pagares*. The spellings *Paxarete* and *Pajarete* also occur.

PALAT, Château
First growth of Saint-Emilion (Claret).

PALATINATE
A plateau on the left bank of the Rhine, South Germany, the vineyards of which produce some of the most luscious and delicious Hocks, as well as a large quantity of both red and white wines of fair to moderate quality. The Palatinate is divided into three parts:

(*a*) Oberland, with Landau as its centre town;

(*b*) Mittelhaardt, from Neustadt to Bad-Dürkheim;

(*c*) Unterland, from Bad-Dürkheim to Frankenthal.

PALERMO
The principal export mart for Marsala and other wines of Sicily.

PALESTINE
The grape-vine is indigenous to Palestine, and wine was made there for thousands of years until the advent of the Turks, who uprooted the Palestinian vineyards. Some of those were replanted towards the end of the last century by Jewish settlers encouraged by Baron Edmond de Rothschild.

PALMA
The wine of Majorca, one of the Balearic Islands. Also the name of wine made in one of the Canary Islands. Also the name of one of the better grades of Sherry.

PALMER, Château
Second *Cru Classé* of the Médoc; Cantenac (Claret).

PALO CORTADO
A mark—a long chalk line with a shorter one across the top—on casks of Sherry in the making, denoting a certain special quality.

PALOMINO
The best white grape grown in the Jerez district for the making of Sherry wine.

PALOUMEY, Château
Bourgeois growth of the Médoc; Ludon (Claret).

PALUS
The low-lying vineyards of the Gironde, producing the cheaper types of Claret (France).

PANTELLERIA
A small island in the Mediterranean between Sicily and Tunis, noted for its sweet Muscat wines (Italy).

PAPE, Château le
Bourgeois growth of the Graves de Bordeaux; Léognan (Claret and a little white wine).

PAPE-CLÉMENT, Château
First growth of the Graves de Bordeaux; Pessac (Claret).

PAREMPUYRE, Château de
Bourgeois growth of the Médoc; Parempuyre (Claret).

PARNAY, Château de
First growth of Saumur; Anjou (white wine).

PAROS
One of the wine-producing islands of the Greek Archipelago.

PASSE-TOUS-GRAINS
A red Burgundy made of mixed grapes, Pinot and Gamay, or grapes not specially selected. It is never a very fine wine but, in good vintages, some Passe-tous-Grains wines are quite good *ordinaires* and good value.

PASSITI
The name of a number of sweet dessert wines made in many parts of Italy.

PASTEURIZATION
The raising of the temperature of newly-made wine to a degree sufficient to kill or render definitely inactive any of the ferments which it may still contain. The pasteurized wine is thus freed from the cause of most diseases likely to affect wine made from grapes that are not quite sound. Safe, i.e. pure, yeast may then be added and fermentation takes place under conditions which are natural, although not Nature's. Pasteurization has saved untold quantities of unsatisfactory wines from the still or from the vinegar butt, but no wine that has been pasteurized will ever reach the same perfection as wine made from sound

grapes and allowed to ferment unchecked with its own self-supplied ferments.

PASTOSO
A sweetish, because imperfectly fermented, new white wine from the Alban Hills (Italy).

PATRAS
One of the best wine-producing districts of Greece. Mostly white.

PATRIMONIO
One of the red beverage wines of Corsica (France).

PAUILLAC
One of the most important wine-producing Communes of the Médoc, 48 kilometres north-north-west of Bordeaux, between Saint-Julien to the south, Saint-Estèphe to the north, and the broad Gironde to the east.

PAVIE, Château
One of the largest of the first growths of Saint-Emilion now divided among a number of different owners.

PAVILLON-CADET
First growth of Saint-Emilion (Claret).

PAXARETE *see* **PAJARETE**

PEACH BRANDY
A Cordial made with Brandy which is flavoured with peaches.

PEACH LIQUEUR
A Liqueur with a Brandy, or any other spirit as a basis, flavoured with fresh or dried peaches and sweetened with sugar or glucose. The best *Peach Liqueurs* are, of course, those made with Brandy, cane sugar and fresh fruit.

PÉCS
The centre of the Villany-Fünfkirchen vineyards, in the Baranya Komitat of

Hungary, noted for their wines and table grapes.

PÉDESCLAUX, Château
Fifth *Cru Classé* of the Médoc; Pauillac (Claret).

PEDRO XIMENEZ or P.X.
The name of a grape which is particularly sweet because it is lacking in acidity, and also the name of a sweet wine which is made from it, chiefly in the south of Spain. The grapes are gathered when fully ripe, left to dry in the sun, on straw mats, for a week or two and then pressed. Their very sweet juice is then run into casks in which there is some Brandy, so that it cannot ferment. It is more a liqueur than a wine and may be drunk as a very sweet liqueur, but it is chiefly used for sweetening high-class Sherries.

PELLETAN, Château
First growth of Saint-Emilion (Claret).

PELURE D'OIGNON
Onion-skin, a term used to describe the peculiar brown sheen which some old red wines acquire with age: some quite young wines made from both red and white grapes can also be tawny or *pelure d'oignon*.

PERALTA
Jullien, in his *Topographie*, mentions this wine as a dessert 'rancio' wine, made from Muscat grapes, at Peralta, in Navarre. As evidence that the wine must have enjoyed a certain measure of popularity there are two labels in the Ionides Collection of Enamel Wine Labels bearing the names of *Peralta* and *Peralte* respectively.

PÉRIGNON, Dom
The Cellarer of the Abbey of Hautvillers who helped to make Champagne more popular in France, at the close of the seventeenth century, by suitably blending wines of different vineyards and intro-

ducing cork stoppers, which made 'Sparkling Champagne' possible. But Dom Pérignon never claimed to have 'discovered' Sparkling Champagne, which was known at an earlier date, in England, where cork stoppers were in common use long before they were obtainable in France.

PERNAND-VERGELESSES
One of the smaller Communes of the Côte d'Or, which produces some fine red Burgundy.

PERNOD
A name that was for many years synonymous with *Absinthe*, in France and Switzerland. The firm of *Pernod*, of Pontarlier, in the Jura Département of France, close to the Swiss frontier, was the oldest and largest to distil *Absinthe*. Since the sale of *Absinthe* has been prohibited in France, they sell an Apéritif under the name of *Pernod*, which has no *Absinthe* but *Aniseed* as its basis.

PERRY
The fermented juice of fresh pears, and usually sweetened as well as filtered before it is bottled. There is both still and sparkling *Perry*, the sparkling kind is the more popular of the two and it is sold as *Medium Dry*, which is sweet enough for most grown-up people, and *Sweet*, which is very sweet.

PERSIA
Once upon a time the country was famous for its wines; today the making and sale of wine is not allowed to Persians, but there are a few Armenians who make and Jews who sell wine.

PERSICO
A Peach Liqueur or Cordial which was well-known under that name, and also as *Persicot* and *Persicoa*, in England, during the eighteenth century. Mrs. Manley mentioned *Persicoa* in her *New Atlantis*.

in 1709, and Addison speaks of 'Cordials, Ratafias, Persico, Orange-flowers and Cherry-Brandy', in the *Spectator* (No. 328, 17 March 1712).

PERUVIAN WINE
The vineyards of Peru are chiefly in the regions of Ica, Locumba, Lima, Pisco and the Sicamba River; their wines are made from European species of grapes; they belong to the *ordinaire* class.

PESSAC
The Commune of the Graves de Bordeaux, the vineyards of which produce some of the finest Clarets.

PESSAN, Château, and
PESSAN, Domaine de
Two of the smaller growths of the Graves de Bordeaux; Portets (Claret and white wine).

PETIT-BOSC, Château
Small growth of the Graves de Bordeaux; Villenave d'Ornon (Claret and white wine).

PETIT-FAURIE de SOUTARD, Château
First growth of Saint-Emilion (Claret).

PETIT-PONTAC, Clos
Small growth of the Graves de Bordeaux, Villenave d'Ornon (Claret).

PETIT VILLAGE, Château
First growth Pomerol (Claret).

PETRUS, Château
First growth Pomerol (Claret).

PEYCHARMANT
A red wine growth of the Upper Dordogne; Bergerac.

PEZINOK (in German *Bösing*)
One of the wine-producing areas of Czechoslavakia, upon the lower Carpathian ridge; mostly white wines.

PFALZ
German for Palatinate (q.v.)

PHÉLAN-SÉGUR, Château
Bourgeois growth of the Médoc; Saint-Estèphe (Claret).

PHÉNIX-HAUT-BRION
Graves de Bordeaux; Pessac (Claret).

PHYLLOXERA
The American vine louse. It was first recorded in Europe at Kew, near London, in 1863, and it has since spread to every continental and island vineyard of the world with but few exceptions. The indigenous North American vines, having become partly immune to this pest, are now largely used in European and other vineyards as the briars upon which the various species of *Vitis vinifera*, the European vine, are grafted.

PIADA, Château
Second *Cru Classé* of Sauternes; Barsac.

PICARD-CANTELOUP, Château
Bourgeois growth of the Médoc; Saint-Estèphe (Claret).

PICARDAN
One of the golden ·sweet dessert wines from vineyards on the French side of the Eastern Pyrenees; it enjoyed a certain measure of popularity in England during the eighteenth century.

PICHON-LONGUEVILLE, Château
Second *Cru Classé* of the Médoc; Pauillac (Claret).

PICHON-LONGUEVILLE-LALANDE, Château
Second *Cru Classé* of the Médoc; Saint-Julien (Claret).

PICPOUL
The name given to a number of light, rather thin and characterless white wines made in the Midi, chiefly in the Aude Département; they are mostly used as

a basis wine in the making of Vermouth. There is, however, a better and sweet dessert wine of that name made in the Pyrénées Orientales Département.

PIEDMONT

Not the largest, but one of the most important wine-producing parts of Italy as regards the quality of the wines it produces. The best wine of Piedmont is the *Barolo*. The next best are the *Barbera*, *Nebbiolo*, *Gattinaza*, *Campiglione* and *Friesa*. All are red wines. One of the few good white table wines of Piedmont is called *Castello di canelli*.

PIERRY

First growth of Champagne; Marne Valley.

PIESPORT

One of the smallest villages of the Moselle Valley (Wittlich district); its vineyards produce some of the finest white wines (Moselle).

PINARD

French Army slang for the ration wine issued to the troops.

PINOT, PINEAU

The variety of grapes, both black and white, from which the best Champagne and the best Burgundies are made. There are a number of different members of the noble *Pinot* family: *Pinot Noir*, *Pinot Blanc*, *Pinot Chardonnay*, etc.

PINT

English standard wine measure, the one-eighth of the gallon, or half the quart. Contents: 34·659 cubic inches, equal to 5·68 décilitres. The old English pint (pre 1826) was only 0·8331 of the present or 'Imperial Pint'; it is still the legal pint in use in the U.S.A. (28·875 cubic inches). There used to be also a Stirling Pint in Scotland, which was equal to nearly 3 Imperial Pints (2·9834).

PIQUÉ

French for *pricked*, wine on the way to the vinegar tub.

PIQUE-CAILLOU, Château

Graves de Bordeaux; Mérignac (Claret and a little white wine).

PIQUETTE

The French name of an imitation wine which is hardly fit to drink: it is usually made out of the husks of grapes, after the juice has been pressed for making wine; they are flooded with water, sweetened with the cheapest available sugar and fermented with brewer's yeast.

PISCO

A very potent and usually immature spirit which is greatly popular in Peru, where it is distilled from wine made in the Valley of the Ica, near Pisco. A milder form is also shipped, from Pisco, to the U.S.A. in porous clay jars.

PLAISANCE, Château

Palus growth of the Médoc; Macau (Claret).

PLAT

French for 'flat', referring to a wine lacking in liveliness and appeal.

PLYMOUTH GIN

A distinctive type of Gin, heavier and richer than London Gin, unsweetened.

PODENSAC

One of the Communes of the Gironde, 32 kilometres, south-south-east of Bordeaux, the vineyards of which produce some red wines of no particular merit but more and better white wines, similar to those of the adjoining Commune of Cérons; they are mostly sold under the name of *Cérons* wines. The best wines of Podensac are those of *Châteaux de Madère* and *de Mauves*.

PODERSDORF

Township of the Burgenland (Austria); its vineyards produce some white wines from middling to fair quality.

POLIGNY

An important wine-producing Commune of the Jura Département, it is chiefly noted for its white wines, more particularly some of the *Vins jaunes* and *Vins de paille* which are similar to those of Château Chalon.

POMÉROL

One of the more important wine-producing Communes of the Gironde. Its vineyards occupy a small plateau between Libourne and Saint-Emilion: they produce no white wine but a large quantity of Claret of high quality, as well as a greater quantity still of wholesome and pleasant but commoner red wines.

POMEYS, Château

Bourgeois growth of the Médoc; Moulis (Claret).

POMIES-AGASSAC, Château

Bourgeois growth of the Médoc; Ludon (Claret).

POMMARD

One of the best-known Communes of the Côte d'Or (Côte de Beaune) which produces a large quantity of red Burgundy, much of it being of very fine quality and much more of little distinction.

POMMARÈDE, Château de

Graves de Bordeaux; Castres (Claret and a little white wine).

POMYS, Château

Bourgeois growth of the Médoc; Saint-Estèphe (Claret).

PONCHE CASTILLO and PONCHE SOTO

Two popular Spanish liqueurs.

PONTAC

The name of several red wines of the Gironde (Claret), none of them of any outstanding merit. But in the seventeenth century Pontac was considered one of the finest Clarets in England. John Locke wrote in 1677: 'The Vin de Pontac, so much esteemed in England, grows on a rising opening to the west . . .', and John Evelyn wrote, on 13th July, 1683, that he had met Monsieur Pontac, 'the son of the famous Bordeaux President, who owns the excellent vineyards of Pontac and Haut-Brion, whence the best Bordeaux wines come from.' Pontac is also the name given to a sweet and highly fortified red wine made at the Cape, where it is highly popular locally, chiefly among 'gentlemen of colour' on Saturday nights.

PONTET-CANET, Château

Fifth *Cru Classé* of the Médoc; Pauillac (Claret).

PORT

Port is a wine made from grapes grown in the valley of the Upper Douro, fortified at the vintage time and shipped from Oporto. When the grapes are pressed, their sweet juice begins to ferment; but before fermentation has transformed the whole of the grape-juice sugar into alcohol, Brandy is added to it and all further vinous fermentation is immediately checked. At that stage, Port is a blend of wine (fermented grape-juice), Brandy, and unfermented grape-juice. But of such materials Time, that great artist, fashions two different and equally seductive wines; Vintage Port and Tawny Port. *Vintage Port* is a wine made in one year, shipped usually two years after it is made, and bottled in England soon after it is received. *Tawny Port* is not a wine made from any one year's grapes, but a blend of wines of a number of years. Tawny Port is kept at Oporto in the Shipper's Lodges for many years and matured in wood. It ages more rapidly than early-bottled Vintage Port, and is shipped when ready for drinking. *Ruby Port* is a compromise between the early-bottled Vintage Port and the matured in wood Tawny Port. Ruby Port may be the wine of one vintage kept in cask long enough to lose some of its 'fire', but not long enough to lose much of its colour. Ruby Port may be a blend of wines of different years and style—a blend which may be made at Oporto by the Shipper, or in England by wine merchants. Although the first duty of Port is to be red, there is such a thing as *White Port*, and it has many admirers, more particularly among the ladies.

The standard gauge of a Pipe of Port is 115 gallons; its average yield, 56 dozens.

PORTETS, Château de
Graves de Bordeaux; Portets (Claret and white wine).

POSSET
One of the most popular forms of hot drinks to prevent or cure a cold. Its basis is hot milk, curdled with hot ale, sweetened with sugar, and flavoured with grated nutmeg. In the *de luxe* edition of the Posset, Sherry is used in place of ale.

POTTLE
English wine measure equal to one-half of a gallon or 4 Imperial Pints. The pre-1826 English Pottle was, and the present American Pottle is, equal to 3·3324 Imperial Pints.

POUGET, Château
Fourth *Cru Classé* of the Médoc; Cantenac (Claret).

POUILLY
There are different French white wines of that name, the better known of which is a white Burgundy from the vineyards of two adjoining villages of the Saône-et-Loire Département, the one called *Pouilly* and the other *Fuissé*; hence the hyphenated name of Pouilly-Fuissé by which the

wine is usually known. The other wine is from the Loire Valley, from the vineyards of the Commune of Pouilly-sur-Loire, in the Nièvre Département; it is made from Chasselas white grapes, The better white wines of the Pouilly-sur-Loire vineyards are made from Sauvignon grapes and sold as *Blanc Fumé* (q.v.).

POUJEAUX, Château
Bourgeois growth of the Médoc; Moulis (Claret).

PRAMNIAN WINE
One of the most famous of ancient Greek wines, the wine that was Nestor's—and presumably Homer's favourite (*Iliad* X. 780). There is every reason to believe, from the descriptions of Pramnian wines which have reached us, that it was not the wine of any particular vineyard, but a wine made from over-ripe grapes, which were not actually pressed, their very sweet juice being collected as it oozed out under the weight of the gathered grapes: if so, it may have been somewhat like some of the *Tokay Essenz*.

PREIGNAC
Commune of the Sauternes district; its vineyards produce some of the best white wines of Bordeaux.

PRÉMEAUX
Commune of the Côte d'Or, immediately south of Nuits Saint-Georges; its vineyards produce mostly red wines, some of them are of fine quality and sold under the name of *Nuits Saint-Georges*.

PRIBAN, Château
Bourgeois growth of the Médoc; Macau (Claret).

PRIEURE, Château Le
Fourth *Cru Classé* of the Médoc; Cantenac (Claret). After the Second World War, this Château was acquired by an American syndicate and re-named Le Prieuré-Lichine.

PRIEURÉ-SAINT-EMILION, Château Le

First growth of Saint-Emilion (Claret).

PROOF SPIRIT

In the U.K. Proof Spirit is 'that which at the temperature of 51°F. weighs exactly twelve-thirteenths of an equal measure of distilled water'. This means that at a temperature of 60°F. Proof Spirit contains 49·28 per cent by weight or 57·10 per cent by volume of alcohol. Any degree or degrees of Proof Spirit over or under 57·10 of alcohol by volume is stated with the mention 'o.p.' or 'u.p.', meaning 'over proof' or 'under proof'. Thus a spirit containing 60·6 of alcohol by volume, and another 53·8 would be described as: the first 6·13 o.p.; and the second 5·78 u.p.

In the U.S.A., what is known as 'Proof Spirit' is a spirit containing 50 per cent by volume of alcohol at 15·6°C. (60°F.) (Trailles alcoholometer). Thus 1 per cent of Proof Spirit equals 0·46 per cent of absolute alcohol by weight and 0·57 per cent of absolute alcohol by volume.

PROVENCE

A former province of France divided into the Alpes-Maritimes, Bouches-du-Rhône, Var, and Vaucluse Départements. It produces a great deal of wine, *rosés*, red and white, those of *Bellet*, *Cassis*, and *La Gaude* being among the best.

PRUNELLE

A French Liqueur, the informing flavour of which is that of fresh sloes.

PRUSSIAN STATE DOMAINS

The vineyards were those owned by the Prussian State, the largest vineyard owners in the Rhinegau, and they spared no expense or trouble to secure the best wine possible. Their stamp, on a Hock bottle: *Original-Abfüllung Preuss. Staatsdomäine*, is a guarantee of quality as well as of authenticity. The Prussian State vineyards were the following:

Hochheim: part of the Domdechaney and Kirchenstuck vineyards.
Rüdesheim: parts of Schlossberg, Burgweg, Roseneck, Bronnen, Zollhaus, Bischofsberg, Hinterhaus.
Steinberg. The whole of Steinberg.
Hattenheim: most of the Engelmannsberg vineyards.
Markobrunn, Rauenthal, and *Kiedrich*. Parts of quite a number of vineyards in each.

PULIGNY-MONTRACHET

A Commune of the Côte d'Or Département, the vineyards of which, with those of the adjoining Commune of Chassagne-Montrachet, produce the finest white wines of Burgundy, and of France.

PULQUE

An intoxicating beverage fermented, chiefly in Mexico, from the sap of the Maguey and other kinds of aloes.

PUNCH

Punch in its oldest and simplest form is Rum and water, hot or iced, with sugar to taste and orange or lemon (for hot *Punch*), or fresh lime (for cold *Punch*). It was in 1655, when they took Jamaica from Spain, that the English were first introduced to Rum and to Punch. During the eighteenth century *Punch* became much more elaborate, in England, as well as the recognized Whig drink: it was 'brewed' or mixed at table in a Punchbowl, by the host, with rum as one of the ingredients, but other spirits as well, brandy nearly always, and either hot water or hot tea, oranges and lemons in thin slices, grated nutmeg and sundry decorations or flavourings to the taste or discretion of the holder of the Punch Ladle.

'Punch cures the Gout, the Cholic, and the Phtisic,
And it is to all men the very best Physic.'

Ale Punch. Put into a bowl 1 quart of mild ale, 1 wine-glassful of sherry, the like quantity of brandy, a tablespoonful of icing sugar, the peel and juice of 1 lemon, a little grated nutmeg, and a small piece of ice; serve in small tumblers.

Army Punch. Two dozen lemons and two dozen oranges. One quart of light rum; three pounds of sugar; bottle and cork it and serve with crushed ice. *Mrs. Wm. H. Thomas, Carrol County.*

Chilean 3-day Punch. First day: pare yellow rind from 9 lemons with sharp knife, so thinly that none of the bitter white adheres. Put in a quart jug and pour on 1 pint fine Jamaica rum. Screw cover right down and set aside for use on third day.

Second day. Put 2 lb. sugar loaf in another jar and squeeze over them the juice of those 9 skinned lemons. Screw cover down and set snugly by the side of the rum-and-rind jar.

Third day. Mix contents of both jars in a big punch bowl, pour in 3 pints rum and 5 quarts distilled water, or water that has been boiled and cooled, with 2 pints boiling hot milk. Let it drain slowly through a flannel bag, without squeezing.

Duke of Norfolk's Punch. To a gallon of rum or brandy take 6 lemons and 6 oranges. Pare them as thin as you can and put the parings into the spirits and let them steep 24 hours. Afterwards take 6 quarts of Spring water and 3 pounds of loaf sugar and boil the water and sugar for ¼ of an hour and clear it with whites of eggs. When the sugar and water is cold, strain the parings from the brandy or rum and squeeze in your juice of oranges, etc., through a strainer to keep out the seeds. Then mix all together and turn it in a vessel where it must remain 6 weeks at least unbottled. (Anne Wynne of Bodewryd, 1675).

Fish House Punch. One pint lemon juice, 3 pints mixture, viz.: 1 pint Jamaica spirits, 1 pint brandy and 1 pint

peach brandy, 4 pounds sugar, 9 pints water. Make lemonade first, then add other liquors. *Mrs. Charles H. Tilghman, Talbot County.*

'Fish House Punch has been the main speciality of the "State in Schuylkill" since this association was founded, in 1732. This drink has made countless thousands happy, including George Washington, Lafayette, and late, General Pershing.'

Loganberry Punch
>   ¼ cup boiling water
>   2 teaspoons orange pekoe tea
>   ¼ cup sugar
>   Few grains salt
>   1 cup loganberry juice
>   Juice 2 lemons
>   1 pint ginger ale
>   Small bunch fresh mint.

Let tea stand in boiling water 2 minutes. Drain. Add sugar and salt, and cool. Add fruit juices and ginger ale. Pour over cracked ice and garnish with mint sprigs.

Milk Punch
>   1 tablespoonful of fine white sugar
>   1 tablespoonful of water
>   1 wine glass of Cognac brandy
>   ¼ wineglass of Santa Cruz or Jamaica rum
>   A little chipped ice

Fill with milk, shake the ingredients well together, and grate a little nutmeg on top.

Mississippi Punch
>   1 wineglass brandy
>   ¼ wineglass Bourbon whisky
>   ¼ wineglass Jamaica rum
>   ¼ wineglass water
>   1½ tablespoons powdered sugar

Mix well and pour over shaved ice. May be garnished with bits of orange and other fruits in season.

Old Medford Punch
>   1 quart Medford rum
>   ¼ pint brandy
>   ¼ pint claret
>   1 cup strong tea

Sweeten to taste and add 3 sliced oranges, 1 sliced pineapple. Stand 24 hours. Chill, and to serve add 2 quarts champagne.

Planters' Punch. The planters' punch, according to one writer, gets its name because it has been drunk by the sugar planters in Jamaica for over a hundred years. Unfortunately, like a mint julep, it is made in a hundred different ways and seems to reflect the idiosyncrasies of the various bartenders. Generally speaking, a planters' punch is made with a good drink of rum (1½ to 2 oz.) in a long glass with cracked ice and water, shaken up with lime juice and sugar and served unstrained with a straw. In some places orange juice is used instead of water.

Planters' Punch
    1 tablespoon sugar
    3 tablespoons water
    2 jiggers (¼ cup) rum
    Juice of 1 lime
    1 slice orange
    1 slice pineapple
    Shaved ice
Use a tall glass, dissolve sugar in water, add rum and lime juice, fill with shaved ice, stir until outside is coated like a mint julep. Garnish with orange and pineapple and perhaps a maraschino cherry.

Peabody Punch
    1 bottle best Jamaica rum
    6 glasses Cognac
    3 glasses Madeira
    1 doz. large limes or 2 doz. small
    1 jar guava jelly
    1 pint green tea
    Sugar to taste
Rub sugar on limes to get the essential oil diffused into the sugar. Dissolve two-thirds of sugar in tea. Then cut the limes, squeeze and add their juice to the remainder of the impregnated sugar. Dissolve the guava jelly in a pint of boiling water. Mix all these until you get the right sweetness; then add the rum, Madeira and Cognac. It should stand for at least 12 hours, and better, 24. Let large lump of ice float in the punch for an hour before serving, which serves two purposes—making the concoction cool and pleasant to the taste, and diluting it to a pleasant consistency. Bottle any punch left over for a future occasion, as it improves with age.

Roman Punch. 6 oranges, 4 lemons, 1 quart whisky or 1 bottle champagne, 8 egg whites, 2 pounds sugar, 1 gallon water. Grate the rinds and add to the juice 1 gallon water, 1 quart whisky and 8 whites of eggs beaten to a froth. Freeze. *Mrs. Robert Goldsborough Henry, Myrtle Grove, Talbot County.*

Royal Punch. One pint of hot green tea, ¼ a pint of brandy, ¼ a pint of Jamaica rum, 1 wine-glass of white Curaçao, 1 wine-glass of arrack, the juice of 2 limes, a thin slice of lemon, white sugar to taste, a gill of warm calf's foot jelly. To be drunk as hot as possible.

Rum Punch. Put into a large tumbler a tablespoonful of icing sugar, a wine-glass of brandy, the like quantity of rum, two teaspoonfuls of arrack, the juice of 1 lemon, quarter of a wine-glass of green tea, a teaspoonful of essence of spice. Half fill the glass with shaved ice, shake well, strain, and add sufficient milk to fill the glass. Dust with nutmeg and cinnamon, and serve with a straw.

Tea Punch: one pint rum, 1½ cups sugar, 6 lemons, 1 tablespoonful brandy, 2 cups strong tea. Peel the lemons thin and pour the tea boiling hot over them. Squeeze the lemon juice on the sugar and let remain an hour or more. Mix altogether and mix over a bowl of crushed ice. This would serve about 6 people before prohibition. *Mrs. Anne Merryman Carroll, Hayfields, Baltimore County.*

Virginia Verder Punch
    9 lemons
    9 oranges
    1 bottle brandy
    3 lb. sugar
    1½ gallons boiling water
    3 pints boiling milk

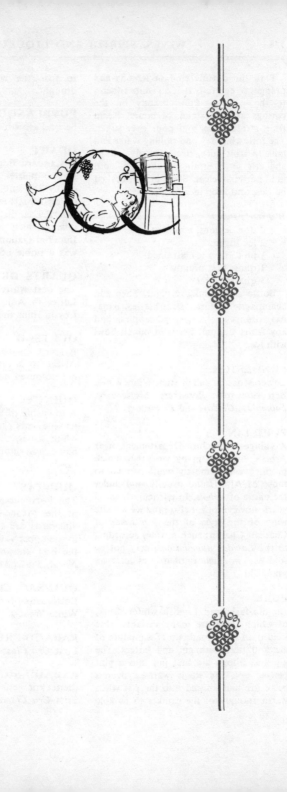

Pare the outside rind of lemons and oranges so carefully that no white adheres to the parings. Pour brandy on the parings and let stand 24 hours. Ream fruit, strain juice, and pour over sugar. The following day add boiling water and milk to fruit juice, strain brandy into it, and stir well. Strain all through cloth until perfectly clear. Store in well corked bottles, and keep in a cool place.

Webster's Punch
   2 doz. lemons, strained
   2 lb. sugar
   ½ pint green tea, strained
   1 quart best brandy
   3 quarts claret
Bottle and stand overnight. Then add champagne to taste, strawberries, bananas, oranges, cherries, pineapples, and any fruits desired. Serve in punch bowl with ice.

PUNDERICH
Lower Moselle. Zell district. White wines. Best vineyards: *Rosenberg, Marienberg, Falkenlay, Golday*, and *Petersberg*.

PUPILLIN
A village of the Jura Département, near Arbois, hemmed in by vineyards which produce wines, mostly white, similar to those of Arbois and usually sold under the name of *Arbois*. In particularly good years, however, they also produce a white wine of the style of the *Vin Jaune* of Château Chalon; such a wine, according to the *Loi des Appellations*, may not be sold as *Vin Jaune* until it is at least six years old.

PURL
An old-fashioned English winter drink, of which there are many variants. One kind used to be made up of a mixture of ale and beer with gin and bitters. The gin and bitters are first put into a pint pewter pot, the ale is warmed over a brisk fire and poured into the pot when warm enough for the drinker to be able to toss the whole down at a single draught.

PUYBLANQUET, Domaine de
Second growth of Saint-Emilion (Claret).

QUART
A standard English wine measure equal to one-quarter of a gallon, 1·136 litres or 69·318 cubic inches. This standard or legal quart is also known as 'Imperial Quart', as distinct from the 'reputed' quart, which is only one-sixth of the Imperial Gallon. The 'Winchester Quart' was a noble bottle holding five pints.

QUARTS DE CHAUME
The best white wines of Rochefort-sur-Loire, in Anjou, where the little River Layon joins the great Loire.

QUETSCH
A spirit distilled from plums, chiefly in Alsace: it is always pure white, as it is not coloured nor matured in wood.

QUINCY
A township of Berry, in the Cher Valley; its vineyards produce some very pleasant white wines, the best being made from Sauvignon grapes and sold as *Quincy fumé*.

QUINTAS
The Portuguese equivalent of *Châteaux* in the Médoc—'Estates' of which the vineyards are the most important part, in the upper valley of the Douro. Among the best known Quintas are *Boa Vista, Noval, Roriz, Malvedos*, etc.

QUINSAC, Château
Entre-deux-Mers; Gironde (Claret and White Wine).

RABAUD-PROMIS, Château
First *Cru Classé* of Sauternes; Bommes.

RABAUD-SIGALAS, Château
(better known as *Château Sigalas-Rabaud*). First *Cru Classé* of Sauternes; Bommes.

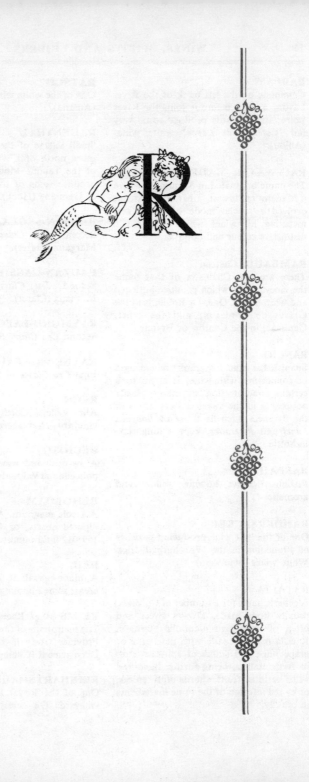

RABLAY
Commune on the left bank of the River Layon, a little before it joins the River Loire; its vineyards produce some very fair *'Coteaux de Layon'* white wines (Anjou).

RAINWATER MADEIRA
The name originated in Savannah, where a Madeira enthusiast, a Mr. Habersham, evolved a special mode of fining and maturing his wines which acquired a distinctive colour and bouquet.

RAMBAUD, Château
There are two Châteaux of that name the vineyards of which produce both red and white wines. One, La Brède, is in the Graves de Bordeaux; and the other, Genissac, in the Canton of Branne.

RANCIO
Spanish for rancid or rank: where used in connection with wine, it refers to a certain concentration of ethers chiefly noticeable in the sweet dessert wines of the Pyrenees, such as those of *Banyuls*, *Lunel* and *Rivesaltes*, kept a long time in bottle.

RASPAIL
French digestive liqueur, yellow and aromatic.

RANDERSACKER
One of the best wine-producing parishes of Franconia in the Würzburg district. White wines (Steinwein).

RATAFIA
A generic name for a number of Cordials, usually home-made, always sweet and often of very high alcoholic strength. Ratafia may be made with new wine or grape juice and sufficient spirit to stop its fermentation, being further flavoured with various fruits, herbs and spices, or by the infusion of the same ingredients in brandy.

RATSCH
One of the white wines of the Steiermark (Austria).

RAUENTHAL
Small village of the Rhinegau, about 2 miles north of Eltville, on the foothills of the Taunus Mountain. Its vineyards produce some of the finest white wines of Germany (Hock).

RAUSAN-SÉGLA, Château
Second *Cru Classé* of the Médoc; Margaux (Claret).

RAUZAN-GASSIES, Château
Second *Cru Classé* of the Médoc; Margaux (Claret).

RAYMOND-LAFON, Château
Second *Cru Classé* Sauternes, Sauternes.

RAYNE-VIGNEAU, Château
First *Cru Classé* of Sauternes; Bommes.

RECH
Ahr Valley. Chiefly red wines. Best vineyard: *Herrenberg.*

RECIOTO
A sweetish red wine made in the Valpolicella and Valpantena, in Veneto (Italy).

REHOBOAM
A treble magnum. A bottle holding six reputed quarts, or 4·80 litres, equal to 169·012 fluid ounces.

REIL
A minor growth of the Moselle (Wittlich area); some middling to fair white wines.

REIMS (*Angl.* **Rheims**)
The metropolis of the former Champagne Province and of the present Marne Département (Champagne).

REINHARTSHAUSEN, Schloss
One of the Royal Prussian castles. Its vineyards (74 acres) are partly in the

Hattenheim and partly in the Erbach area: their finest wines are sold as *Schloss Reinhartshausener 'Cabinet' Erbacher Markobrunnen*; they are always 'Château bottled' and the bottles bear a white label with a narrow red border.

REMICH

One of the more important growths of the Moselle during its passage through the Grand Duchy of Luxembourg (white wines).

RESPIDE, Château de

One of the more important growths of Saint-Pierre-du-Mons, a short distance east of Langon (White wines of the Sauternes type). To the west of Langon there is a Château Respide (not *de*), the red and white wines of which are entitled to the *Appellation Contrôlée Graves Supérieures*.

RETSINA

The generic name of the *ordinaire* table wines of Greece which have been 'resinated' or treated with pitch.

RHEINGAU (*Angl.* Rhinegau)

The district on the right bank of the Rhine which produces the finest German wines, both red and white, but chiefly white. The principal wine-producing parishes of the Rhinegau, as one goes up the Rhine, will be found in the following order: *Assmannhausen, Rüdesheim, Geisenheim, Johannisberg, Winkel, Oestrich, Hallgarten, Hattenheim, Kiedrich, Erbach, Eltville, Rauenthal*, and, farther on, *Wiesbaden* and *Hochheim*.

RHENISH

The name by which the wines of the Rhine were known in England from a very early date down to the eighteenth century, when they began to be called Hocks (q.v.) Rhenish is mentioned by Shakespeare:

Portia. Therefore, for fear of the worst, I pray thee set a deep glass of

Rhenish wine on the contrary casket: for, if the devil be within and that temptation without, I know he will choose it. . . .
> *The Merchant of Venice*,
> Act I, Scene ii.

Salarino. There is more difference between thy flesh and hers than between jet and ivory; more between your bloods than there is between red wine and Rhenish.
> *The Merchant of Venice*,
> Act III, Scene i.

Hamlet. The king doth wake tonight, and takes his rouse,
Keeps wassail, and the swaggering up-spring reels;
And, as he drains his draughts of Rhenish down,
The kettle-drum and trumpet thus bray out
The triumph of his pledge.
> *Hamlet*, Act I, Scene iv.

1st Clown. A pestilence on him for a mad rogue! 'a poured a flagon of Rhenish on my head once. . . .
> *Hamlet*, Act V, Scene i.

RHINEHESSE

The district on the left bank of the Rhine, practically opposite the Rhinegau, which produces the largest quantity of German red and white wines of fine quality; chiefly white. The principal wine-producing districts of Rhinehesse are: *Alzey, Bingen, Mayence, Oppenheim* and *Worms*.

RHODES

One of the isles of the Greek Archipelago, which has been famed for the excellence of its wines for the past two thousand years.

RHÔNE

A fine river with vineyards more or less the whole of its course. The Rhône vineyards produce some fair white wines in the Valais Canton of Switzerland and in Savoy (Seyssel), but the best red wines are those from vineyards below Lyons and before Avignon. The most celebrated are the wines of *Côte Rôtie*, *Hermitage* and *Châteauneuf-du-Pape*. Many others are sold under the name of *Côtes-du-Rhône*.

RIBEAUVILLÉ
One of the best white wines of Alsace come from the vineyards of this picturesque little town, the German name of which is Rappoltsweiler.

RICAUD, Château de
An important growth of the Entre-deux-Mers area; Haut-Loupiac (white wines).

RICHEBOURG
A red Burgundy wine of superlative excellence from a vineyard (20 acres) of the Commune of Vosne-Romanée (Côte de Nuits). The Richebourg and Romanée-Conti vineyards are near neighbours and their wines are considered by many good judges the finest of all red Burgundies, but whilst the smaller Romanée-Conti vineyard belongs to one owner, the larger Richebourg vineyards are divided among three owners, a fact which accounts for possible differences in the *Richebourgs* of the same vintage.

RIESLING
The finest white grapes for the making of high-class white wines in Alsace, Austria, Germany and Hungary. It is very similar to, but not identical with, the *Pinot Blanc*.

RIEUSSEC, Château
First *Cru Classé* of Sauternes; Fargues.

RIGAILHOU, Château
Graves de Bordeaux; Léognan (Claret and White Wine).

RILLY-la-MONTAGNE
First growth of the Montagne de Reims (Champagne).

RIOJA
A district of Aragon, in Spain, which has been famous for centuries past for the excellence of its fruits and vegetables. It was, however, rather less than a hundred years ago that its vineyards were developed, and they have since gained the reputation of producing the best Spanish table wines, mostly red. They have more body than charm and greater alcoholic strength than 'finesse'.

RIONS
A Commune of the Gironde, 33 kilometres south-south-east of Bordeaux, on the right bank of the River Garonne, the site of Ryuncium, an important Gallo-Roman city. Its vineyards produce both red and white wines of fair quality but of no outstanding merit.

RIPEAU, Château
First growth of Graves de Saint-Emilion (Claret).

RIVESALTES
A picturesque little town on the lower slopes of the Pyrenees, at their Mediterranean end: it is surrounded by vineyards the best wine of which is a white, sweet dessert wine, not unlike *Lunel*.

ROCHECORBON
One of the better growths of Touraine; Vouvray area.

ROCHEMORIN, Château
Graves de Bordeaux; Martillac (Claret).

ROCHET, Château
Fourth *Cru Classé* of the Médoc; Saint-Estèphe (Claret).

ROEDELSEE
One of the smaller wine-producing townships of Franconia (Steinwein).

ROMANÈCHE-THORINS
A well-known growth of the Beaujolais (Lower Burgundy). One of the best wines of the district is that of the *Hospices de Romanèche-Thorins*, which, since 1926, have always been bottled at the Hospices.

ROMANÉE, La
The smallest of the *Romanées* vineyards (2 acres) in the Commune of Vosne-Romanée (Côte de Nuits), but responsible for some of the finest Red Burgundies.

ROMANÉE-CONTI
A small vineyard (4½ acres) of the Commune of Vosne-Romanée (Côte de Nuits), responsible for the finest of all Red Burgundies.

ROMANÉE SAINT-VIVANT
The largest of the *Romanée* vineyards (24 acres), in the Commune of Vosne-Romanée (Côte de Nuits); they are responsible for very fine, even if not the finest, Red Burgundy.

ROMER, Château
Second *Cru Classé* of Sauternes; Fargues.

ROSÉ, Vin
Pink wine. The best natural *vin rosé* is that of Tavel (Rhône Valley) but *vins rosés* are made elsewhere, both still and sparkling, either with red grapes which are not left long to ferment on their husks, or white wines coloured with cochineal or blended with red wine. The cochineal colouring is harmless enough and the colour is more stable, but its use is not to be encouraged, since it introduces into the wine an animal dye quite foreign to it.

ROSEMONT, Château
Bourgeois growth of the Médoc; Labarde (Claret).

ROSSOLIO
Also known as Rossolis. One of the oldest of all French liqueurs, now all but forgotten. It used to be home-made always, brandy and sugar being the basis of the liqueur, which was flavoured with any and every kind of fresh fruit available at different times and places. *Rossolio*, or *Rossoglio* or *Crème de Rose* is a bright red liqueur, coloured with cochineal and flavoured with oil of roses, made chiefly in Zara. In Turin they distil an Orange Rosoglio, also red in colour, and flavoured with Tangerine rind and orange juice as well as orange blossom.

ROTENFELS
The name of high red rocks overlooking the River Nahe and of some vineyards, at the foot of those rocks, which produce some very fair white wines (Hocks).

ROUMIEUX, Château
Second *Cru Classé* of Sauternes; Barsac.

ROUSSETTE
The most popular white wine of Seyssel, Savoy; the best come from the Ain, or right bank of the Rhône.

ROUSSILLON
One of the southernmost former Provinces of France which produces a great deal of strong, dark, red wines. Its vinous reputation, however, rests on the vineyards of three of its main valleys: (1) Vallée du Tech, the vineyards of which are responsible for the wines of *Banyuls*, *Picardan* and *Collioures;* (2) Vallée du Têt, from which come mostly red and white beverage wines; and (3) Vallée de l'Agly, the vineyards of which produce the wines of *Corbières* and the Muscat of *Rivesaltes.*

ROXHEIM
One of the Nahe Valley growths; Kreuznach (Hocks).

ROYAL-MÉDOC
A registered brand used for the sale of the 'second' wine of Château Cantemerle.

RÜDESHEIM

The westernmost town of the Rhinegau proper; its 650 acres of vineyards produce some of the great Hocks as well as white wines from fair to fine in quality.

RUEDA

A township of the Valladolid district, the vineyards of which produce some fair red table wines.

RULLY

The Commune of the Côte Chalonnaise which produces some of the most attractive of the moderately priced white Burgundies, as well as some fair red wines.

RUM

A spirit distilled from molasses; it can be, has been and still is, distilled from the fermented juice of the sugar cane, but it is not a commercial proposition. There are many types and styles of *Rum*, most of which may be classed in one or the other of the following three main categories: (1) the very dry, light-bodied *Rum*, of which the Cuban *Rum* is the prototype; (2) the rich, full-bodied *Rums*, of which the *Jamaica Rum* is the acknowledged standard; (3) the more aromatic *Rums* such as are made in the Dutch East Indies; Martinique, Puerto Rico, Trinidad, Barbados, Demerara and many other islands and mainland sugar cane districts all produce *Rums* which possess some characteristics of their own.

Rum Collins. The juice of half a lemon, half a tablespoonful powdered sugar, 1 glass Jamaica Rum. Shake well and strain into long tumbler. Add 1 lump ice and soda water.

Rum Daisy. 1 teaspoonful sugar, a teaspoonful raspberry syrup, juice of half an orange, juice of half a lime, juice of half a lemon, 75 per cent Medford Rum. Fill glass with cracked ice. Shake, strain, and fill glass with fizz water and serve.—J.M.

Rum Flip. Prepare grated ginger and nutmeg with a little fine dried lemon peel rubbed together in a mortar; to make a quart of *Flip*, heat rather more than a pint and a half of ale; beat up 3 or 4 eggs with 4 oz. of moist sugar; a teaspoonful of grated nutmeg or ginger; and a gill of good old rum or brandy; and when it is nearly boiling, put it into a pitcher and the rum and eggs, etc., into another. Mix and pour it from one pitcher to the other till it is as smooth as cream.

Rum Shrub. Put 3 pints of orange juice and 1 pound of loaf sugar to a gallon of rum. Put all into a cask, and leave it for 6 weeks, when it will be ready for use.

Spiced Rum (*Hot*). 1 lump sugar, ½ teaspoonful mixed allspice; dissolve with a little water; 100 per cent Jamaica rum. Fill glass with hot water. Stir, grate a little nutmeg and serve.

Rum Toddy. 1 lump of sugar and 1 jigger of Jamaica rum. Fill glass with boiling water. Insert one small piece of cinnamon, 1 slice of lemon garnished with 4 cloves and a thin slice of lemon rind twisted over glass and inserted. Stir mixture a little and serve with a spoon. Also serve a small pitcher of hot water on the side.

RUPPERTSBERG

A village of the Palatinate, half a mile from Deidesheim. Its vineyards produce much *ordinaire* red wine and much less white wine of superlative excellence (Hocks).

RUWER

A small river which joins the Moselle a short distance north of Trier. The vineyards of the Ruwer produce some very delicate white wines, usually sold in England as 'Moselles'.

SAAR

A small tributary of the River Moselle. Many vineyards grace both banks of the

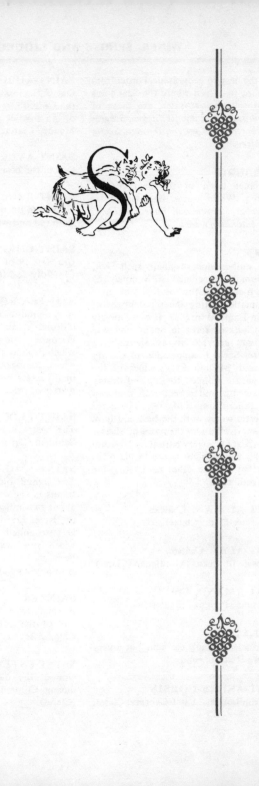

Saar, the best, in geographical order from Saarburg to Filzen where the Saar joins the Moselle below Trier, are those of *Saarburg, Ockfen, Ayl, Wiltingen, Scharzhof, Oberemmel, Canzem, Wawern, Serrig* and *Filzen.*

SAARBURG

The chief town of the Saar (Rheinprovinz). White wines. Best vineyards: *Mühlenberg, Leyenkaul, Rausch, Schlossberg, Antoniusbrunnen.*

SACK

A dry, amber wine, originally spelt *Seck,* occasionally sweetened with honey or sugar, mentioned for the first time in a Proclamation fixing the retail prices of wine in England in 1532. It came mostly from Cadiz or Jerez in Spain, and was sometimes referred to as Sherris-Sack (or Jerez-Sack) in opposition to Canary Sack and Malligo Sack, wines of the same nature shipped to England during the sixteenth and seventeenth centuries from Teneriffe and Malaga. The Jerez or Sherris wines were the best and have alone survived under the name of Sherry. Shakespeare was very partial to Sack and it is the wine which occurs in his plays more than all the other names of wine put together.

SAINT-AIGNAN, Château

Entre-deux-Mers (Claret).

SAINT-ALBE, Château

Graves de Bordeaux; Gradignan (Claret).

SAINT-AMAND, Cru

Sauternais; Preignac (Sauternes).

SAINT-AMOUR

Mâconnais. Not a great wine but a very pleasing Red Burgundy.

SAINT-ANDRÉ-CORBIN

Saint-Emilionnais; Saint-Georges; Claret.

SAINT-AUBIN

One of the least important Communes of the Côte d'Or; red Burgundy. Also one of the smaller Communes of the Haut-Médoc; Claret.

SAINT-AVERTIN

One of the best red wines of Touraine.

SAINT-BRIS, Château

Graves de Bordeaux; Villenave d'Ornon. Both red and white wines.

SAINT-CHRISTOLY, Château

Cru Artisan of the Haut-Médoc; Saint-Christoly-de-Médoc (Claret).

SAINTE-CROIX-du-MONT

A Commune of the Entre-deux-Mers (Gironde), on the right bank of the Garonne facing the Sauternes country, which produces some very pleasing white wines, comparable to those of Sauternes in sweetness but not in breed nor in the matter of price.

SAINT-ELIE

The best known wine of the island of Santorin (Greece).

SAINT-EMILION

The quaint old City of Saint-Emilion stands in the centre of a cluster of hills, about two miles from the right bank of the River Dordogne above Libourne. It is surrounded by extensive vineyards which run into some fifteen different parishes, but all the wine they produce is known as Saint-Emilion wine.

SAINTES

A small town rich in Roman remains, one of the commercial centres of the Cognac Brandy trade.

SAINT-ESTÈPHE

One of the most important wine-producing Communes of the Haut-Médoc (Claret).

SAINT-GEORGES, Les
Some of the best vineyards of the Commune of Nuits-Saint-Georges, Côte d'Or (Red Burgundy).

SAINT-GEORGES-CÔTE-PAVIE, Château
First growth of Saint-Emilion (Claret).

SAINT-GEORGES-DE-MONTAGNE, Château *and*
SAINT-GEORGES-MACQUIN, Château
Commune of Saint-Georges; Saint-Emilionnais (Claret).

SAINT-GERMAIN, Domaine de
Premier *Cru bourgeois*; Blayais (Claret).

SAINT-GERMAIN, Domaine de
Entre-deux-Mers (White Bordeaux).

SAINT-GERMAIN, Château
The largest estate of the Commune of Saint-Germain-de-Grave; white wine of moderate quality.

SAINT-GERMAIN, Château
Commune of Donzac; Entre-deux-Mers. (Claret and white wine).

SAINT-GERMAIN-DE-GRAVE
A Commune of the Entre-deux-Mers district of Bordeaux, producing some white wine of fair quality.

SAINT-JEAN-D'ANGÉLY
A small but ancient town of the Charente district, one of the commercial centres of the Cognac Brandy trade.

SAINT-JEAN-DE-BRAYE
One of the best *Vins de pays* of the Orléans district.

SAINT-JULIEN
There are a number of Communes in France bearing the name Saint-Julien, one in the Bouches-du-Rhône, and another in the Meuse Départements, both producing chiefly red wines of no real merit. But, of course, *the* great and famous Commune of Saint-Julien is in the Gironde Département.

SAINT-JULIEN, Château
There is no Château Saint-Julien in the Médoc, but part of the yield of the Château Lagrange is sold under the name of *Château Saint-Julien*.

SAINT-JULIEN, Château
First growth of Saint-Emilion (Claret).

SAINT-LAURENT
There are quite a few wine-producing Communes in France bearing the name of Saint-Laurent—two in the Gironde Département and one each in the Dordogne, Jura, Var and Gard Départements, but the most famous of all, and the only one to produce wines of real merit, is in the Médoc (Gironde Département).

SAINT-NICHOLAS-DE-BOURGUEIL
One of the best red wines of Touraine.

SAINT-PÉRAY
One of the wine-producing Communes of the Ardéche (Rhône Valley) that has been famous for centuries past for its white wines, both still and sparkling.

SAINT-PIERRE-BONTEMPS, Château
Saint-Julien. Fourth *Cru Classé* of the Médoc (Claret).

SAINT-PIERRE-DE-MONS
A Commune of the Gironde, some eight miles to the east-north-east of Sauternes, renowned for its white wines, which are now legally entitled to the name of Sauternes.

SAINT-PIERRE-SEVAISTRE, Château
Saint-Julien. Fourth *Cru Classé* of the Médoc (Claret).

SAINT-POURÇAIN

A Commune of the Allier (Loire Valley), famous for its still, white wines; the white wines of the adjoining villages of Louchy, Saulcet and Montord are also sold under the better-known name of *Saint-Pourçain*.

SAINT-SATUR

One of the best white wines of the Sancerre district (Berry).

SAINT-RAPHAËL

One of the more popular French Aperitifs.

SAINT-SAUVEUR

One of the lesser wine-producing Communes of the Haut-Médoc, the wines of which have acquired by long usage the right to be sold under the name of the neighbouring and better known Commune of *Saint-Estèphe*.

SAINT-SEURIN-DE-CADOURNE

One of the lesser wine-producing Communes of the Haut-Médoc the wines of which have acquired by long usage the right to be sold under the name of the neighbouring and better-known Commune of *Saint-Estèphe*.

SAINT-THIBAULT

One of the best white wines of the Sancerre district (Berry).

SAINT-VIVANT

The largest of the four Romanée vineyards, Vosne-Romanée, Côte d'Or (Red Burgundy).

SAINT-YZANS

A Commune of the Médoc, 68 kilometres north-north-west of Bordeaux, the vineyards of which produce a good deal of sound red wine and a small quantity of white wine as well.

SAKÉ

A Japanese rice beer obtained by two consecutive processes of fermentation of a brew mostly of rice, but occasionally of other grain. Its alcoholic content is usually from 14 to 16 per cent of alcohol by volume; it is colourless, quite still, and is served warm in tiny porcelain bowls holding little more than an ounce. The first taste of *Saké* is rather sweet but its after-taste is bitter. Its name is supposed to come from Osaka, which has long been famous for its *Saké*. *Saké* is sometimes served in specially made little bowls with an air tube so devised that one draws air when sipping the *Saké* in the bowl, thus producing a whistling sound: these little bowls are called singing *Saké* cups.

SALMANAZAR

A large glass bottle for show more than for use: it is supposed to hold 12 reputed quarts (9·60 litres) or 338.012 fluid ounces.

SAMOS

One of the Greek islands producing some of the most popular tawny dessert wines sold in the Netherlands and Scandinavian countries.

SAMSHU

The Chinese *Saké*, a kind of beer brewed from rice that is treated with a special yeast, *Aspergillus oryzae*, which converts the starch of the rice into sugar.

SANCERRE

A picturesque old City of the Cher Département of France; its vineyards produce chiefly white wines, which are consumed locally. They also produce a noted white wine which is sold in bottles quite distinctive in shape, under the name of *Château de Sancerre*.

SANGAREE

The name given to long, mixed, iced drinks in some parts of the tropics: whether wine or spirits be used as a basis, and if so which sorts and in what proportion, are left to the ingenuity or imagination of the mixer.

SAN GIMIGNANO
One of the better red table wines of Italy (Chianti).

SANGIOVESE
A ruby red wine, rather coarse by itself but refreshing when diluted with water; it is the only vinous glory of the miniscule Republic of San Marino. It is also made in the adjoining Italian Province of Emilia.

SANGUE DI GUIDA
One of the 'blood-red' table wines of Lombardy, similar to *Broni*.

SANKT GEORGEN
A white wine from the vineyards of Freiburg-im-Breisgau is sold under this name; also both red and white wines from the vineyards of Pressburg.

SANKT MAGDALENER, SANTA MADDALENA
German and Italian names of the same wine, the red table wine of Bozen or Bolzano, in the South Tyrol.

SANKT MARGARETHEN (Austria)
Burgenland; mostly white wines.

SANKT MARTIN (Palatinate)
Landau district; white wine.

SAN LUCAR DE BARRAMEDA
One of the chief centres of the Sherry-producing district.

SAN LUIS OBISPO
One of the wine-producing counties of the State of California, U.S.A.

SAN SADURNI DE NAYA
One of the wine-producing parishes of Villafranca del Panades (Barcelona Province) where sparkling Spanish white wines are manufactured on an important scale.

SANSONNET, Château
First growth of Saint Emilion (Claret).

SANTA BARBARA
One of the wine-producing counties of the State of California, U.S.A.

SANTA GIUSTINA
A red table wine from Bolzano, South Tyrol, formerly Bozen; it used to be known, until after the War, as Leitacher.

SANTENAY
The southernmost Commune of the Côte d'Or (Burgundy); its vineyards produce a good deal of red wine of fair quality as well as a little of real merit.

SANTORIN
One of the minor and the most volcanic of the Cyclade islands, formerly called Thera and, even earlier, Calliste. It produces a number of different types of wine, red and white, dry and sweet. Its best dry white wine is called *Saint-Elie* and its best sweet, a golden dessert wine, *Vinsanto*. They also make at Santorin a rich, strong, deep-purple wine which they call *Lachryma Christi*.

SARANSOT-DUPRÉ, Château
Bourgeois growth; Listrac (Claret).

SARDINIA
Sardinia produces a quantity of wine, mostly of the sweet or dessert type; the best known are *Giro, Monica, Moscato di Cagliari* and *Vernaccia*.

SARMSHEIM
Kreuznach district (Nahe Valley); white wine.

SARTÈNE
The largest wine-producing Commune of Corsica.

SASBACH
Kaiserstuhl ridge, in Brisgau (Baden); white wine.

SASSARI
One of the red wines of Sardinia (Italy).

SASSELLA
One of the best red wines of the Valtellina (Lombardy).

SAULCET
One of the best wines of the Allier Département of France: it is usually sold under the better-known name of the adjoining Commune of *Saint-Pourçain*.

SAUMUR
The chief city of the chief wine-producing part of the old Province of Anjou; it is the centre of vineyards which produce an abundance of white wines and a little red wine. Some of the white wines are quite suitable for the making of sparkling wines, but the best white wines of the district are still wines.

SAUTERNES
The Sauternes district comprises not only the vineyards of the Commune of Sauternes, but those of the adjoining Communes of Bommes, Barsac, Preignac and Fargues. The Sauternes district adjoins that of Graves, but its soil is different and the wine-making conditions are also different.

SAUVIGNON
One of the noblest white-grape species of vines, responsible for the excellence of the best Sauternes and other white wines, together with the *Semillon*.

SAVERNE
Alsace; white wine of moderate quality.

SAVIGNY
One of the Communes of the Côte d'Or which produces much red Burgundy of fair quality and some of outstanding merit, similar to the wines of the adjoining Communes of Aloxe-Corton and Pernand-Vergelesses.

SAVOY
The French part of the mountainous country between the Rhône Valley, Switzerland and Italy, or Savoy. There are many vineyards in Savoy which produce wines, both red and white, still and sparkling, of local fame, but none of superlative quality, nor any made in sufficiently large quantities to be sold in other parts of France or overseas. The *Rousette* is the name both of the grapes mostly used in the Seyssel district and of the white wine best known in Savoy. A fair white wine is made near Evian, at *Féternes;* at Jongieux, the *Marétel*. Near Thonon, the *Ripaille blanc* has many admirers, as has the *Crépy Blanc*, at Douvaine. The *Marignan*, at Sciez, and the wine of the *Coteau d'Altesse*, to the left of the Lac du Bourget. Among red wines, the *Montmélian*, from vineyards in the vicinity of Chambéry, is one of the best; whilst the red *Chignin* is the most popular of the red wines.

SCHAFFHAUSEN
One of the less important wine-producing Cantons of Switzerland. Its best white wine is the *Siblinger* and the best red the *Osterfinger*, from the vineyards of Hallau.

SCHARZBERGER
One of the best wines of the Saar and Moselle Valleys, from the vineyards of Scharzhof, in the valley of the Saar.

SCHARZHOF
A small township of the Saar Valley, also known as Scharzhof-Wiltingen. Its vineyards produce some of the most delicate white wines of Germany; the finest are those sold under the names of *Scharzhofberger* and *Scharzberger*.

SCHIEDAM
The Gin distilled at Schiedam, one of the oldest centres of Gin distillation in Holland. It is pure white and the best known brand of Schiedam Gin is sold in black bottles with flat sides, known in the vernacular as *Square-face*.

SCHILLERWEIN
The more ordinary beverage wines, chiefly of Württemberg and Baden, light red in colour, usually made of both black and white grapes mixed in the pressing.

SCHIRAZ
The cradle of viticulture, in Persia, if not, as has been claimed, of the world. There is wine still made in the Schiraz district, but its quality cannot be said to deserve Omar's and other poets' praises.

SCHLOSS
German for 'Castle', 'Château'.

SCHLOSSABZUG
German for 'Château bottled'.

SCHLOSSBERGER
White wine from Villingen in Aargau (Switzerland).

SCHLOSS BÖCKELHEIMER
Nahe Valley; Kreuznach district. White wine. Best vineyards: *Kupfergrube, Felsenberg, Mühlberg.*

SCHLOSS JOHANNISBERG
See *Johannisberg.*

SCHLOSS NEUWEIER
See *Neuweier.*

SCHLOSS REINHARTS-HAUSEN
See *Erbach.*

SCHLOSS STAUFENBERG
See *Durbach.*

SCHLOSS VOLLRADS
See *Winkel.*

SCHNAIT
Württemberg. White wines.

SCHOPPEN or SEIDEL
German wine measure; the same as Nössel, half a litre or 0·11 gallon. In Switzerland, the Schoppen equals 0·08 gallon.

SCHOZACH
Württemberg. White and red wines, mostly white.

SCHRIESHEIM
Baden. Mannheim district; white wines.

SCHWABSBURG
Rhinehesse. Oppenheim district; white wine. Best vineyards: *Ebersberg, Schlossberg, Birkenauer, Federberg, Schnappenberg, Niersteiner Weg* (also known as *Orbel*).

SCHWAIGERN
Württemberg; 25 per cent white wine; 60 per cent red wine; 15 per cent Schillerwein.

SCOPELO
One of the minor Greek Islands of the Eastern Mediterranean, north of Euboca, where they make a rich Malmsey type of wine of some repute: it must have been known in England formerly, since there is, in the Ionides Collection, a wine-label bearing the name *Scopoli.*

SCOTCH WHISKY
The most popular of grain spirits all the world over, but since the latter part of the nineteenth century only. Up to 1814 every laird in the Highlands had his own still and never bought whisky, nor did he sell any. In 1814, no still was permitted under 500 gallons and the distillation of whisky became a commercial proposition which has been exploited ever since with such vigour and intelligence that whisky has earned fortunes and peerages for distillers. The four main regions of Scotland chiefly concerned in the production of Malt Whisky are the Highlands, the Lowlands, Campbeltown and Islay. Scotch Whisky is made from barley. (Scotch-grown or any other barley),

which is (1) malted; (2) mashed; (3) fermented; (4) distilled in pot stills. The spirit thus obtained was the only one to answer to the name of Scotch Whisky until 1853, when an all-important innovation was introduced: the blending of 'straight' malt whisky with plain grain spirit, distilled from barley or other grain, unmalted and from a patent still, which is not only a much cheaper method of distillation, but one which produces a lighter type of spirit which appeals to Lowlanders in general and Englishmen in particular. The differences in the flavour of different brands of whisky are chiefly due to the differences in the types and proportion of any of the four above-mentioned Malt Whiskies which have been blended with plain grain spirit. Their alcoholic strength is a matter of added water, their colour is naturally white but it can be and is made golden, light or dark, according to taste.

The finest Malt Whiskies are those of the Highlands, chiefly Banffshire, and within Banffshire, the Glenlivet and Speyside districts are reputed the best. Next in importance comes Moray. Campbeltown malts are heavy and smoky; Islay malts, heavier still and more pungent; Lowland malts the least smoky of all. All whiskies must be matured for at least three years before the law allows them to be sold. They are matured in well-seasoned oak casks and often kept longer than three years. The blending of malt whisky and plain grain spirit is done after whisky and spirit have been matured; it is the last as well as the most difficult and the most important step to be taken by the distiller to transform barley into a spirit of exactly the same strength, colour, flavour and taste as has been bottled by him for years and years in any particular shape of bottles and under any particular label.

SEC
French for 'dry', in the vernacular, but for 'sweet' on the label of a Champagne bottle. *Sec* is not as sweet as a wine labelled *Demi-Sec*, which is very sweet, but it is sweeter than another labelled *Extra-Sec*, which is but slightly sugared.

SECCHIO
Italian wine measure equal to 2·377 gallons.

SÉCHET
One of the second growths of Chablis (White Burgundy).

SEDIMENT
The 'lees' or organic matter discarded by wine kept in bottle, Red wines have more sediment than white wines, because the colour pigment in the skins of the black grapes is responsible for very minute particles of mucilage being held in suspension in the wine for quite a long time; eventually, however, many such particles and others of vegetable character are fixed upon some of the wine's tartrates or other salts and fall upon the glass inside the bottle in the form of crust or sediment.

White wines throw no 'crust', but sometimes small flakes of tannin or gelatine, which are not hurtful to the taste of the wine and do not affect its limpidity. The 'blue' sediment in white wines, similar to tobacco smoke, is due to iron oxides and spoils both the look and the taste of the wine.

SEEWEINE
The wines from the vineyards of Lake Constance (Germany).

SEGONZAC
One of the best Brandy-producing Communes of the Cognac district.

SÉGUR, Château
Cru bourgeois; Médoc. (Claret).

SÉGUR, Cru de
Isle d'Ares; *Cru bourgeois*; Parempuyre; Médoc. (Claret).

SEGUR, Le Clerc de
Palus de Parempuyre; Médoc (claret).

SEIDEL
Austrian wine measure equal to 0·6224 gallon, also used in Germany where it is equal to 0·11 gallon.

SEKT
German sparkling white wine.

SELZEN
Rhinehesse. Oppenheim district; white wine. Best vineyards: *Eichelstein, Hohenberg, Göttersgarten, Platte, Rosengarten, Osterberg.*

SEMEILLAN, Château
Bourgeois growth; Listrac; Médoc (claret).

SEMILLON
One of the best white-grape species of vines. It is responsible, together with the *Sauvignon*, for some of the finest white wines made in France and elsewhere.

SÉNANCOLE
A digestive liqueur of the Chartreuse type made by the Trappists of the Abbey of Senantes, in France.

SÉNÉJAC, Château
Cru bourgeois; Le Pian-Médoc.

SENHEIM-SENHALS
Moselle Valley; Zell district; white wines.

SERCIAL
One of the finest and most distinctive types of Madeira wine; it has a dry finish and great breed as well as power, when made, as it should be, from Sercial grapes, which have become very rare in Madeira since the phylloxera disaster of the late 'seventies.

SERRIG
One of the wine-producing parishes of the Saar Valley, in the Saarburg district.

White wines. Best vineyards: *Vogelsang, Heiligenborn, Hindenburgslay, Herrenberg, Marienberg* and *Wurtzberger.*

SERRIGNY
One of the lesser Communes of the Côte d'Or, the vineyards of which produce some fair red Burgundy.

SÈTE, *formerly* **CETTE**
The chief wine-mart of the Hérault Département.

SETIER
Old French wine measure equal to one-eighteenth of the *Muid.*

SETUBAL
A Portuguese Muscatel wine from Estremadura, amber in colour.

SEUREY, Les
One of the best vineyards of Beaune, Côte d'Or (red Burgundy).

SÈVE
French for 'sap'. A wine full of *sève* is a wine full of life and full of goodness.

SEXTARIUS
The old Roman 'pint' or about half a litre. The one-sixth of the *Congius.*

SEYSSEL
The name of two villages separated by the Rhône, the one in Haute-Savoie, on the left bank of the Rhône; the other in the Ain Département. Both are surrounded by vineyards, the best wine of which is known as *Roussette*, the best *Roussettes* being that which is made in the Ain. Some of the white wines of the district are sold as sparkling wines.

SHANDYGAFF
A long drink made up of a bottle of ginger beer and a pint of good ale.

SHEBEEN, SIBIN
A shop or bar, chiefly in Ireland and some parts of Scotland, where excisable liquor is sold without a licence.

SHERBERT
A refreshing semi-liquid concoction usually having some form of water-ice as its foundation, and flavoured with any variety of fruit. The finest *Sherbert* is said to be that flavoured with the Soursop (*Granabana*).

SHERRY
Sherry is a wine made from white grapes grown in the Jerez district, in the south of Spain. The grapes from which Sherry is made are pressed, when ripe, at the vintage time and their sweet juice is allowed to ferment in its own sweet way. After a time this grape juice becomes wine, but it is not yet Sherry. Sherry is made from the best wine of each vintage, to which some Brandy is added, after which it is kept for many years with the best wine of other vintages. Sherry is a blended wine—the blend of many wines of different years kept together long enough for each to lose its individuality and for all to become an harmonious whole.

Sherry is pale amber in colour and dry, but it can be made dark and sweet by adding to it a particular dark and very sweet liqueur wine made specially for the purpose.

The best pale, dry, delicate Sherries are usually those sold under the names of *Amontillado*, *Fino*, *Vino de Pasto*, and *Manzanilla*. The best dark, rich and full Sherries are usually those sold under the names of *Oloroso* and *Amoroso* and *Brown Sherry*, but there are a great number of other names of Sherry, mostly brands registered by shippers and merchants.

The standard gauge of a butt of Sherry is 108 gallons, its average yield 52 dozens.

SHIVOWITZA
A plum liqueur made in Southern Hungary from the *Shiva* plum.

SHRUB
A bottled home-made cordial kept in the store cupboards for emergencies.

SICILY
The southernmost Province of Italy and one of the more important for the extent of its vineyards and the variety of the wines which they produce. The best known wine of Sicily is that of *Marsala*, whilst the *Moscato* of Syracuse is one of the sweetest and best Muscatel wines, and the *Zucco* of Palermo is also an attractive dessert wine. Of Sicilian table wines, the best are the white *Corvo di Casteldaccia* and of *Ætna*; also rather heady *Albanello*, some of which is dry and some sweet.

SIERRE
A white-wine parish of the Valais (Switzerland), the most renowned wine of which is a *Vin de Paille* called *Soleil de Sierre*.

SIGALAS-RABAUD, Château
Bommes; first growth Sauternes.

SILBERBERG
Steiermark district (Austria); white wine.

SILLERY
One of the Communes of the Marne (Champagne), which was made famous by its wines, still and sparkling, a very long time ago. The still white wines of Sillery continued to be made and to be shipped long after sparkling Champagne had become first favourite in the world's markets.

SIMARD, Château
Second growth Saint-Emilion (Claret).

SIMARD, Clos
Second growth Saint-Emilion (Claret).

SION
Canton of Valais, Switzerland. The best white wine of Sion is the *Fendant de Sion*

and the best red is the *Dôle de Sion*, *Fendant* and *Dôle* being the names respectively of the white and red species of grapes chiefly cultivated.

SIRÈNE LAGRANGE
The name under which is sold some of the white wine of Château Lagrange, Saint-Julien; Médoc.

SISTOWH
One of the wines of Bulgaria.

SITGES
A small port of Catalonia (Spain), the vineyards of which produce the best sweet Muscatel wine of Spain.

SLINGS
The name of a number of cold mixed beverages, more particularly popular in the tropics.

Singapore Sling. 1 ounce lime juice; 1 ounce cherry brandy; 2 ounces dry gin. Shake well and ice. Top with seltzer and decorate with slice of orange and fresh mint. Then add through middle with a medicine dropper: 4 drops of Bénédictine and 4 drops of Brandy.—H. J. G.

SLIVOVITZ
The name of the spirit which is distilled from plums, in Hungary, Yugoslavia and Roumania; it is very similar to the Alsatian *Plum Brandy* called *Quetsch*.

SLOE GIN
A Cordial the basis of which is *Gin* and the informing flavour that of *Sloes*, the berries of the Black Thorn.

4 quarts sloes; 1 gallon gin; 2½ lb. sugar candy; ¼ oz. bitter almonds. Put into a 2-gallon jar, shake twice a week for three months, then strain.

Sloe Gin, like Van der Hum and many other liqueurs, is cloyingly sweet and sticky to the palate if drunk too soon after being made. It becomes deliciously clean and mellow if kept for about nine or ten years after bottling.

Sloe Gin Fizz. To one glass of Sloe Gin, and half a glass of lemon juice and a teaspoonful of powdered sugar; shake well and pour over cracked ice in a tumbler; then add as much soda water or seltzer as may be desired.

Sloe Gin Rickey. Put in a tumbler 2 cubes of ice, the juice and rind of half a fresh lime and a glassful of *Sloe Gin*. Fill the glass (more or less according to taste) with soda water or seltzer, stir and sip through straws.

SMASHES
Mixed iced drinks always with a spirit foundation and some mint flavouring:

Brandy Smash. Crush half lump of Sugar with 3 sprigs of mint, 1 jigger brandy, 1 lump ice; stir in old-fashioned glass and serve.

Gin Smash. Same as *Brandy Smash*, using Gin instead of Brandy.

Whisky Smash. Muddle one lump of sugar with a half jigger of water and a few sprigs of mint in glass. Add two cubes of ice. Pour in 1 jigger of whisky. Decorate with 4 or 5 sprigs of mint. Serve with small barspoons, and a glass of charged water on the side.

SMITH-HAUT-LAFITTE, Château
One of the important Châteaux of the Graves district, near Bordeaux (Commune of Martillac).

SOAVE
One of the best of Italian table wines (white). It is made from grapes grown in Venetia; it is dry but not harsh and has a pleasing and delicate bouquet.

SOLEIL DE SIERRE
A noted *Vin de Paille* from Sierre, in the Valais (Switzerland).

SOLERA
Solera is not a type of Sherry: it is really equivalent to 'Blend' or 'Vatting'. A

Sherry described as 'Solera 1860', for instance, is, or should be, a wine from a vat first laid down in 1860; it is a blend of wines of which the oldest dates back to 1860.

SOLITUDE, La
Martillac; Graves (Claret).

SOLUTRÉ
One of the best of the cheaper descriptions of white Burgundies, from the Saône-et-Loire Département. The parish of Solutré adjoins Pouilly and Fuissé and its wines are usually sold as *Pouilly-Fuissé.*

SOMA
The Italian equivalent of the French Hectolitre, or 22 gallons.

SOMERSET WEST (South Africa)
A wine-producing district of Cape Province.

SOMLOI FURMINT
One of the best white wines of Somlyó (Hungary).

SOMLAUER AUSLESE
The usual description of the white Somlyó wine (Hungary).

SOMLYÓ
The best white wine district of Hungary.

SOMMERACHER (Franconia)
Steinwein. Best vineyards: *Katzenkopf, Wilm, Berg, Tieftal, Rotenbühl.*

SONDRIO
A Lombardy village, near the Swiss frontier, the vineyards of which produce some good red wine (Valtellina).

SONOMA
One of the wine-producing counties of the State of California (U.S.A.).

SONTHEIM (Württemberg)
Neckar Valley; white and red wines, mostly white.

SOPRON
A village of Hungary, the vineyards of which produce a good dessert wine known as *Valtellin.*

SOURS
Alcoholic long drinks for thirsty days; they are really *Sweet-sour.*

Apple Jack Sour. Put into a large tumbler, with half a tablespoonful of icing sugar, the juice of half a lemon, and dissolve the same with a squirt of seltzer water from a syphon; add one wine-glass of old cider brandy. Nearly fill the glass with shaved ice, stir well, strain, ornament with a little fruit, and serve.

Brandy Sour. Juice of half a lemon; 1 barspoon sugar; 1 jigger Cognac; shake, strain, dress with fruit and serve.

Brunswick Sour. Juice of 1 small lemon; 1 barspoon sugar; 1 jigger Rye whisky; shake, strain and float Claret on top. Decorate with a slice of orange, a slice of pineapple and 1 cherry.

Champagne Sour. Juice of half a fresh lemon; 1 lump of sugar, dissolved; fill with Champagne, stir well and dress with fruit.

Egg Sour. Juice of half a lemon; 1 barspoon sugar; yolk of 1 egg; 1 dash Anisette; 1 jigger Brandy; shake well and serve.

Gin Sour. Juice of 1 small lemon; 1 barspoon sugar; 1 jigger Dry Gin, Old Tom Gin or Sloe Gin; shake, strain and dress with fruit.

Hancock Sour. 1 jigger Bourbon Whisky; 4 dashes rock candy syrup; 2 dashes rum; juice of lime. Stir, strain, splash with seltzer, and dress with fruit slices.

Jersey Sour (or *Teddy Roosevelt Sour*). 1 jigger Applejack; 1 teaspoon sugar;

juice of half a lemon; 1 slice lemon. Shake, strain, and garnish with lemon juice.

Whisky Sour. Half a glass of lemon or lime juice; 1 glass of Rye or Bourbon Whisky; 1 teaspoonful of sifted sugar; well shaken with some cracked ice; then strained and poured in glass decorated with a maraschino cherry and a slice of orange.

SOUSSANS

One of the lesser wine-producing Communes of the Médoc. The wines of Soussans have acquired by long usage the right to be sold under the name of the neighbouring and better-known Commune of Margaux.

SOUTARD, Château

First growth of Saint-Emilion (Claret).

SOUTARD-CADET, Cru

First growth Saint-Emilion (Claret).

SOUTH AFRICA

Vines grow, and wine is made, in the Transvaal and elsewhere, within the borders of the Union of South Africa, on a very limited scale, It is only in the Cape Province that viticulture attains to real importance and wine is made on a sufficiently large scale to supply a growing export demand. The oldest and most famous South African vineyards are those nearest to Cape Town, at and near Wynberg, which produced the renowned wines of Constantia so much in demand during the early half of the nineteenth century. Wine is still made on an important scale at Wynberg, at 'Groot' Constantia itself, which is a South African Government property.

The finest stretch of vineyards is further inland, from French Hoek to Wellington, along the Paarl Valley, and in the Stellenbosch district close by. Further inland still, at Worcester, Robertson, Montagu, Ladysmith and Oudtshoorn, larger quantities of wine are obtained from grapes grown on richer soil, but wine of inferior quality.

South Africa can, and does, produce a very large quantity of different wines, some very fair, dry beverage wines, both red and white, and some palatable sweet fortified wines, as well as some sparkling wine.

SOUTH AMERICA

The two most important wine-producing Republics of South America are Argentina, for quantity, and Chile, for quality. There are vineyards and there is wine made also in Brazil, Uruguay, Peru and Bolivia, but not nearly on the same important scale.

SPAIN

The largest European wine-producing country after France and Italy, with an average production of about 500 million gallons of red and white wines per annum. The principal provinces of Spain, in order of vinous importance are:

1. La Mancha	9. Andalucia East
2. Catalonia	(Malaga)
3. Valencia	10. Andalucia West
4. Old Castile	(Jerez)
5. Galicia	11. Estremadura
6. Aragon (Rioja)	12. Basque Provinces
7. Castile	13. Balearic Islands
8. Leon	14. Canary Islands

SPALATO

A Dalmation wine, known as *Split* previous to the post-war Treaty of St. Germain.

SPARKLING WINES

That is effervescent wines. All sparkling wines owe their effervescence to the presence of carbonic acid gas, which, in the act of escaping out of the wine, once the cork has been removed, carry with them fine bubbles of wine beaten up to a 'foam' by the out-rushing carbon dioxide. There are two main categories of sparkling wines: first, those with their own carbonic acid gas in solution, owing to the fermentation of the wine having been completed after bottling; secondly, those with carbonic acid gas pumped into the bottle. The finest sparkling wine in the world is Champagne, when good. But sparkling wines that are most acceptable are also made in many other parts of France and of all wine-producing countries.

SPÄTLESE
German for 'late vintaged', that is, a wine made from the last grapes and the ripest to be picked in a good year.

SPIRITS (Potable)
Alcoholic liquids obtained by distillation from some wholesome materials such as wine in the case of Brandy, molasses in the case of Rum, grain in the case of Gin and Whisky, rice in the case of Arrack and Saké, etc. In all spirits the nature, but not the proportion, of ethyl alcohol is the same. The great differences between them are due to the by-products or impurities, which vary according to the nature of the 'mash' or fermented liquid from which they were distilled. Some of those impurities can be, and often are, poisonous, but present in quantities that are too small to be injurious. Thus spirits distilled from potatoes (Vodka) and cider (Applejack) can be quite injurious if consumed in more than very small doses. But spirits distilled from sawdust and all kinds of other materials are usually *rectified* in such a way that they consist in the end of merely ethyl alcohol and water.

SPRENDLINGEN
One of the wine-producing Communes of Rhinehesse, in the Alzey district. White wines. Best vineyards: *Geyersberg, Wiesberg* and *Horn.*

SPRITZIG
German for 'lively wine', denoting the presence in a still white wine of just a little carbonic acid gas, the result of a very limited secondary fermentation of the wine in the bottle, which gives a pleasant impression of liveliness on the palate.

SPRUCE BEER or BLACK BEER
A brew which is concocted without any barley but with black spruce branches, cones and bark, which are boiled for several hours then put into a cask with molasses, hops and yeast. It is left to ferment and is considered fit to drink in twenty-four hours by the fishermen of Newfoundland, Labrador and the Gulf of St. Lawrence.

SPUMANTE
Italian for 'sparkling' or effervescent.

STANISLAUS COUNTY
One of the wine-producing counties of the State of California.

STARS
One, two and three stars have been used upon Cognac labels for a great many years to denote the age of the Brandy in the bottle. One star denotes that the Brandy is not less than three years old, two stars four years old, and three stars five years old.

STEINBERG (Rhinegau)
The finest growth of Hattenheim. The vineyard consists of about sixty acres and belongs to the Prussian State. The grapes are pressed and the wine is kept at Kloster Eberbach. The Steinberg wines are always sold by public auction in an ascending scale of excellence, from the plain *Steinberger* to the *Auslese, Spätlese, Feine Auslese, Hochfeine Auslese, Beeren Auslese* and *Trockenbeeren Auslese. Steinberg Cabinet* used to be the finest of all the Steinberg wines made in any one year; it was placed—or fit to be placed— in the 'Kabinet', or Special Reserve, of the then owners of Steinberg, the Dukes of Nassau.

STEINBRUCHER
White wine from Villingen, in Aargau (Switzerland).

STEIN WEIN
The white wine of Würzburg, usually sold in Bocksbeutels. Genuine Stein wine, or Steinwein, is the produce of the Steinmantel vineyards, north of Würzburg, about 350 acres in all.

STELLENBOSCH
One of the most important wine-producing districts of the Cape Province. Noted for its red and white wine and its Brandy.

STILLS
The apparatus used to distil spirits, i.e. to separate the alcohol contained in any alcoholic liquid from the water contained therein. There are two main classes of Stills: Pot Stills and Patent Stills. From the Pot Stills, the alcohol in the mash is vaporized by the application of heat and collected by condensation. There are direct or single-action Stills. Patent Stills are continuous Stills, gradually freeing the alcohol in the mash from all else and ending in pure spirit or plain alcohol, pure or plain because without any by-products, hence also without taste or distinctive merit.

STIRRUP CUP
The last or parting drink.

STOCKHEIM (Württemberg)
Zabergäu; the best wine is that of *Schloss Stocksberg.*

STOF, STOFF and STOOF
Russian and Latvian liquid measure: one-tenth of the *Vedro,* or a little more than the Imperial Quart (British).

STOOP
Dutch drinking term; approximately two quarts (British).

STOUP
An antiquated English name for a large draught.

STOUT
Stout is the darkest ale or beer brewed: it is also sweeter, both the colour and sweetness being due to the amount of kilning and degree of roasting of the malt used. The quality of the water also has a great deal to do with the quality of Stout, as it has with the quality of all ales and beers.

STRAW WINES
French *Vins de paille.* Sweet wines made from very ripe grapes which, after being picked, are left in the sun, laid on straw mats to become almost like raisins before they are pressed.

STREGA
One of the more popular liqueurs made in Italy.

STROMBOLI
One of the small islands off the coast of Sicily which produces some of the sweet *Malvazia di Lipari* (Italy).

STÜBCHEN
German wine measure equal to 6·374 pints at Altona, 6·846 pints in Hanover and 7·614 pints at Worms.

STÜCK
The standard Rhine tun of 1200 litres is practically never seen; the *Halbstüke,* of 600 litres, is rare, and the *Viertelstücke,* of 300 litres, is the more commonly used.

STUTTGART (Württemberg's capital)
Red and white wines, mostly white.

STUTZEN or STOTZ
Baden wine measure equal to 3·3 gallons.

SUAU, Château
Barsac; second growth Sauternes.

SUDUIRAUT, Château
Preignac; first growth Sauternes.

SUKINDOL
One of the wines of Bulgaria.

SULPHUR
The trusted friend of vine-growers and wine-merchants. It is used in powder form and sprayed over the vines in order to 'gas' a number of the vine's enemies; in the form of fumes, by burning sulphur matches in casks and vats, to dry up moulds; in the liquid form of various acids, to check fermentation or to 'bleach' white wines which are considered too dark in colour. Sulphur is acceptable so long as it does not make its presence felt. Many sulphured white wines, unfortunately, are left with no bouquet of their own; one finds nothing but the smell of sulphur.

SUTTER COUNTY
One of the wine-producing counties of the State of California (U.S.A.).

SWEDISH PUNSCH
A cordial with Arrack as its basis; it is highly spiced and may be drunk neat as a liqueur or with hot water, by way of a chest-protector in cold weather.

SWEETS
According to English law, the name of 'any liquor made from fruit and sugar, mixed with any other material, and which has undergone fermentation in the manufacture'.

SWEET WINES
These are mostly dessert wines; their sweetness is due to the original grape-sugar of the *must* which was prevented from fermenting by added spirit, but much less than is customary or necessary for 'fortified' wines. Some 'sweet wines' are made from such sweet grapes that some of the grape-sugar in the *must* is unable to ferment, even if there is no spirit added. The best sweet wines are made from Muscat grapes in the South of France, Italy, Spain, Portugal and some of the Greek islands.

SWITZERLAND
The Swiss Cantons in which vineyards are cultivated on a large scale and where important quantities of wines are made, both red and white but mostly white, are the Cantons of Bern, Geneva, Neuchâtel, Schaffhausen, Thurgau, Ticino, Valais and Vaud.

SWIZZLES
Cocktails which instead of being shaken in a 'shaker' are mixed with a swizzle-stick, acting as a whisk. The ice is omitted from the swizzle, but the other ingredients may be the same as for any cocktail.

SYLLABUB
Season rich milk with sugar and wine, but not enough to curdle it. Fill the glasses nearly full and crown them with whipped cream, seasoned.

SYLVANER
A free-bearing white-wine grape grown extensively in Germany and in Alsace. Much Alsatian wine (white) made from Sylvaner grapes is marketed under the name of *Sylvaner*.

SYNTHETIC WINE
Synthetic wine is artificial wine. A 'wine' made up of water, spirit, glucose, glycerine and colouring matter is a synthetic wine, artificially made from materials some of which are artificial insomuch as they are never present in any real wine.

A 'wine' made from concentrated *must* to which water and yeast are added in order to provoke fermentation, as is the case with the majority of 'British wines', is artificially made but not from any artificial materials. It may, on analysis, be found to contain no substance that might not be found in real wine. It may

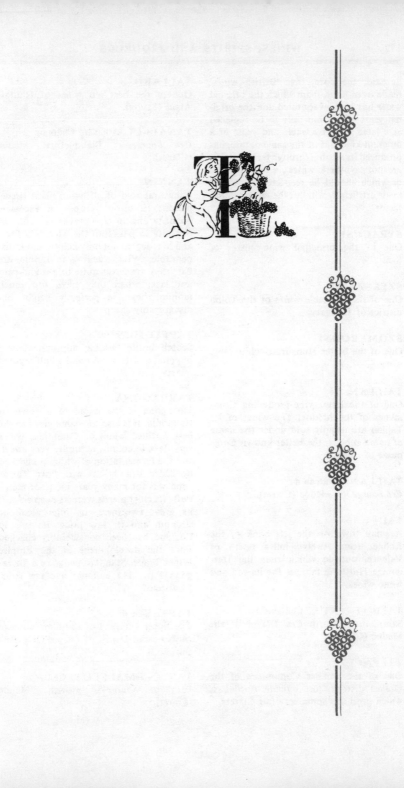

be said, therefore, that 'British wines' made from *must*, from which the original water has been evaporated and the original yeast killed, but only to be replaced at a later stage by water and yeast of a different kind but of the same nature, has produced its alcohol through fermentation are not 'synthetic wines', a term the use of which should be restricted to 'wines' made artificially without the fermentation factor.

SYRACUSE
One of the principal wine-centres of Sicily.

SZEKSZÁRD
One of the red table wines of the Tolna district of Hungary.

SZOMERODNI
One of the better Hungarian white table wines.

TAILLAN, Le
One of the lesser vine-producing Communes of the Médoc. The wines of Le Taillan are usually sold under the name of its neighbour, the better-known Commune of Ludon.

TAILLAN, Château du
Cru bourgeois; Médoc (Claret).

TAIN
A small town on the left bank of the Rhône, some twelve miles north of Valence, outside which rises the Hermitage Hill long famous for its red and white wines.

TALBOT-D'AUX, Château
Saint-Julien; fourth *Cru Classé* of the Médoc (Claret).

TALENCE
One of the smaller Communes of the Graves district, just outside Bordeaux, which produces some very fair Clarets.

TALLARD
One of the best red wines of Hautes-Alpes (Savoy).

TANAIS-CLAPEAU, Château
Cru bourgeois; Blanquefort; Médoc (Claret).

TANNIN
A natural acid of all living plant tissue, present in unripe grapes in excessive quantity and in ripe grapes in sufficient quantity to pass into the wine in a form and to a degree not only helpful but indispensable. Wines lacking in tannin are flat; they are never quite bright and cannot last; when they have too much tannin, they are perfectly bright but disagreeably sharp.

TAPPIT-HEN
Scotch bottle holding approximately 3 imperial quarts or four and a half reputed quarts.

TARRAGONA
Tarragona is the name of a town of Catalonia. It is also the name given to the best fortified wines of Catalonia, wines very dark in colour, naturally very sweet, and the fermentation of which is checked by added Brandy—as with Port. Tarragona was for many years the poor man's Port. Its chief merits were its deep colour, its great sweetness, its high alcoholic strength and its low price. Its sale in England has been considerably checked since the development of the Empire Wines Trade. Standard gauge of a Tarragona Pipe, 115 gallons; average yield, 56 dozens.

TART, Clos de
The finest vineyard of the Commune of Morey-Saint-Denis, Côte d'Or (Red Burgundy).

TASTINS-MALECOT, Château
Pauillac; *bourgeois* growth; Médoc (Claret).

TATACHILLA
One of the best vineyards of the Maclaren Vale (South Australia).

TAUPINE, La
One of the best vineyards of Monthélie, Côte d'Or (Red Burgundy).

TAUZIA, Château de
Gradignan; Graves (Claret).

TAVEL
Gard Département. A village on the right bank of the Rhône, the vineyards of which, together with those of the adjoining Commune of Lirac, produce the best *Vin Rosé* of France.

TAWNY
The peculiar brownish-red colour of Ports matured in wood. Also the name of Port matured in wood until it has acquired a tawny complexion.

TEMPERATURE
All white wines are better served cool or cold, that is to say, at the temperature of the ideal white wines cellar, i.e. 48°F., and all red wines at the temperature of the ideal red wines cellar, i.e. 55°F. There is no great harm in cooling white wines rather quickly in a frigidaire or ice bucket if they come from too warm a cellar, but there is a very grave danger of ruining red wines past all hope of redress by bringing them up to a higher temperature than that of the cold cellar out of which they come. To put a red wine in front of the fire, or to plunge it into hot water, to 'take the chill off', is a sin that cannot be forgiven because there is no atonement for it. If your red wine comes from too cold a cellar, leave it in the dining-room long enough, and it will soon acquire the temperature of the room, which is all that is desirable. If you cannot leave it long enough in the room, warm the wine-filled glass in the hollow of your hands and you will soon have the wine at the right temperature.

TENERIFFE
The most important of the seven Cape Verde Islands; its vineyards now produce only a small quantity of wines, mostly white.

TENT or ROTA TENT or TINTILLA DE ROTA
The name of the darkest of all Spanish red wines. Mostly used for blending with lighter red wines.

TEQUILA
A fiery spirit which is distilled from *Pulque*, an intoxicating beverage fermented, chiefly in Mexico, from the sap of the Maguey and other kinds of aloes.

TERLANER, TERLANO
The German and Italian names of the same wine, a white wine of the Tyrol.

TERMO
The name of a plain, white Portuguese table wine made from the vineyards of the Lisbon region.

TERRANO
The name of an Italian black grape and the name of the best red wine of Istria (*Italy*).

TERTRE, Château du
Arsac; fifth *Cru Classé* of the Médoc (Claret).

TERTRE-DAUGAY, Château
First growth Saint-Emilion (Claret).

TERTRE-DE-DAUGAY
First growth Saint-Emilion (Claret).

TEURONS or THEURONS, Les
One of the best vineyards of Beaune, Côte d'Or (Red Burgundy).

THANAN
Siamese for Litre, or 0·22 gallon.

THORINS
One of the best red wines of the Beaujolais. The name of Thorins may be given to all the wines made from the vineyards of Romanêche-Thorins and some of those in the Commune of Chénas. But only the wine made from 46 named vineyards in the Commune of Romanêche-Thorins may be sold as *Thorins Grand Cru*.

THOUARCÉ
Anjou; Coteaux du Layon. White wines.

THURGAU
One of the minor wine-producing Cantons of Switzerland. Its best wine is the red wine from vineyards between Worth and Ittingen; it is sold as *Karthauser*.

TICINO
One of the more important wine-producing Cantons of Switzerland. Both red and white wines of moderate quality.

TIÉLANDRY
One of the best vineyards of Beaune, Côte d'Or (Red Burgundy).

TIERCE
An English wine measure: the third of a pipe or butt.

TIERÇON
French measure corresponding to the English Tierce.

TIERZE
German measure corresponding to the English Tierce.

TISCHWEINE
The German equivalent of Piquette, or poor, acid wines made in sunless years.

TO
A Japanese liquid measure equivalent to 3·97 gallons (British) or one-tenth of the Kôku.

TODDY
The name of two distinct types of drinks. In tropical and sub-tropical countries Toddy is the name of the sap of various palms, and also of the beverages which are fermented from such sap. The name is also sometimes given to some iced long drinks of fairly high alcoholic strength. In northern latitudes, a Toddy is a hot drink usually made with sugar, spirits ànd hot water, with a squeeze or a slice of lemon. Here are two examples of Hot Toddies, one simple and one not so simple. Also a hot weather American iced Toddy.

Hot Apple Toddy. This is used and useful on a cold winter's night and is made as follows: Bake in an earthenware dish 13 Newton Pippin apples. Do not core, but remove eyes and stems. Put baked apples in a 2½- or 3-gallon jug and add 2 quarts of Jamaica Rum, 1 quart of Brandy, 12 to 15 lumps of sugar and 2 quarts of boiling water. Cover jug with plate and place near an open fire to steam for at least two hours before serving. Stir gently with a wooden spoon occasionally while brewing.

Pendennis Toddy. Crush ½ lump of sugar with a little water in an old-fashioned glass; 1 jigger Bourbon Whisky; 1 lump of ice.

Rum Toddy. 1 lump of sugar; 1 jigger of Jamaica Rum. Fill glass with boiling water. Insert 1 small piece of cinnamon, 1 slice of lemon garnished with 4 cloves and 1 thin slice of lemon rind twisted over glass and inserted. Stir mixture a little and serve with a spoon. Also serve a small pitcher of hot water on the side.

TOKAY
The wines of Tokay take their name from the small village of Tokaji, in the Hegyalja district of north-eastern Hungary, at the foot of the Carpathians. The best Tokay wine is known as *Tokaji Essencia*, the next best as *Tokaji Aszu*, which is not quite so rich but very sweet and of greatly concentrated flavour. Both will keep

longer than any other wine but they both deserve Professor Saintsbury's verdict: 'No more a wine but a prince of liqueurs'. The next grade is called *Tokaji Szamorodner* and is more of a table wine, being fairly dry, unless made in a great vintage when it is also quite rich: it is then labelled *Tokaji édes szamorodner*. Wines sold under labels such as *Tokay Forditás* or *Tokay Maslas* are commercial wines not in the same class as the others. They are made from the lees of the pressings of the real Tokay wines. These are always made from the Furmint grape and from over-ripe grapes, called *trockenbeeren*. They are gathered in wooden vessels known as *puttony*, holding about 25 quarts, and it is the number of these *puttony* full of over-ripe Furmint grapes per cask which determines the quality of the wine. When the label on the bottle records '1 puttony', it means that about 10 per cent of the grapes used were *trockenbeeren* when that particular cask of wine was made; if '3 puttony', the proportion was 30 per cent, and if '5 puttony', as much as 50 per cent, which is the richest and finest *Tokay Aszu* made, except in the exceptional years, such as 1920, when a '6 puttony' wine was made. When the *Tokay Aszu* is offered under the German name of *Tokay Ausbruch*, the German for *puttony* is *büttig*.

TOM COLLINS

A wonderful thirst quencher in hot weather. It is made of a glass of dry Gin, half a glass of lime juice or lemon juice, and a teaspoonful of powdered sugar, well shaken with some cracked ice and then strained in a long glass, a cube or two of ice then added, and the glass filled with soda or selzer water. There are also a number of bastard Tom Collins known as:

Bourbon Collins, made with Bourbon Whisky;

Brandy Collins, made with Brandy;

Irish Collins, made with Irish Whiskey;

John Collins, made with Hollands Gin;

Rum Collins, made with Rum;

Rye Collins, made with Rye Whisky;

Scotch Collins, made with Scotch Whisky.

TONDE

A Danish measure equal to 28·9 gallons (Britain).

TONELADA

The Portuguese equivalent of Tun.

TONNE or TONNEAU

The French equivalent of Tun, or four hogsheads, approximately 200 gallons.

TONNERRE

The metropolis of the Wine Trade of the Yonne Département, Lower Burgundy.

TOOP

Esthonian wine measure equal to 1·08 quart (Britain).

TORO

The best red wine of Zamora (Spain).

TORREDOS

One of the red wines of Greece.

TORRE GIULIA

One of the best table white wines of Italy; it is made from the vineyards of Foggia, in Apulia; it is quite a dry wine, it has a good *bouquet* and is full-bodied.

TORRES VEDRAS

Plain beverage Portuguese wines from the parishes of Lourinha and Mafra, near Lisbon.

TOURAINE

One of the fairest of the old Provinces of France, chiefly noted for its Châteaux and its wines. The best white wines of Touraine are those of *Vouvray*, and its best red wines those of *Joué* and *Bourgueil*.

TOURNON
An ancient little city on the right bank of the Rhône, immediately facing Tain-l'Hermitage; its vineyards produce both red and white table wines, the red wines being the better as well as the more plentiful of the two.

TOURNUS
One of the most important wine-producing centres of the Saône-et-Loire Département (Red Burgundy).

TRABEN-TRARBACH
Twin villages on opposite banks of the Moselle; Zell district. Good white wines. Best vineyards of Traben (left bank of the Moselle): *Königsberg, Würzgarten* and *Kräuterhaus.* Best vineyards of Trarbach (right bank of the Moselle): *Schlossberg, Hühneberg* and *Burgberg.*

TRAMINER
A species of white grape extensively grown in Alsace and Germany for the making of high-class wines.

TRANI
One of the red wines of Apulia (Italy).

TRARBACHER
The wine of Trarbach (Moselle).

TREIS
Lower Moselle; Cochem district. White wines. Best vineyards: *Castel, Greth, Steilchen, Kapellenberg.*

TREUX, Les
One of the best vineyards of Flagey-Echézeaux, Côte d'Or (Red Burgundy).

TREYTORRENS
One of the white wines of Dézaley (Switzerland).

TRIER or TRÈVES
Moselle Valley. The most interesting city, from a wine-lover's point of view, and one of the oldest in Germany. Unique Wine Museum. White wines of moderate quality. Best vineyards: *Neuberg, Herrenberg, Klosterberg, Augenscheiner.*

TRITTENHEIM
A wine-producing parish of the Middle Moselle, in the Trier district. The best vineyards of Trittenheim are *Laurentiusberg, Falkenberg, Olk* and *Apotheke.*

TROCKENBEEREN AUSLESE
The German name of a wine made from a special selection of over-ripe grapes, from which the richest, sweetest and finest German white wines are made.

TROIS-MOULINS, Château
First growth Saint-Emilion (Claret).

TROMPETTE, Château
Palus de Parempuyre; Médoc (Claret).

TROPLONG-MONDOT, Château
First growth Saint-Emilion (Claret).

TROTANOY, Château
First growth Pomerol (Claret).

TROTTEVIEILLE, Château
First growth Saint-Emilion (Claret).

TULARE COUNTY
A Californian County, south of Fresno County; they are both very important producers of fortified wine.

TUN
An English wine measure for a large cask containing 210 Imperial gallons or 252 U.S. gallons or 954 litres.

TUNISIA
That part of Northern Africa immediately east of Algeria; its vineyards produce mostly red wines.

TUQUET, Château du
The only important Estate of the Commune of Beautiran, in the Graves de Bordeaux district. It produces on an

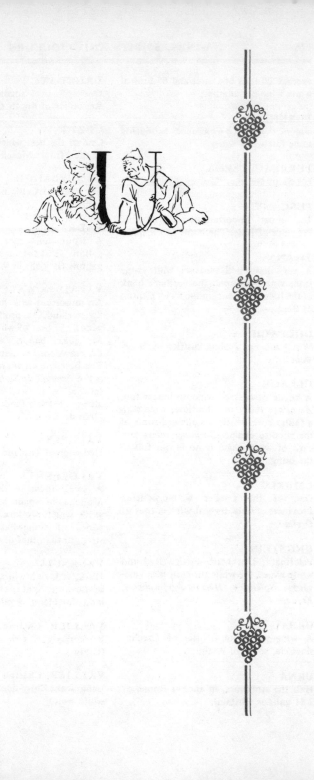

average 20 tuns of Claret and 65 tuns of white wine per annum.

TURKHEIM
One of the Alsace Communes producing some fair white wines.

TURPEAU, Château
Isle-Saint-Georges; Graves (Claret).

TUSCANY
The most important wine-producing Province of Italy. The home of *Chianti*.

TWANN
A very light and pleasant white wine from vineyards upon the northern bank of the lake of Bienne, in the Swiss Canton of Bern.

UHLBACH
Württemberg; Essling district. *Schiller-wein* only.

ULLAGE
A bottle or cask of wine no longer full. *An ullage* refers to a bottle of wine with a faulty cork which has allowed some of the wine to escape. *On ullage* refers to a cask of wine which is no longer full to the bung.

UMBRIA
One of the smaller wine-producing Provinces of Italy. Its best wine is that of *Orvieto*.

UNGSTEIN
Palatinate; Dürkheim district. Red and white wines, the white the best. Best vineyards: *Spielberg, Herrenberg, Kobnert, Kreuz*.

URBAU
A wine-producing district of Czechoslovakia, south of Znaim.

URNA
Half the Amphora, in ancient Rome, or 2·81 gallons (Britain).

URUGUAY
One of the smaller wine-producing Republics of South America.

ÜRZIG
One of the best wine-producing parishes of the Middle Moselle (Wittlich district).

USQUEBAUGH
The original Celtic name of the modern Whisky.

VADRA
A Roumanian measure equal to 3·34 gallons (British) in Moldavia, and 2·83 gallons (British) in Wallachia.

VALAIS or WALLIS
An important wine-producing Canton of Switzerland. It produces mostly white wines, the best of which are the wines of *Molignox, Baliot, Les Murets de Sion, Clos de Montibeux*, and *Château Conthey*. The best-known white wine of the Valais is the *Fendant de Sion*. Also the *Gletscher* (glacier) wine from Sion. A red wine is also made from Pinot noir which is called Dôle de Sion.

VALDELSA
Red wine of Tuscany of the Chianti type.

VALDEPEÑAS
A small town in the Province of La Mancha, in Spain, surrounded by vineyards which produce both red and white wines of somewhat higher alcoholic strength than that of most table wines.

VALENCIA
Dark, red, rich wines from the Province of Levante, Spain; chiefly used, in England, for blending purposes.

VALLIER, Château Le
Parempuyre; *Cru artisan;* Médoc (Claret).

VALLIER, Château du
Langoiran; Entre-deux-Mers (Claret and white wine).

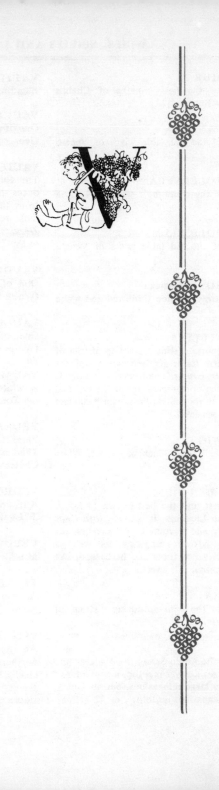

VALMUR
One of the best growths of Chablis (White Burgundy).

VALPANTENA
One of the red table wines of Veneto (Italy).

VALPOLCEVERA
One of the white table wines of Liguria (Italy).

VALPOLICELLA
One of the red table wines of Veneto (Italy).

VALROSE, Château
Île Patiras; Médoc (both red and white wine).

VALTELLINA
An important wine-producing district of northern Italy; its best wines are the *Sassella, Grumello* and *Inferno*. It extends from the northern shores of the Lake of Como to the Stelvio Pass, over 9,000 feet above sea-level.

VALWIG
Moselle Valley; Cochem district. White wines.

VAN DER HUM
The best and the best known of South African Liqueurs. It is made with Cape Brandy and flavoured with *naartjes*, the South African tangerine, as well as various other fruits and herbs and, like all liqueurs, it is sweet.

VARNA
One of the wine-producing districts of Bulgaria.

VAT
From the Anglo-Saxon *faet*—a large tub. In English, a vat is a tub, a container of usually large dimensions, but, in Dutch, vat means one hectolitre, or 22 gallons.

VATTING
Blending.

VAUCRAINS, Les
One of the best vineyards of Nuits-Saint-Georges, Côte d'Or (Red Burgundy).

VAUD, Canton of, or WAADT
The Canton of Switzerland which produces the best Swiss white wines, mostly from the *Fendant Vert* grape. The two most renowned wines of Vaud are the *Dézaley, Yvorne, Epesses* and other wines of the Lavaux ridge.

VAUDÉSIR
One of the best vineyards of Chablis (White Burgundy).

VAULORENT
One of the first growths of Chablis (White Burgundy).

VAUMORILLONS
A white wine resembling Chablis from the Tonnerre (Yonne) district.

VÉDRINES, Château
Barsac; second growth of Sauternes. This estate was originally part of the Château Doisy.

VEDRO
Russian and Latvian measure equal to 2·71 gallons.

VELDENZ
Moselle. Bernkastel district. White wines.

VELTE
An old French measure equal to 1·64 gallon (British), still used in Mauritius.

VENETIA
An important wine-producing district of northern Italy (Lombardy), producing chiefly red wine of common quality, with the exception of the wines grown on the slopes of the Colli Berici and Euganei.

VENETO
One of the important wine-producing Provinces of northern Italy.

VENEZIA TRIDENTINA
The northernmost Province of Italy, formerly Austrian South Tyrol. It produces some good dry white wines.

VENTURA COUNTY
One of the wine-producing counties of the State of California, U.S.A.

VERDELHO
One of the white fortified wines of Madeira, which used to be made from the Verdelho grape, now all but extinct.

VERDIGNAN, Château
Saint - Seurin - de - Cadourne; *bourgeois* growth; Médoc (Claret).

VERDISO
Italian white table wine of Conegliano (Veneto).

VERGELESSES
Some of the best vineyards of Pernand-Vergelesses and Savigny, Côte d'Or (Red Burgundy).

VERGENNES, Les
One of the best vineyards of Serrigny, Côte d'Or (Red Burgundy).

VERJUICE
The acid juice of green, unripe grapes. Latin: *Omphacium*. Italian: *Agresto*. Spanish: *Agrazo*. Portuguese: *Agraço*. French: *Verjus*.

VERMENTINO
White table wine of Liguria (Italy).

VERMOUTH
A white wine, almost a medicinal wine, possessing certain tonic properties owing to the aromatical Alpine herbs and various ingredients, which are cooked in the wine before it becomes Vermouth. The Italian Vermouth is usually darker in colour and sweeter than the French.

VERNACCIA
A red wine from grapes of that name made in different parts of Italy from Sardinian vineyards.

VERSEUIL, En
One of the best vineyards of Volnay, Côte d'Or (Red Burgundy).

VERTHEUIL
One of the lesser wine-producing Communes of the Médoc, the wines of which have acquired by long usage the right to be sold under the name of the adjoining and better-known Commune of *Saint-Estèphe*.

VERTUS
One of the wine-producing Communes of the Marne Valley (Champagne).

VERZENAY
One of the most important wine-producing Communes of the Montagne de Reims (Champagne).

VERZY
One of the more important Communes of the Montagne de Reims (Champagne).

VESUVIO
One of the white wines of Sicily.

VEYRIN, Château
Listrac; *bourgeois* growth; Médoc (Claret).

VEYRIN-DOMECQ, Château
Listrac; *bourgeois* growth; Médoc (Claret).

VIDONIA
A dessert wine which used to come chiefly from Teneriffe in pre-phylloxera days and enjoyed a very fair measure of popularity in England.

VIEILLE CURE
A popular French liqueur, distilled at Bordeaux; its basis is Brandy and it is highly aromatic, somewhat on the same lines as *Bénédictine*, although not so sweet.

VIERTEL
A German and Danish wine measure equal to 1·713 gallon. Also a Swiss wine measure equal to 3·30 gallons.

VIEUX CHÂTEAU CERTAN
First growth Pomerol (Claret).

VIEUX MOULIN-DU-CADET
First growth Saint-Emilion (Claret).

VIGNE-AU-SAINT, La
One of the best vineyards of Aloxe-Corton, Côte d'Or (Red Burgundy).

VIGNE BLANCHE, La
The only white vineyard of Vougeot, Côte d'Or (White Burgundy).

VIGNE DU DIABLE
Red wine of Cortaillod (Switzerland).

VIGNES FRANCHES, Les
One of the best vineyards of Beaune, Côte d'Or (Red Burgundy).

VILA NOVA DE GAYA
Oporto's twin city, on the left bank of the Douro, where most Port Shippers have their wine stores.

VILLAFRANCA DEL PANADES
One of the most important wine-producing districts of Northern Spain (Barcelona Province).

VILLANY-PÉCS
One of the most important wine-producing districts of Hungary. The best white wine is known as *Villanyer Riesling* and the best red as *Villanyer Auslese*.

VILLEDOMMANGE
One of the wine-producing Communes of the Montagne de Reims (Champagne).

VILLEMAURINE, Château
First growth Saint-Emilion (Claret).

VILLENAVE-D'ORNON
One of the more important wine-producing Communes of the Graves (Gironde).

VILLERS-MARMERY
One of the wine-producing Communes of the Montagne de Reims (Champagne).

VIN
French for Wine.

Vin blanc, white wine;

Vin bourru, new wine, before it has fallen bright;

Vin chaud, mulled wine;

Vin cuit, grape-juice boiled to the consistency of a syrup;

Vin de côtes, wine from hillside vineyards.

Vin de coule, wine of the first pressing of the grapes;

Vin de cuvée, wine of the first pressing (Champagne);

Vin de garde, a well-balanced wine suitable for laying down;

Vin de goutte, wine from the last squeezings of the grapes;

Vin de liqueur, grape-juice the fermentation of which has been checked by the addition of Brandy;

Vin de messe, altar wine;

Vin de paille, a sweet, golden wine made from grapes which are left on straw mats when picked, to dry in the sun, before they are pressed;

Vin de palus, Claret from the vineyards nearest the banks of the rivers Garonne, Dordogne and Gironde;

Vin de pays, local wine; wine with a

local reputation but not made in sufficiently large quantities to be exported.

Vin de paysan, homely wine; the poorer quality of *Vin de pays*;

Vin de plaine, wine from plain vineyards, never so good as that from the hillsides;

Vin de presse, an inferior wine made from the pressed husks of the grapes;

Vin doux, grape-juice before it ferments and becomes wine; also used for a 'sweet' wine;

Vin gris, light red wine of Lorraine and Alsace, usually made of mixed black and white grapes;

Vin jaune, the best wine of Château Chalon, Jura;

Vin mousseux, sparkling wine;

Vin nature, unsweetened wine;

Vin non-mousseux, still wine;

Vin ordinaire, the more homely type of table wine;

Vin rosé (1) a pink wine made from very ripe black grapes, the skins of which are not allowed to ferment with the wine, so that they only impart to it a pink tinge instead of a dark red colour; (2) A pink wine made from black and white grapes mixed in the pressing; (3) A white wine coloured with cochineal to the degree of pink required.

Vin rouge, red wine.

VINEGAR

An acid liquid prepared from various substances by acetous fermentation of the alcohol present in all alcoholic beverages, which becomes, in the presence of oxygen, acetic acid. In all wine-producing countries wine vinegar is the rule; in the others, it is malt vinegar. Vinegar is also made from cider, and to a much less extent from perry, honey, rice, maize and all manner of other vegetable substances which are susceptible to produce alcohol by fermentation.

VINHO

Portuguese for Wine.

Vinho claro, unfortified wine;

Vinho generoso, fortified wine;

Vinho spumoso, sparkling wine;

Vinho verde, the more homely sort of table wine; new wine;

Vinho estufado, Madeira wine matured in an *estufa* (q.v.);

Vinho trasfugado, the *Vinho estufado* after it has been racked.

VINO

Spanish for Wine.

Vino blanco, white wine;

Vino corriente, ordinary table wine;

Vino de anada, young Jerez wine before it is blended;

Vino de color, grape-juice boiled to the consistency of a sweet syrup;

Vino de cuarte, a *Rosé* wine from the Province of Valencia;

Vino de la tierra, local wine;

Vino de pasto, dinner wine, a 'utility' type of Sherry;

Vino maestro, a very sweet and strong wine used for blending with harsh or weak wines;

Vino rojo, red wine;

Vino spumoso, sparkling wine;

Vino tierno, another name for *Vino maestro*;

Vino tiuto, red wine.

VINO, VINI

Italian for Wine and Wines.

Vini bianchi, white wines;

Vini di lusso, expensive dessert wines;

Vini rossi, red wines;

Vini rosati, *Rosés* wines;

Vini tipici, standard wines;

Vino cotto, grape-juice boiled to the consistency of a sweet syrup;

Vino della riviera, wines from the Lombardy side of the Lake Garda;

Vino de arrosto, wine of breed;

Vino frizzante, cheap fizzy wine;
Vino spumante, sparkling wine.

VINTAGE
The gathering of the grapes. Also the particular year when the grapes were gathered and the wine made. There is a Vintage every year but the quality of the grapes vintaged varies from year to year. There are wines shipped under the date of their vintage and others shipped without any such date; all were made alike from grapes gathered in one or more years. The chief difference between dated (Vintage) and undated (non-Vintage) wines is that the first show greater promise of improving with age and should be kept, whilst the others are ready for immediate consumption and may—but need not—be kept.

VINZELLES
One of the lesser wine-producing Communes of Saône-et-Loire (Burgundy). Mostly white wine, usually sold as *Pouilly - Vinzelles*, *Vinzelles - Lochê*, or *Pouilly-Loché*.

VIRÉ
One of the lesser wine-producing Communes of Saône-et-Loire (Burgundy).

VIRELADE
One of the smaller Communes of the Graves (Gironde).

VIRELADE, Château de
Graves (Claret and white wine).

VISPTHAL
The highest vine-growing valley in Europe; from Visp to Zermatt, Valais (Switzerland).

VITERBO
One of the white wines of the Latium (Italy).

VODKA
The national Russian spirit. It is as nearly 'plain' as a spirit can be, being distilled from the cheapest material at hand, mostly potatoes or grain, and neither flavoured nor coloured nor matured. It is served very cold and swallowed at one gulp, there is no need for nose or palate to waste any time over Vodka.

VOLNAY
One of the best-known Communes of the Côte d'Or, producing much red Burgundy of very fair quality.

VOLLRADS, Schloss
One of the finest growths of the Rhinegau. The castle dates back to the fourteenth century. It stands in a little valley at the back of the twin villages of Winkel and Mittelheim, and has been for generations the property of the Matuschka-Greiffenklau family.

VOSLAU
One of the best wine-producing districts of Austria for both red and white wines.

VOSNE-ROMANÉE
One of the most important Communes of the Côte d'Or, in which are situated vineyards producing the most celebrated red Burgundy, chief among them being the small *Romanée Conti* vineyard, also the other *Romanées*, *La Romanée*, *Saint-Vivant*, and *La Tâche*; also *Les Richebourg*.

VOUGEOT
One of the most famous Communes of the Côte d'Or, where is the celebrated Clos de Vougeot.

VOUGEOT, Clos de
The finest vineyard of Burgundy but now divided among a large number of different owners who do not all give the same care to their share of the vines, hence differences in quality of the wines sold under and entitled to the name of *Clos de Vougeot*. The wines of Vougeot are mostly red wines, but there is a little

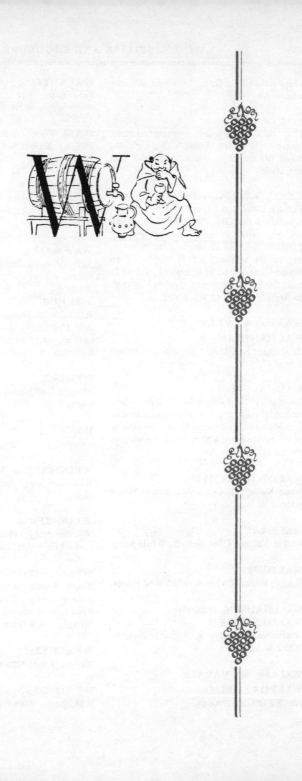

white wine made from the *Vigne Blanche* vineyard.

VOUVRAY
The most important wine-producing centre of Touraine (Loire Valley), chiefly noted for its white wines, both still and sparkling.

V.S.O., V.S.O.P., V.V.S.O.P.
These initials stand for: V for Very, S for Special, O for Old and P for Pale. They are generally accepted in the Brandy Trade to refer to the age of the Brandy, not to its quality, V.S.O. referring to Brandy from 12 to 17 years old; V.S.O.P. from 20 to 25 years old, and V.V.S.O.P. to Brandy about 40 years old.

WAADT, see VAUD

WACHENHEIM
Palatinate; Bad-Dürkheim district. White wines.

WACHSTUM
German for 'The property of'. It precedes, on the labels of the best growths of Hocks and Moselles, the name of the proprietor of the estate from which came the wine in the bottle.

WALDBÖCKELHEIM
Nahe Valley; Kreuznech district. White wine.

WALDRACH
Ruwer Valley; Trier district. White wine.

WALDUM
Baden; Baden-Baden district. Red wines.

WALLHAUSEN, formerly
WALDENHUSEN
Gräfenbach Valley. Kreuznach district. White wines.

WALLIS, see VALAIS
WALPORZHEIM
Ahr Valley. Red wines.

WALSHEIM
Palatinate; Landau district. Red and white wines of moderate quality.

WASENWEILER
Baden; Kaiserstuhl ridge, in Brisgau. White wine.

WATERVALE
South Australia. The wine-producing district in which are situated the Spring Vale vineyards.

WAWERN
Saar Valley; Saarburg district. White wines.

WEEPER
A bottle showing the first signs of a defective cork; one that should be re-corked, or, preferably, drunk, before it becomes an Ullage.

WEHLEN
Moselle Valley; Bernkastel district. White wines.

WEIN
German for Wine.

WEINMASS or WEINGEMASS
Bavarian wine measure equal to 2·515 pints.

WEINSBERG
Württemberg; Heilbronn district. Red and white wines, mostly red.

WELLINGTON
South Africa. One of the most prolific wine-growing districts of the Cape Province, at the end of the Paarl Valley, farthest away from French Hoek.

WERTHEIM
Baden. White wines; Steinwein type.

WESTHOFEN
Rhinehesse; Worms district. White wines.

WHISKEY. WHISKY

A grain spirit distilled from barley, rye and other cereals which are first of all malted and then fermented. The strength, colour, flavour and 'quality' of different Whiskies depend upon the grain used in the first instance, the manner and degree of the malting, fermentation and distillation, the length of time of maturing and the skill of the blender. Some indication of the main differences resulting from all such factors is given under the headings of the principal Whiskies of commerce, which are, in alphabetical order: *Bourbon*, *Canadian*, *Irish*, *Rye* and *Scotch*.

WILTINGEN

Saar Valley; Saarburg district. White wines.

WINCHERINGEN

Upper Moselle. Saarburg district. White wines. Best vineyards: *Fuchsloch* and *Mühlenberg*.

WINE

Wine is the suitably fermented juice of freshly gathered ripe grapes. The colour, bouquet, flavour, strength and 'quality' of any wine depend upon a number of factors, chief among them being: (1) the species of grapes from which the wine is made; (2) the nature of the soil and aspect of the vineyard in which the grapes were grown; (3) the incidence of rain and sunshine responsible for the quality and ripeness of the grapes when gathered at the time of the vintage; (4) the care given to the cultivation of the vines and to the gathering of the grapes; (5) to the manner and degree of the pressing of the grapes, the fermentation of their sweet juice, and the treatment accorded to the newly made wine; (6) to the methods adopted for blending and maturing; the time and manner of bottling, packing, despatching, binning, uncorking, decanting and serving.

Fermentation may be slow or rapid, complete or partial, satisfactory or not, but it is as inevitable as it is natural, and it transforms part or the whole of the sugar present in fresh grape juice into alcohol: the sweeter the grape, the stronger the wine. Fermentation may be checked by the addition of spirit or of chemicals, but there cannot be any such thing as a 'non-alcoholic wine': it is a contradiction in terms.

Light beverage wines, which are 'natural' wines, contain an average of 12 per cent of alcohol by volume; fortified wines twice as much; water always is the bulk of the wine (from 66 to 90 per cent), but there are also minute quantities of quite a large number of other substances which are responsible for the colour, bouquet, flavour and keeping quality of every wine. There are as many types of wine as there are types of men and women in the world, a few are very good, some are very bad but the great majority are neither good nor bad, just 'ordinaires'. Some are long lived, they are the exception; some are short lived; some are sound and others are sick, but all must die. A wine need not be rare, nor costly to be enjoyable: it must be suited to the food that is served with it, to the occasion and mood of the moment, and, whatever its price, name or pedigree, it is quite indispensable that it should be *sound*. A sound wine is a wine that is pleasant to look at, sweet smelling and intensely clean on the palate; it is a wine that has got over the distemper of youth, but shows as yet no signs of decay, of approaching its end.

WINKEL

One of the best-known villages of the Rhinegau (Hock).

WINNINGEN

Lower Moselle Valley; Coblence district. White wines.

WINTRICH

Moselle Valley; Bernkastel district. White wines.

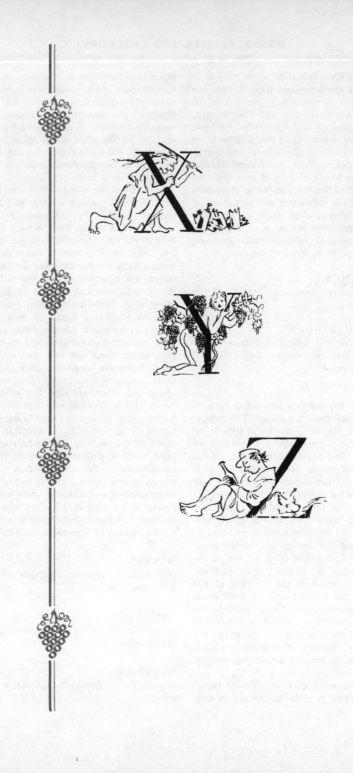

WINZENHEIM
Nahe Valley; Kreuznach district. White wines.

WOLFENWEILER
Baden; Freiburg district. White wines.

WOLLMESHEIM
Palatinate; Landau district. *Ordinaire* white wines.

WOLXHEIM
One of the best white wines of Alsace.

WOODY
A wine or spirit having acquired the smell of the cask in which it has been lodged too long. If one of the staves of a cask is mouldy, the wine or spirit in it soon acquires a musty taste which renders it undrinkable. But 'woodiness' is the smell of *sound* oak; it is unwelcome but not unwholesome, and it can, as a rule, be remedied.

WORCESTER
One of the important wine-producing districts of Cape Province, South Africa.

WORMS
An important centre of the Rhinehesse Wine Trade.

WÜRZBURG
The chief centre of the Franconia Wine Trade (Stein wines). Best vineyards: *Steinmantel*, formerly known as *Jesuiten-Stein*, *Stein*, *Innere Leiste*, *Leisten*, *Rossberg*, *Harfe*, *Abstleite*, *Schalksberg*, *Ständerbühl*, and *Neuberg*.

WYNBERG
The oldest wine-producing district of the Cape Peninsula (South Africa).

XÉRÈS
French for Jerez, as well as for Sherry.

YAYIN
One of the Hebrew names of Wine.

YIN
A Chinese measure equal to 45·56 gallons (British).

YOLO COUNTY
One of the wine-producing counties of the State of California, U.S.A.

YON-FIGEAC, Château
Graves de Saint-Emilion (Claret).

YON-FIGEAC, Clos
Graves de Saint-Emilion (Claret).

YONNE
A wine-producing Département of France noted for its white wines, the best of which is that of *Chablis*.

YQUEM, Château d'
Sauternes. The finest of all naturally sweet wines.

YUBA COUNTY
One of the wine-producing counties of the State of California, U.S.A.

YUGOSLAVIA
One of the new Balkan States born of the First World War. Its average annual production of wine is about 80 million gallons.

YVORNE
One of the best Swiss white wines from Aigle, in the Upper Rhône Valley.

ZACO
The best white wine of the Rioja district (Spain).

ZANTE
Dessert wine from the Ionian island of that name. One of the Zante wines was known formerly by the name of *Jenorodi*.

ZELL

Palatinate (Unterhaardt). White wines. Best vineyards: *Schwarzer Herrgott, Schnepfenflug, Osterberg, Philippsbrunnen*. There is also a village of the same name in the valley of the Middle Moselle. White wines. Best vineyard: *Schwarze Kazt*.

ZELTINGEN

Middle Moselle. Bernkastel district. White wines. Best vineyards: *Kirchenpfad, Stefanslay, Steinmauer, Schlossberg, Himmelbreick, Sonnuhr* and *Rotlay*.

ZOMBIE

¾ oz. lime juice; ¾ oz. pineapple juice; 1 teaspoonful Falernum or simple syrup; 1 oz. White Label Rum; 2 oz. Gold Label Rum; 1 oz. Jamaica Rum; ¼ oz. 151° proof Demerara Rum; ¼ oz. apricot liqueur. Shake well and strain into 14 oz. Zombie glass, quarter filled with ice. Garnish with slice of orange and several sprigs of mint. Serve with straws.

ZUBROWKA

A Russian spirit which is just as 'raw' as Vodka, but not quite so plain. It is Vodka (q.v.) in which some Zubrowka grass is steeped, so that it has a little colour, aromatic bouquet and bitterish taste, whereas Vodka is colourless and free from all bouquet or taste.

ZUCCO

A dessert wine from Sicilian vineyards, chiefly those of Palermo.